LOEB CLASSICAL LIBRARY
FOUNDED BY JAMES LOEB 1911

EDITED BY
JEFFREY HENDERSON

CATO
I

LCL 551

CATO

TESTIMONIA

ORIGINES

EDITED AND TRANSLATED BY

GESINE MANUWALD

HARVARD UNIVERSITY PRESS
CAMBRIDGE, MASSACHUSETTS
LONDON, ENGLAND
2023

First published 2023

Library of Congress Control Number 2022039357
CIP data available from the Library of Congress

ISBN 978-0-674-99752-3

*Composed in ZephGreek and ZephText by
Technologies 'N Typography, Merrimac, Massachusetts.
Printed on acid-free paper and bound by
Maple Press, York, Pennsylvania*

CONTENTS

GENERAL INTRODUCTION

CATO'S BIOGRAPHY

M. Porcius Cato (234–149 BC; *RE* Porcius 9)[1] is one of the best known figures of the middle Roman Republic, famous for his political and military career, austere morality, literary works, and pithy sayings.[2] In fact, he is "the earliest Roman for whom we possess any significant biographical information," a great deal of which ultimately goes back to his own writings.[3] Moreover, since Cato was already a noteworthy figure in antiquity, a number of references to him as well as more extended treatments can be found in ancient authors, particularly the biographies of Cornelius Nepos, of which a shortened version survives

[1] On Cato's biography, features of his portrait, and the sources, see, e.g., Fraccaro [1910a; 1910b; 1911] 1956; Marmorale 1949; Pastorino 1951, 43–195; Gelzer and Helm 1953; Della Corte 1953, v–viii, x–xiv; 1969, 9–122; Forde 1975; Astin 1978; Kienast 1979; Gehrke 2000; Suerbaum 2002, 380–418; on the historical context of Cato's activities, see Scullard 1973 *passim*.

[2] For bibliography on Cato, see Till 1937, i–viii (early period); Kroymann in Peter, *HRR* (repr.) 1:389–91; Suerbaum 2004 (esp. on twentieth century); see also Zuccarelli 1952 (on 1940–1950); Sblendorio Cugusi and Cugusi 1996 (on 1978–1993).

[3] Cornell 2009, 18–19 (quotation on p. 18). On Cato and the origins of Roman autobiography, see Cornell 2009.

(T 26), and Plutarch (excerpts at T 55–64), a short summary in the work *De viris illustribus* (T 82), as well as the portrayal in Cicero's dialogue *Cato maior de senectute* (excerpts at T 18–23), supplemented by information in Livy's historical account and the biographies of contemporaries of Cato. Thus, in addition to the external facts of Cato's life, such as the dates of his political career, there is ample material on his life, lifestyle, character, and literary output. Since it seems, however, that Cato intended to create a certain portrait of himself in his writings, Cicero developed this portrayal for the purposes of creating a literary and political framework for himself, and later authors built on and expanded the developing literary historical tradition, all notices concerning details of Cato's life have to be approached with the appropriate caution and should not be regarded as unequivocal statements of facts, while they continue to be regularly adduced by scholars as a basis.[4]

Cato, born in 234 BC (T 19), came from an equestrian family in Tusculum, in the Alban Hills of Latium, near modern Frascati (T 12, 15, 26, 36, 55, 77, 82; *Orat.* F 146, 174); he was thus a *homo novus* ("new man") in Roman terminology (T 9, 55). In his youth he ran estates in the Sabine country that were left to him by his father (T 26, 55, 63), and he served as a soldier (T 19, 21, 26, 55); in 214 BC he was a military tribune in Sicily (T 26, 82; *MRR* 1:261), and he fought in the battle at Sena Gallica in 207

[4] On "Cato's aristocratic self-fashioning" through his writings, see Reay 2005. On the sources and tendentiousness of Plutarch's biography of Cato, see, e.g., Kienast 1979, 10–24.

BC (T 26). After Cato had come to Rome, encouraged by L. Valerius Flaccus (T 26, 82), he began a political career (*MRR* 1:307, 327, 330, 339, 344, 354, 363, 374–75): he was quaestor to (proconsul) P. Cornelius Scipio Africanus maior (cos. 205, 194; censor 199 BC; *ORF*^{4} 4)[5] in Africa and Sicily in 204 BC (T 13, 19, 26, 30, 82), plebeian aedile in 199 BC (T 26), praetor in Sardinia in 198 BC (T 26, 82), and consul in 195 BC together with L. Valerius Flaccus (T 13, 21, 26, 32c, 64, 82). He was then assigned the province of Hither Iberia and celebrated a triumph in 194 BC for his achievements there (T 3, 26, 32a, 32c, 44, 57; *Orat.* F 53). In 191 BC he was a successful general with consul M'. Acilius Glabrio in the fight against Antiochus III the Great (T 21, 59, 64, 82). Two years later, in 189 BC, he was a legate for the consul M. Fulvius Nobilior (*Orat.* F 130). Then, in 184 BC, he became censor, again with L. Valerius Flaccus (T 26, 33, 44, 64, 79, 82; *Op. cet.* F 69); this censorship was proverbially strict and led to the reduction of status for some senators and equestrians (T 26, 33, 82). Cato died in 149 BC, at the advanced age of eighty-five (T 13, 14, 44; *Op. cet.* F 5), though wrongly given as extending to eighty-six and ninety years in some sources (T 32b, 37, 60).

Because of the noteworthy censorship, Cato later (at-

[5] Roman Republican politicians, of whose oratorical interventions fragments and/or testimonia remain and who are therefore included in the edition *Oratorum Romanorum Fragmenta* (*ORF*^{4}) by E. Malcovati and thus in the *Loeb Classical Library* volumes *Roman Oratory* in *Fragmentary Republican Latin* (*FRL*), are identified by their serial numbers in these editions after their full name.

tested from Seneca the Younger onward) received the epithet "Censorius" (lit., "ex-censor"), to distinguish him from other family members of the same name (Sen. *Ep.* 87.9 [T 39]; *Vit. beat.* 21.3 [*Fals.* F 1]). Cicero often designates Cato as *sapiens*, "wise" (Cic. *Div. Caec.* 66; *Verr.* 2.2.5, 2.5.180; *Leg.* 2.5 [T 12]; *Div.* 1.28 [*Orig.* F 132]; for a discussion of the connotations, see T 7; see also Quintilian, at T 20b) or *senex* ("old in age" or "of old": e.g., Cic. *Sull.* 23; *Arch.* 16; *Rep.* 2.1 [T 10]; *Off.* 1.37 [*Op. cet.* F 35]; 1.104 [*Op. cet.* F 51]; 2.89 [*Op. cet.* F 52]).[6]

Cato's outward appearance is sketched by Plutarch (T 55).[7] His lifestyle is generally presented as frugal (e.g., T 32a, 32b, 39, 56, 57, 63). In his personal life Cato had two sons from different wives: from his first marriage with Licinia, there was an elder son, M. Porcius Cato Licinianus (*RE* Porcius 14; ca. 192/90–152 BC), who is said to have been well educated by his father, won merits as a soldier in his youth (in the battle of Pydna in 168 BC), and later married Aemilia (*RE* Aemilia 152; a daughter of L. Aemilius Paullus, cos. 182, 168 BC [*ORF*^{4} 12], and a sister of P. Cornelius Scipio Aemilianus Africanus, cos. 147, 134; censor 142 BC [*ORF*^{4} 21]). This son wrote about law,[8] and he died, as praetor-elect, before his father, who is said to have given him a simple funeral (T 7c, 61, 62, 79, 97; *Op.*

[6] On the names/epithets applied to Cato and their various nuances, see Pasco-Pranger 2012; on the question to what extent these descriptions may have been part of the name, see also Ruebel 1972, 130–32.

[7] On a potential ancient portrait of Cato, see Hafner 1999.

[8] On the son's activity as a jurisconsult and his writings, see Wieacker 1988, 539.

cet. F 36; Liv. *Epit.* 48). From Cato's second marriage, with Salonia (after his first wife's death), there was a much younger son (allegedly born when Cato was in his eighties), M. Porcius Cato Salonianus (*RE* Porcius 15; T 41, 62, 79, 82; *Op. cet.* F 75).

While Cato was active as a public speaker throughout his life, he is said to have devoted time to literary activity proper only in old age (T 26). Cato probably knew the Greek language from an early stage; it is claimed that he could have delivered a speech in Greek in 191 BC, though he chose not to do so (*Op. cet.* F 67a); and he knew about Greek philosophers early (T 22, 56). Yet he is said to have engaged with Greek literature more intensively in old age (T 18, 20, 22, 37, 56, 89a, 94).

Cato's attitude to Greek learning and culture is perhaps best characterized as determined by qualified caution and a drive to champion Roman national character and traditions, challenged by Greek rhetoric and philosophy, while such a stance does not mean that he was not familiar with the concepts.[9] Like some of his contemporaries, he opposed luxury and unqualified dedication to all Greek influences, as it could be observed among some Romans of his time; he voiced strong criticism of Greek doctors (*Op. cet.* F 5) and contributed to expelling Greek philosophers from Rome (cf. T 50; *Op. cet.* F 74; *Inc.* F 14), while he became acquainted with Greek philosophy and advised

9 See Gruen 1992, 52–83; on the tension between Roman tradition and Greek culture and Cato's reaction to this situation, see also Klingner [1934] 1961; Fuhrmann 1988; Jehne 1999; Torres 2006. On some of the perceived "contradictions" in Cato's behavior and between his life and works, see Vogt-Spira 2000.

his son to dip into Greek literature, though not to study it too much (*Op. cet.* F 5). Some of Cato's political maxims align with aspects of Greek philosophy.[10] Plutarch claims a general impact of Greek literature and mentions Thucydides and Demosthenes (T 56); influence of Polybius, Timaeus, and Eratosthenes has been assumed by modern scholars;[11] reminiscences of Xenophon (*Orig.* F 2; cf. Cic. *Sen.* 59) and Herodotus (*Orig.* F 76; cf. T 77)[12] have been suggested.

Cato developed into a highly regarded figure, while it was already noted in antiquity that he liked to praise himself and created a "brand" for himself (T 39, 89b, 95; *Orig.* F 133; *Op. cet.* F 71), for instance by ostentatiously demonstrating his devotion to frugality.[13] Cato's accomplishments covering a variety of roles, as a politician, orator, advocate, soldier and general, farmer, legal expert, and writer, are frequently mentioned (T 5, 8, 10, 15, 20b, 21,

[10] On the ambivalence toward Greek culture within a broader context, see Gehrke 1994, esp. 599–607. On Cato's reaction to Greek philosophers and elements in the fragments potentially reflecting Greek philosophy, see Garbarino 1973, 138–43 (fragments), 313–48 (discussion).

[11] See, e.g., Moretti 1952.

[12] See Krebs 2006.

[13] On Cato presenting himself as a moral exemplar, see Pasco-Pranger 2015. Ruebel (1972) argues that in the early part of his career Cato's advances were based on his successful military activity and that he only later discovered that he could create a particular image of himself by speeches and literary activity, that he then switched tactics and started to build the now famous image of himself from the time of this first (unsuccessful) candidature for the censorship.

26, 32b, 36, 37, 42, 44, 51, 55, 60, 64, 82). He became famous for his integrity of character, moral strictness, modest way of life, corresponding political beliefs, opposition to Carthage, pithy sayings, and matter-of-fact style.

CATO'S LITERARY WORKS: OVERVIEW

Especially if viewed through the lens of later ancient authors and then modern scholars, Cato occupies an important position in the development of Roman literary history, marking the beginning of Latin prose literature in several genres: he is the author of the earliest extant piece of prose writing in Latin; he is the first Roman to write a historiographical work and an agricultural treatise in Latin; and he is the first Roman orator of whom authentic written speeches were available to later generations since at least for some of them written versions existed (cf. T 13, 14, 32b).[14]

Like his contemporary Q. Ennius (239–169 BC), Cato was a Latin author active in a range of literary genres, in his case in the area of prose writing and with an emphasis on Roman history, politics, traditions, and values: Cato composed a historical work entitled *Origines*; a treatise on agriculture called *De agricultura*; more than 150 political and forensic speeches; a piece addressed to his son covering at least the topics of medicine, oratory, and agriculture; a work on military science; (perhaps) a piece on law; a *Carmen de moribus*; letters; a number of sayings (re-

[14] On Cato's role at the beginning of Latin prose literature within the contemporary cultural context, see Sciarrino 2011.

ferred to as *Dicta memorabilia*); a notebook with prescriptions for the treatment of illnesses; and more informal texts for his young son.[15] When Quintilian identifies Cato as the first Roman who wrote on rhetorical theory (T 48), this might refer to observations on oratory included in the work addressed to Cato's son or to scattered comments and noteworthy sayings in other contexts; it does not need to indicate a specific work on rhetoric (cf. *Op. cet.* F 15). At any rate, Cicero did not know of a separate rhetorical treatise by Cato.[16] As the advice to the son reveals, Cato seems to have been concerned more with the requirements of a practicing orator than with rhetorical theory, though he would have been aware of rhetorical discussions available in his time. Cato is said to have delivered speeches from a young age, while the *Origines* is defined as a work of his old age (T 22, 26). All of Cato's writings seem to be linked to his personal, public, and political activity and his life experiences (e.g., based on his roles as leader of a household, farmer, general, advocate, and politician):[17] this context makes them appear authentic and suggests the author's personal engagement. Still, autobiographical interpretations need to apply the appropriate caution.

Of the certain items by Cato, *De agricultura* (T 23, 25, 38, 44, 45, 63, 72, 98) is the first treatise on agriculture in Latin and also the only work of Cato's to have survived in

[15] On Cato's literary output, see, e.g., Gelzer and Helm 1953; Astin 1978, 182–239; Suerbaum 2002, 387–413.

[16] For a discussion of the potential nature of Cato's statements on oratory, see Calboli 1982, 41–45.

[17] On this aspect of Cato's historiography, see Schmal 2002.

more or less complete form (though its structure and publication history are debated). Thus, it is the only extant prose work in Latin from the early phase of Republican literature prior to the first century BC.

All other works by Cato are known through testimonia and fragments. For the *Origines* and the speeches these are more numerous and meaningful.[18] The material on the other works is limited, and details concerning their precise character, title, content, and extent are often unclear. Both in antiquity and in subsequent periods, the image of Cato the writer has been dominated by the *Origines*, the *De agricultura*, the speeches, and perhaps the memorable sayings.

At least some of Cato's literary works were available in the ancient world and are quoted and referred to by later writers; how they were "published" and to what extent Cato intended "publication" is uncertain. Cicero presents Cato engaged in literary activity in old age, editing speeches and finalizing the *Origines* (T 22): such a scenario could have been influenced by the conventions of Cicero's own time, the intended portrayal of Cato, and the aim to create a parallel for Cicero's own practices. Statements attributed to Cato suggest that he composed texts for the use of himself and his family, including a medical manual (*Op. cet.* F 5; *Inc.* F 14), a historical work for his son (*Inc.* F 12), and records of some of his speeches (*Orat.* F 173), while there is no clear evidence on any public dimension.

All of Cato's more formal works not fully preserved and

[18] For a brief discussion of Cato's place in the development of early Roman historiography, see Badian 1966.

instead attested by testimonia and fragments are included in this edition; more information on each work can be found in the introductions to each of them preceding the presentation of the texts.

CATO'S LANGUAGE AND STYLE

Cato became highly regarded because of his character and his political and military achievements; among writers in later periods he was also valued as an early historiographer and an early orator (T 13, 35, 70a). People engaging with his works acknowledged that his writing was accomplished for his time, while it was equally seen as old-fashioned and not very polished by the standards of later periods, though not quite as basic as that of his scattered predecessors (T 4, 6, 8, 11, 13, 15, 16, 47, 52, 53, 54). Cato's works were not widely read and appreciated in Cicero's time (T 13), though wrongly in Cicero's view (T 13); they were promoted by Cicero and later would again find favor with the archaists (T 69, 70, 71, 72, 75, 77). Ancient readers felt that they could detect an individual style characteristic of Cato and a particular use of certain expressions (T 69, 73, 77). He was credited with introducing new words into the Latin language (T 27).

For Cato's speeches, Cicero claims that they already include the main characteristics of oratory (with others still lacking); their brevity, a number of standard rhetorical figures, and a basic form of prose rhythm are identified by later ancient readers (T 13, 16, 17, 46, 84; *Orat.* F 59, 133, 151, 166, 173, 214, 236–37; see Introduction to Orations). Because of the fragmentary nature of all of Cato's works except *De agricultura*, it is difficult to confirm or fal-

sify the views of ancient authors or to provide a comprehensive and more objective description of Cato's writing style.[19] This difficulty applies in particular to broader questions of structure. More can be discerned about individual stylistic features, observable in the text of longer fragments. There are clearly stylistic differences between the different literary genres (e.g., the style of the speeches and *Origines* being more elevated than that of *De agricultura*); additionally, the style varies in each genre depending on the character of sections.

Generally, the available texts point to a concise, plain, and down-to-earth style, yet also including poetic elements and solemn archaic features,[20] with little use of grammatical subordination and a more linear mode of expression, made effective sometimes by pleonasm and sometimes by brevity. Longer fragments (cf. *Orat.* F 169A) display rhetorical figures and forms of expression, such as alliteration (e.g., *Orig.* F 116; *Orat.* F 19, 58, 59, 60, 66, 72, 111, 128, 152, 163, 169, 174, 178, 196, 200, 246), anaphora (e.g., *Orig.* F 143; *Orat.* F 28, 34, 58, 146, 155, 173), homoioteleuton / epiphora (e.g., *Orig.* F 97, 99; *Orat.* F 28, 59, 66, 106, 115, 133, 163, 177, 178, 204), asyndeton (e.g., *Orig.* F 116; *Orat.* F 20, 35, 44, 58, 72, 98, 106, 115, 146, 183, 196, 224), polysyndeton (e.g., *Orat.*

[19] On aspects of Cato's language, style, and prose rhythm, see Till 1935 / 1968; Leeman 1963, 44–49; Fraenkel 1968, 123–57; Primmer 1970; Sblendorio 1971; Sblendorio Cugusi 1987, 31–44; Habinek 1985; Traglia 1985; Calboli 1996, 17–22, 27–28; von Albrecht 2012, 15–36; for a comparison between the style of Cato and that of Terence, see Goldberg 1983.

[20] For the use of archaisms, see Mariotti 1991.

F 21, 59, 163), accumulation of synonyms (e.g., *Orat.* F 21, 59, 163), pair of words and tricolon (e.g., *Orig.* F 97, 99, 116, 143; *Orat.* F 21, 35, 50, 58, 59, 61, 72, 108, 128, 163, 178, 183, 196, 224; *Op. cet.* F 21), figura etymologica (e.g., *Orig.* F 103; *Orat.* F 28, 182, 185, 246), climax (e.g., *Orat.* F 58, 59), antithesis (e.g., *Orat.* F 106, 163, 173), parallelism (e.g., *Orat.* F 17, 58, 106, 173), chiasmus (e.g., *Orig.* F 42; *Orat.* F 146), poeticism (e.g., *Orat.* F 29), fictional dialogue (*Orat.* F 173), enthymeme (*Orat.* F 165), use of rhetorical questions, metaphor, and neologisms, including new words, new constructions, and new meanings. The word order typically is not random and instead contributes to stressing important words and ideas (e.g., initial position of verb: *Orat.* F 58, 114, 173), which is sometimes repeated in subsequent sentences. A straightforward structure and a clear progression of thought seem to be adduced to aid the impact of the argumentation and the presentation. A basic rhythmical structure of main cola, showing similarities to structures in the poets Ennius and Plautus and often used for effect and for underlining contrasts or parallelisms, can be discerned, while there are not yet long, sophisticated periods.

Modern scholars have pointed out that Cato employed expressions also used in spoken speech (sometimes for lack of alternatives), but nothing deliberately colloquial.[21] At the same time, technical language is chosen where appropriate. Despite the (apparent) professed opposition to all things Greek, Cato was obviously sufficiently familiar with Greek material to include Greek loanwords, quotations, and stories in his writings; he also takes up elements

21 See especially Briscoe 2010.

of Greek and Roman popular philosophy as well as well-known sayings and alludes to stories from Homer's *Odyssey* (cf. T 56; *Orat.* F 189; *Op. cet.* F 64). It is now assumed that Cato knew about the basic principles of Greek oratory, but that he did not let his style be completely governed by it.

However biased some of these assessments are, it is clear from them, and confirmed by some of the fragments, that Cato's writings had a certain amount of rhetorical polish, were deliberately shaped, and might have incorporated elements of Greek rhetoric; at any rate, Cicero was able to present Cato (without this appearing as implausible) as working on editing his speeches and finalizing the *Origines* in his old age (T 22).

In view of these observations, it is debated to what extent the stylistic character of Cato's writings is based on the influence of earlier literature, especially Greek models and Greek literary theory, or on Cato's ability, experience, and techniques. While longer sections, especially from the speeches, can be analyzed according to Greek theory (as has been attempted by ancient and modern scholars), that such a terminology can be applied does not prove that the texts were deliberately arranged in line with the corresponding principles; the result could be a coincidence if certain structures or styles of argument suggest themselves as the most appropriate for the subject matter. While Cato must have been aware of Greek theory, his famous statements on the qualities and principles of an orator (esp. *Op. cet.* F 1, 8) might point to a more independent approach.

Overall, it seems, in line with what can be inferred for Cato's character, that he did not indulge in unnecessary

embellishment and rather deployed language and style for the purposes of furthering his argument and of enhancing the impact of the presentation.

CATO'S AFTERLIFE: THE RECEPTION IN OTHER ROMAN AUTHORS

As the number of references to Cato in later ancient authors demonstrates (see Testimonia), he became an important and widely recognized figure in Roman consciousness, though this status was linked less to his writings and rather based on his personality and political activity.[22] Cato was seen as a manifestation of traditional Roman virtues, a symbol of Roman Republican character, and a paradigmatic strict censor; he was known for his moral sternness, his parsimony, his opposition to Greek luxury and other Greek influences, and his hard line against Carthage. Later, his portrait was influenced by his presentation in Cicero's dialogue with Cato as the protagonist (see excerpts at T 18–23) and also by the relevant narratives in Livy and in the biographies of Cornelius Nepos (T 26) and Plutarch (excerpts at T 55–64).[23]

Cicero in his early writings (T 2) and also the author of

[22] On Cato's reception in antiquity and the image(s) of him created by later ancient authors, see (with references), e.g., Wójcik 1965; Haffter 1967; Della Corte 1969, 123–281; Agache 1980; Ducos 2010. On his reception in Cicero, Plutarch, the Middle Ages, and the Renaissance, see Wulfram 2009; on his presentation in Cicero, see Hermand 2010; in Livy, see Fraccaro [1934] 1956; in Plutarch, see Carsana 2014.

[23] For an overview on scholarship on Plutarch's biography and a discussion of the use of availability of sources on Cato, see Scardigli 1979, 43–51 (with notes on pp. 170–73).

the *Rhetoric to Herennius* (T 1) mention Cato as one of the paradigmatic orators influential on successors, though there is no engagement with particular passages.[24] Additionally, Cicero presented him as a precursor of a *homo novus*, who became a successful orator and politician.[25] In the *Brutus*, Cicero acknowledges that Cato's orations are not widely read in his time, while he claims that he has identified and read more than 150 speeches, although he does not engage with individual examples (T 13). In the discussion in the *Brutus*, Cato's speeches are characterized as worth reading as a model, especially in the context of the controversy between Atticism and Asianism, illustrated by a comparison between Cato and Lysias; it is acknowledged, however, that they are archaic and not as rhetorically polished as contemporary ones (T 13, 15; cf. T 56, 57).[26]

Moreover, Cicero offers a portrayal of Cato's personality in *Cato maior de senectute*, a dialogue dedicated to Atticus (cf. T 18–23). Atticus in turn encouraged Cornelius Nepos' biography (T 26). And Cicero's contemporary Varro adduces Cato as a source in his works. Cicero's freedman M. Tullius Tiro produced a detailed critique of one of Cato's most famous speeches, which was analyzed and commented on by Gellius in the second century AD (*Orat.* F 163–69). For after the wave of interest among

24 On parallels between Cato's and Cicero's speeches, see Cugusi 1986. On Cato developing into a model for "archaic" style, see Calboli 1986.

25 See van der Blom 2010 *passim*. On Cicero's attitude to Cato as an individual and as a writer as well as its development over time, see Gnauk 1936, 70–104.

26 On Cicero's portrayal of Cato in the *Brutus*, see, e.g., Desmouliez 1982.

Cicero and his acquaintances and contemporaries (also noticeable in stylistic reminiscences to Cato in Sallust's historiographical works), Cato found favor again among the archaists, such as Gellius and Fronto (e.g., T 67–77, 88). Fronto, for instance, values Cato above Cicero and praises Cato for the sophisticated and careful selection of words (T 71). Later, the archaic language of his works was studied by grammarians and lexicographers. The increased attention to Cato in Cicero's later works and among his contemporaries might be connected with Cicero rediscovering Cato's speeches in preparation for writing the *Brutus* in the context of contemporary rhetorical debates. From that time onward, those orations seem to have been more easily available, and there are more specific references from the following periods.[27]

Cato appears to have exerted some influence on successors in the literary genres he was active in.[28] In historiography he was followed by L. Cassius Hemina (*FRHist* 6), L. Coelius Antipater (*FRHist* 15), Sallust, and Livy. Sallust was known for adopting elements of Cato's style and presentation for his historical works (T 49, 65, 66, 71, 81). Livy seems to have used Cato's works as sources for the relevant parts of his narrative and gives reports on Cato's activities presumably inspired by Cato's presentation (T 30–34).[29] Cato's writings provided sources for Dionysius of Halicarnassus (T 28, 29) and Pliny the Elder (T 40); he was regarded as a diligent and trustworthy his-

27 See Baumgart 1905, 20–34.

28 On Cicero's reception of Cato's historical work in comparison with Ennius' *Annales*, see Elliott 2020.

29 On Livy's use of Cato's works as a source, see Tränkle 1970; 1971.

torian (*Orig.* F 13a, 17, 52, 80). Servius' commentary on Virgil often refers to Cato's writings for information on the early history of Rome. Frontinus (*Op. cet.* F 18) and Vegetius (*Op. cet.* F 27–29) still have recourse to Cato's piece on military matters. Varro and Columella draw on material from Cato for their works on agriculture; Varro also uses Cato's writings or the same sources for his works dealing with Roman history, and he quotes examples from Cato's pieces in his discussions about the Latin language.

Features of archaic vocabulary, morphology, and syntax attract the attention of lexicographers and grammarians, from Varro to Pliny the Elder (*Inc.* F 45), Statilius Maximus (*Orig.* F 143; *Orat.* F 235, 247, 248; *Inc.* F 46, 47, 48, 50), Verrius Flaccus (*Orat.* F 158), and the grammarians of late antiquity. Even Christian authors of late antiquity mention Cato and maxims of his, though it is not always clear how direct their knowledge is.

The *Disticha Catonis* is a late antique collection of brief proverbs in verse; although the work is not authentic, it was regarded in the Middle Ages as having been authored by Cato. It became popular, was translated into many vernaculars, and shaped the view of Cato's character and writings.[30]

ORGANIZATION OF THIS EDITION

The fragments and the testimonia documenting Cato's works have been edited previously as part of editions of

30 For an edition of the Latin text of the *Disticha Catonis*, see Boas 1952. For an edition of the Greek translation by Maximus Planudes, see Ortoleva 1992. For a brief discussion, including the generic and cultural context, see Roos 1984.

all of Cato's (fragmentary) writings or of those of the literary genres to which some of his writings belong.[31]

The reference edition for all of Cato's works for a long time was, and to some extent still is, the one by H. Jordan (1860; reprint, 1967); it is still frequently cited, especially as regards the "minor" or "other works," and its numbering is widely used. This edition has now been complemented by a more recent comprehensive edition of all of Cato's works by P. Cugusi and M. T. Sblendorio Cugusi published in 2001, also including an Italian translation and notes.

In addition, the standard reference work for the *Origines* for a long time was the edition of all fragments of the Roman historiographers by H. Peter (1914–1916; reprint, 1967). That edition has now been superseded by the multivolume work *Fragments of the Roman Historians* (*FRHist*), edited by T. Cornell and others (2013). The fragments of the speeches are found in the edition of all the fragments of the Republican orators, in E. Malcovati's *Oratorum Romanorum Fragmenta liberae rei publicae* (*ORF*^{4}, 1976) and also in the separate edition of Cato's speeches by M. T. Sblendorio Cugusi (1982).

In line with the conventions of the Loeb Classical Library, this edition does not aim to introduce a new numbering of fragments where it is not necessary or helpful in view of existing numbering systems, while providing readers with the most widely used and most scholarly up-to-date arrangement of the fragments.

For these reasons, this edition has adopted for the

[31] For a survey of manuscripts including sections of Cato's works, see Munk Olsen 1982, 57–59.

Origines the ordering and numbering of the fragments in *FRHist*, and for the speeches that of *ORF*^{4}, as also for the fragmentary speeches of other Roman Republican orators in the separate Loeb volumes on *Oratory* (LCL 540, 541, and 542) as part of the series *Fragmentary Republican Latin* (*FRL*); on characteristics of *ORF*^{4} see the Introduction to the *Oratory* volumes.[32] A consequence of this principle—since both editions aim to include as many fragments potentially belonging to their respective literary genres, even if they are transmitted just for Cato, but not to a particular work—is that some fragments may be attributed to both works, and some fragments assigned to *Incerta* in complete editions of Cato are tentatively attributed to the *Origines* and/or the speeches in these editions. This situation cannot be avoided if the numerical sequence of the reference editions is not to be disrupted, but introductions to each section, cross-references, and notes on the relative certainty of attribution (where it is not obvious from the texts of fragments and their contexts) clarify the arrangement, signal the basis for the positioning, and indicate whether different attributions have been suggested; for greater clarity, these notes replace the system of adding one or more asterisks to fragment numbers in *FRHist* to indicate the level of attribution in the transmission. Fragments hypothetically assigned to a particular work are not repeated in the *Incerta* section, where they would belong according to strict editorial criteria; instead, a headnote to the section lists them, so that it is obvious

[32] Since *ORF*^{4} numbers testimonia and fragments consecutively, the fragments of Cato's speeches start at number 17 (thus, in this Loeb edition, F 1–16 of Cato's speeches do not exist).

at a glance which fragments have not been assigned explicitly to a particular work in the transmission.

Both *FRHist* and *ORF*[4] present a selection of testimonia, preceding the fragments. Understandably, these testimonia focus on information relevant for the respective works included in these editions. Therefore, on the one hand, they do not provide a complete set of relevant testimonia; on the other hand, they overlap, as some passages offer information on Cato's writings in different literary genres. For that reason, in the present edition these testimonia have been combined into one continuous section and supplemented by additional ones on Cato's life and literary works, so as to conveniently provide all the information about Cato the man and the writer in one place. Consequently, the passages had to be renumbered and are now arranged in chronological order according to the dates of the transmitting authors, as are the testimonia for Ennius in the respective volume of *FRL* (LCL 294). Since Cato was a well-known figure (in a number of roles, not only as a writer), later ancient authors refer to him frequently. The testimonia given in this edition therefore do not include every mention of him, if it merely includes a laudatory or distinguishing epithet (like "wise" or "old" or "ex-censor"), and rather aim to collate all the sources providing substantial information.

The distinction between "testimonia" and "fragments" partly follows the model of previous editions and is partly determined by pragmatic considerations. The main criterion thus is whether a passage offers information about the author's life or works in general (assigned to "testimonia") or on a particular section of a work (assigned to "fragments"). This means that not all texts presented in the

"fragments" section are fragments in the narrow sense of literal quotations of passages from the original text. They may also consist of reports in indirect speech or the simple statement that Cato made a certain comment or talked about a particular topic in a particular work. Such passages are not testimonia in a strict sense either; thus it seemed best to list them with the "fragments." In order to highlight fragments in the narrow sense, everything that can fairly certainly be identified as a literal quotation has been enclosed in quotation marks. For historiographical fragments, *FRHist* has established a system of using different kinds of typeface (roman, italic, bold, and combinations of these) as a shortcut for indicating the different status of various types of "fragments." While such a method is helpful in principle, it complicates the layout and signals a false certainty for borderline cases. Therefore, this system has not been adopted, while notes on the status of fragments have been added where appropriate.

In line with the principles of *FRHist*, the fragments of the *Origines* have been arranged as follows: fragments assigned to a particular book and to be inserted into a chronological sequence are arranged within that book in that sequence. Fragments assigned to a particular book, but too unspecific to be ordered chronologically follow after the appropriate chronological sequence, arranged by citing sources. The order determined by quoting authors is also applied to the fragments of Books 2 and 3 as it is unclear how these books were organized. The section "From Books 1–3" includes fragments (in citation order) dealing with Italy but without attribution to a specific book (and sometimes even to the *Origines*); it is likely that they come from this part of the work (probably mostly Book 2

or 3), but the precise position cannot be determined. Fragments cited from Books 4 through 7 are placed within each book in chronological order where identifiable, followed by the remaining fragments in citation order. The next section gives the fragments cited for the *Origines* without book numbers that cannot be placed in context (arranged according to the chronology of the sources). The final section (also in that order) provides those of the many fragments attributed to Cato without an indication of a particular work that might come from the *Origines* due to their content.

On the basis of *ORF*^{4}, the fragments of the speeches are presented in the assumed chronological order of the orations established by the editor E. Malcovati, followed by speeches that cannot be assigned to a particular date, and then fragments from oratorical contexts but not assigned to specific speeches. *ORF*^{4} provides a Latin title for each speech, mostly developed from one of the ancient sources for the speech. These titles have been replaced by English descriptions, to avoid the impression that all of them are transmitted and established designations. In *ORF*^{4} each speech is given a Roman numeral, and the title is followed by a date wherever possible. The numbers for orations have not been taken over: the numbering of the source texts seems sufficient to identify particular oratorical occasions and to enable cross-references, while the numbering of orations might suggest a false sense of completeness in terms of the overall number of speeches known and of certainty about their sequence. Potential dates for speeches for which there is sufficient evidence are discussed in the introductions to each speech.

All other fragments have been compiled from various existing editions, particularly those of H. Jordan, and P. Cugusi and M. T. Sblendorio Cugusi.[33] The assignment to specific works and the phrasing of their titles follows what seems to be the latest *communis opinio* in scholarship. For those works—because there is not an established reference edition to the same extent as for the *Origines* and the orations and because the material has been compiled from various sources—the fragments have been reorganized: within each category the fragments are presented according to the chronology of transmitting authors. So as to avoid having too many separate sequences of fragment numbers, all the other works with titles or generic descriptions have been combined into a section entitled *Opera cetera* with continuous numbering, followed by separate sections for the fragments that cannot be assigned to any works, those whose attribution to Cato is dubious, and those that are probably falsely attributed to Cato. For other arrangements and numbering systems, see the Concordances.

EDITORIAL CONVENTIONS

The Latin texts of the testimonia and fragments have not been taken from the editions of Cato's works adduced as a basis for the arrangement of the material but rather from the most recent and/or most reliable editions of the source authors (listed in the Bibliography), along with precise

[33] For testimonia and fragments relating to Cato's engagement with agriculture, see Speranza 1974, 16–29.

indications of the locations of the passages printed.[34] For all pieces of evidence, as much of the context is given as is necessary for a full understanding and evaluation of the information.

The textual apparatus of the editions consulted has not been copied in full. What is provided here are brief notes on major issues in the transmission affecting the sense and/or the attribution as well as indications as to whether an emendation or conjecture has been accepted into the text or a particular reading of a manuscript is followed. Because of the wide range of source authors, individual manuscripts are not identified by specific sigla; instead, they are referred to as "*cod.*" or "*codd.*," as appropriate.

For source authors represented elsewhere in the Loeb Classical Library, those existing English translations have provided helpful starting points (with thanks to their respective translators), though they have all been updated and adapted for the purposes of this edition. The texts from source authors not (yet) included in the Loeb Classical Library have been newly translated.

Overall, the translations intend to offer readable versions in English and at the same time to retain as much as possible of the individual styles of the many different Greek and Latin sources. Thus, they aim to stay as close as possible to the original version and explicate the meaning of condensed passages by explanatory notes rather than by a free translation.

34 Where references are to the page numbers of a particular edition, the abbreviated last name of the editor is supplied for identification; full details are given in the Bibliography.

Notes on the individual texts confine themselves to points of detail necessary for the understanding of the passage.

For cross-references to other fragments of Cato, F + fragment number are used for fragments of the same literary genre or category; the abbreviated form of the title or category is added for references to fragments in other sections (*Orig.*; *Orat.*; *Op. cet.*; *Inc.*; *Dub.*; *Fals.*). T + number refers to a passage in the Testimonia section.

If the surrounding texts mention other Roman historiographers or orators and speeches, these writers are identified by their full names, their numbers in *FRHist* and *ORF*[4] (on which the volumes on *Oratory* as part of *Fragmentary Republican Latin* in the Loeb Classical Library are based), respectively, and the numbers of specific texts in these editions (T or F + number) where relevant.

In the Latin text, { } indicates deletions, < > marks additions (by modern scholars), and [ ] encloses explanations. Words to be deleted are rarely translated; if so, they are also enclosed in { } in the English version. Meaningful additions to the Latin (beyond individual letters to create a grammatical text) have also been marked in the English by < > (apart from very corrupt texts discussed in notes). Substantial additions to the English version for the sake of clarity have been enclosed in [ ], and square [ ] brackets are again used for explanations.

NOTE ON SCHOLARSHIP

A comprehensive and concise source of information on Cato's life and works (including testimonia and bibliography) is provided by Suerbaum 2002 (in German). A de-

tailed bibliography, especially on scholarship of the twentieth century (including a reprint of the key parts of Suerbaum 2002), is found in Suerbaum 2004 (in German). A complete bibliography (especially of older works) is therefore not attempted in this edition (for bibliographies see also references in note 2).

Standard works on Cato's biography and his literary output are still Astin 1978 and Kienast 1979 (in German); a more recent discussion of Cato's writings can be found in Sciarrino 2011.

An up-to-date introduction to Cato and especially his historiography can be found in *FRHist*. *FRHist* also provides a detailed commentary on all fragments of the *Origines*. Here, only notes necessary for the immediate understanding of the respective fragments are given; thus, scholarly discussion on issues such as the potential meaning, position, or assignment to particular historical events of individual fragments, and the possible implications for Cato's compositional technique, are only offered where required. For such discussions (including references to further bibliography), *FRHist* should be consulted. The presentation of the fragments of the *Origines* in this edition is indebted to the material and discussion in *FRHist* throughout (while other commentaries and annotated editions have also been taken into account).

For the speeches, background information can be found in *ORF*^{4} (in Latin) and in Cugusi and Sblendorio Cugusi 2001 (in Italian). The arrangement of the fragments follows the order in *ORF*^{4}; both editions have been consulted throughout. Again, introductions to the speeches and notes on individual fragments aim to provide what is necessary for an immediate understanding,

but refrain from often speculative detailed discussion. Here, since the standard editions are less comprehensive and up to date, more references to scholarship on details are provided where relevant.

The minor works have received less attention in scholarship. The reference edition for these is still that of Jordan (1860), now supplemented by that of Cugusi and Sblendorio Cugusi (2001). Brief discussions of the current state of play can be found in the introduction to *FRHist* (2013) and especially in Suerbaum (2002, in German, with further references to bibliography) as well as a few scattered articles, noted where appropriate.

ABBREVIATIONS AND SYMBOLS

TYPES OF NUMBERS

T + number (e.g., T 1): testimonium
F + number (e.g., F 4): sequentially numbered "fragment" in a particular category
T or F + number + lower-case letter (e.g., T 11a or F 1b): different sources for the same piece of information or "fragment"
F + number + capital letter (for speeches) (e.g., F 17A): "fragment" added to those given in *ORF*[4]

CROSS-REFERENCES

F + number (e.g., F 4): cross-reference to a "fragment" in the same category
abbreviated title of category + F + number (e.g., *Orig.* F 135 or *Orat.* F 155): cross-reference to a "fragment" in another category

NUMBERING

Origines: F numbered according to *FRHist*
Orationes: F numbered according to *ORF*[4]

Testimonia and other works: new arrangement according to the chronology of transmitting authors for each category (see Concordances) and new sequential numbering for each major group (Testimonia; *Opera cetera*; *Incertorum operum reliquiae*; *Fragmenta dubiae auctoritatis*; *Fragmenta Catoni falso attributa*)

REFERENCE WORKS

CCMR Pina Polo, Francisco. *Las contiones civiles y militares en Roma*. Zaragoza, 1989.

LPPR Rotondi, Giovanni. *Leges publicae populi Romani. Elenco cronologico con una introduzione sull'attività legislativa dei comizi romani. Estratto dalla Enciclopedia Giuridia Italiana*. Milano, 1912. Reprint, Hildesheim, 1966; with supplement from Giovanni Rotondi. *Scritti Giuridici I*. Milano, 1922.

MRR Broughton, T. R. S. *The Magistrates of the Roman Republic.* 3 vols. Philological Monographs XV, vols. 1–3. New York, 1951–1986.

RE Pauly, August Friedrich, Georg Wissowa et al., eds. *Real-Encyclopädie der classischen Altertumswissenschaft*. Stuttgart, 1893–1980.

TLRR Alexander, Michael C. *Trials in the Late Roman Republic, 149 BC to 50 BC*. Phoenix Suppl. XXVI. Toronto / Buffalo / London, 1990.

COLLECTIONS OF FRAGMENTS AND OF GRAMMATICAL AND RHETORICAL TEXTS

FGrHist — *Die Fragmente der griechischen Historiker*, ed. Felix Jacoby. Berlin, 1923–.

FPL[4] — *Fragmenta poetarum Latinorum epicorum et lyricorum praeter Enni Annales et Ciceronis Germanicique Aratea*, post W. Morel et K. Büchner editionem quartam auctam curavit Jürgen Blänsdorf. Berlin, 2011.

FRHist — *The Fragments of the Roman Historians*, ed. T. J. Cornell. Oxford, 2013.

FRL — *Fragmentary Republican Latin*. Loeb Classical Library. Cambridge, MA / London, 2018ff.

GL — *Grammatici Latini*, ex recensione Henrici Keilii. 7 vols. Leipzig, 1855–1880.

GRF — *Grammaticae Romanae fragmenta*, collegit, recensuit Hyginus Funaioli. Leipzig. 1907.

HRR — *Historicorum Romanorum reliquiae*, iteratis curis collegit, disposuit, recensuit, praefatus est Hermannus Peter. 2 vols. Leipzig, 1914–1916. Reprint, with bibliographical editions, by J. Kroymann. Stuttgart, 1967, 1993.

ORF[4] — *Oratorum Romanorum Fragmenta liberae rei publicae quartum edidit H. Malcovati. I—Textus*. Corpus Scriptorum Latinorum Paravianum. Aug. Taurinorum / Mediolani / Patavii / Bononiae / Florentiae / Aterni / Romae / Neapoli / Barii / Panormi, 1976.

RLM — *Rhetores Latini minores. Ex codicibus maximam partem primum adhibitis emendabat*. Carolus Halm. Leipzig, 1863.

TrRF — *Tragicorum Romanorum fragmenta*. Vols. I–II. Göttingen, 2012.

BRACKETS

{ } deletions (by modern scholars)

< > additions (by modern scholars)

[ ] explanations and substantial additions to the English version

BIBLIOGRAPHY

1. EDITIONS INCLUDING FRAGMENTS OF CATO

Beck, Hans, and Uwe Walter, eds. *Die frühen römischen Historiker. Band I. Von Fabius Pictor bis Cn. Gellius. Herausgegeben, übersetzt und kommentiert*. Texte zur Forschung 76. Darmstadt, 2001.

Calboli, Gualtiero, ed. *Marci Porci Catonis Oratio pro Rhodiensibus. Catone, l'oriente greco e gli impenditori romani. Introduzione, edizione critica dei frammenti, traduzione e commento*. Edizioni e saggi universitari di filologia classica 18. Bologna, 1978, [2]2003.

Chassignet, Martine, ed. *Caton, Les origines (fragments). Texte établi, traduit et commenté*. CUF. Paris, 1986.

Cornell, T. J., ed. *The Fragments of the Roman Historians*. 3 vols. Oxford, 2013 [*FRHist*].

Courtney, Edward, ed. *Archaic Latin Prose*. American Philological Association, American Classical Studies 42. Atlanta, 1999.

Cugusi, Paolo, ed. *Epistolographi Latini minores. Vol. I, Aetatem Anteciceronianam amplectens*. 2 vols. Corpus Scriptorum Latinorum Paravianum. Aug. Taurinorum / Mediolani / Patavii / Bononiae / Florentiae / Aterni / Romae / Neapoli / Barii / Panormi, 1970.

Cugusi, Paolo, and Maria Teresa Cugusi Sblendorio, eds. *Opere di Marco Porcio Catone Censore*. 2 vols. Classici latini. Torino, 2001.

Della Corte, Francesco. *Plutarco. Detti e Vita di Catone. Introduzione e commento. Seconda edizione*. Collezione di Classici Greci e Latini. Torino, 1953.

Garbarino, Giovanna, ed. *Roma e la filosofia greca dalle origini alla fine del II seccolo a. C. Raccolta di testi con introduzione e commento*. 2 vols. Historica, Politica, Philosophica. Il pensiero antico—Studi e testi 6. Torino / Milano / Genova / Padova / Bologna / Firenze / Pescara / Roma / Napoli / Bari / Palermo, 1973.

Horsfall, Nicholas, ed. *Cornelius Nepos. A selection, Including the Lives of Cato and Atticus. Translated with Introductions and Commentary*. Clarendon Ancient History Series. Oxford, 1989.

Iordan [Jordan], Henricus, ed. *M. Catonis praeter librum De re rustica quae extant Henricus Iordan recensuit et prolegomena scripsit*. Leipzig, 1860. Reprint, Stuttgart 1967.

Malcovati, Henrica, ed. *Oratorum Romanorum Fragmenta liberae rei publicae quartum edidit. I—Textus*. Corpus Scriptorum Latinorum Paravianum. Aug. Taurinorum / Mediolani / Patavii / Bononiae / Florentiae / Aterni / Romae / Neapoli / Barii / Panormi, 1976 [*ORF*[4]].

———, ed. *Oratorum Romanorum Fragmenta liberae rei publicae quartum edidit. II—Index verborum, e scidulis ab † Helmut Gugel collectis compositus ab Helmuth Vretska adiuvante Carolo Vretska*. Corpus Scriptorum Latinorum Paravianum. Aug. Taurinorum / Mediolani / Patavii / Bononiae / Florentiae / Aterni / Romae / Neapoli / Barii / Panormi, 1979 [*ORF*[4]: index].

Meyer, Henricus, ed. *Oratorum Romanorum Fragmenta ab Appio inde Caeco et M. Porcio Catone usque ad Q. Aurelium Symmachum. Collegit atque illustravit. Editio auctior et emendatior*. Zürich, 1842.

Pastorino, Agostino. *Plutarco. Detti e Vita di Catone Maggiore. Introduzione, testo e commento*. Torino, 1951.

Peter, Hermannus, ed. *Historicorum Romanorum reliquiae, iteratis curis disposuit, recensuit, praefatus est*. 2 vols. Leipzig, 1914–1916. Reprint, with bibliographical editions, by J. Kroymann. Stuttgart, 1967, 1993 [*HRR*].

Sansone, David, ed. *Plutarch. The Lives of Aristeides and Cato. Edited with Translation and Commentary*. Warminster, 1989.

Sblendorio Cugusi, Maria Teresa, ed. *M. Porci Catonis orationum reliquiae. Introduzione, testo critico e commento filologico*. Historia, Politica, Philosophica. Il pensiero antico. Studi e testi 12. Torino / Milano / Genova / Padova / Bologna / Firenze / Pescara / Roma / Napoli / Bari / Tropea / Catania / Palermo, 1982.

Schönberger, Otto, ed. *Marcus Porcius Cato. Vom Landbau, Fragmente. Lateinisch-deutsch. Hg. u. übers.* 2., überarb. Aufl. Sammlung Tusculum. Düsseldorf / Zürich, 2000.

Schröder, Wilt Aden, ed. *M. Porcius Cato. Das erste Buch der Origines. Ausgabe und Erklärung der Fragmente*. Beiträge zur Klassischen Philologie 41. Meisenheim am Glan, 1971.

Speranza, Felicianus, ed. *Scriptorum Romanorum de re rustica reliquiae collegit, recensuit. Volumen prius*. Biblioteca di Helikon, Testi e studi 8. Messina, ^{2}1974.

Wagener, Augustus, ed. *M. Porcii Catonis Originum fragmenta emendata disposita illustrata*. Diss., Bonn, 1849.

2. EDITIONS OF TRANSMITTING AUTHORS

2.1. Ammianus Marcellinus (Amm. Marc.)

Seyfarth, Wolfgang, ed. *Ammiani Marcellini Rerum gestarum libri qui supersunt. Ed. Wolfgang Seyfarth, adiuvantibus Liselotte Jacob-Karau et Ilse Ulmann. Vol. I. Libri XIV–XXV*. Stuttgart / Leipzig, 1999 (ed. stereotypa editionis anni MCMLXXVIII).

2.2. Ampelius (Ampel.)

Assmann, Erwin, ed. *Lucii Ampelii liber memorialis*. Stuttgart, 1976 (ed. stereotypa editionis anni MCMXXXV).

2.3. Appian (App.)

Mendelssohn, Ludwig, and Paul Viereck, eds. *Appiani Historia Romana. Ex recensione Ludovici Mendelssohnii*. 2 vols. Leipzig, 1879–1881. *Editio altera correctior curante Paulo Viereck. Volumen alterum*. Leipzig, 1905.

2.4. Apuleius (Apul.)

Helm, Rudolf, ed. *Apulei Platonici Madaurensis opera quae supersunt. Vol. II, Fasc. 1. Pro se de magia liber (apologia)*. Editio stereotypa editionis alterius cum addendis. Leipzig, 1959 [^{1}1905, ^{2}1912, ^{4}1963, repr.].

2.5. Aurelius Augustinus (August.)

Martin, Ioseph, and K.-D. Daur, eds. *Sancti Aurelii Augustini De doctrina Christiana, De vera religione*. CCSL XXXII, Aur. Aug. Op. Pars IV,1. Turnhout, 1962.

2.6. Pseudo-Augustinus (Ps.-August.)

Mai, Angelus, ed. *Novae Patrum Bibliothecae Tomus Primus, continens Sancti Augustini novos ex codicibus Vaticanis Sermones, item eiusdem speculum et alia quaedam cum diversorum patrum scriptis et tabulis XVI.* Roma, 1852.

2.7. *Carmina Latina Epigraphica* (CLE)

Buecheler, Franciscus, and Alexander Riese, eds. *Anthologia Latina sive Poesis Latinae Supplementum. Pars posterior: Carmina epigraphica. Conlegit Franciscus Buecheler. Fasciculus II*. Leipzig, 1897.

2.8. Cassiodorus (Cassiod.)

Mommsen, Theodorus, ed. *Cassiodori senatoris Variae. Recensuit T. M. Accedunt I. Epistulae Theodericianae variae. Ed. T. M. II. Acta synhodorum habitarum Romae A. CCCCXCVIIII. DI. DII. Ed. T. M. III. Cassiodori Orationum reliquiae. Ed. Lud. Traube. Accedunt Tabulae duae*. MGH, AA XII. Berlin, 1894.

2.9. Flavius Sosipater Charisius (Charis.)

Barwick, Carolus, ed. *Flavii Sosipatri Charisii artis grammaticae libri V.* Edidit C. B. Addenda et corrigenda collegit et adiecit F. Kühnert. Leipzig, 1964. Reprint, Stuttgart / Leipzig, 1997.

Keil, Henricus, ed. *Grammatici Latini. Vol. I. Flavii Sosipatri Charisii Artis grammaticae libri V, Diomedis Artis grammaticae libri III, ex Charisii arte grammatic excerpta*. Leipzig, 1857.

2.10. M. Tullius Cicero (Cic.)

Clark, Albertus Curtis, ed. *M. Tulli Ciceronis orationes.* [*IV*]. *Pro P. Quinctio, Pro Q. Roscio comoedo, Pro A. Caecina, De lege agraria contra Rullum, Pro C. Rabirio perduellionis reo, Pro L. Flacco, In L. Pisonem, Pro C. Rabirio Postumo. Recognovit brevique adnotatione critica instruxit.* Oxford, 1909 (repr.).

———, ed. *M. Tulli Ciceronis orationes* [*VI*]. *Pro Tullio, Pro Fonteio, Pro Sulla, Pro Archia, Pro Plancio, Pro Scauro. Recognovit brevique adnotatione critica instruxit*. Oxford, 1911.

Giomini, Remo, ed. *M. Tulli Ciceronis scripta quae manserunt omnia. Fasc. 46. De divinatione, de fato, Timaeus*. Leipzig, 1975.

Giusta, Michelangelus, ed. *M. Tulli Ciceronis Tusculanae disputationes*. Torino, 1984.

Kumaniecki, Kazimierz F., ed. *M. Tulli Ciceronis scripta quae manserunt omnia. Fasc. 3. De oratore*. Leipzig, 1969.

Malcovati, Henrica, ed. *M. Tulli Ciceronis scripta quae manserunt omnia. Fasc. 4. Brutus*. Leipzig, 1965.

Peterson, Gulielmus, ed. *M. Tulli Ciceronis Orationes* [*III*]. *Divinatio in Q. Caecilium, In C. Verrem. Recognovit brevique adnotatione critica instruxit. Editio altera, recognita et emendata*. Oxford, 1917 [[1]1907].

Powell, J. G. F., ed. M. *Tulli Ciceronis De re publica, De legibus, Cato maior de senectute, Laelius de amicitia. Recognovit brevique adnotatione critica instruxit*. Oxford, 2006.

Stroebel, Eduard, ed., *M. Tulli Ciceronis scripta quae*

manserunt omnia. Fasc. 2. Rhetorici libri duo qui vocantur de inventione. Leipzig, 1915.

Westman, Rolf, ed. *M. Tulli Ciceronis scripta quae manserunt omnia. Fasc. 5. Orator*. Leipzig, 1980.

Winterbottom, Michael, ed. *M. Tulli Ciceronis De officiis. Recognovit brevique adnotatione critica instruxit*. Oxford, 1994.

2.11. L. Iunius Moderatus Columella (Columella)

Rodgers, R. H., ed. *L. Iuni Moderati Columellae Res rustica, Incerti auctoris Liber de arboribus. Recognovit brevique adnotatione critica instruxit*. Oxford, 2010.

2.12. *De adtributis personae et negotio*

Halm, Carolus, ed. *Rhetores Latini minores. Ex codicibus maximam partem primum adhibitis emendabat*. Leipzig, 1863.

2.13. *De dubiis nominibus*

Keil, Henricus, ed. *Grammatici Latini. Vol. V. Artium scriptores minores. Cledonius, Pompeius, Iulianus, Excerpta ex commentariis in Donatum, Consentius, Phocas, Eutyches, Augustinus, Palaemon, Asper, De nomine et pronomine, De dubiis nominibus*. Leipzig, 1868.

2.14. *De scientia politica*

Mazzucchi, Carolus Maria, ed. *Menae patricii cum Thoma referendario De scientia politica dialogus quae exstant in codice Vaticano palimpsesto*. Milano, 1982.

2.15. *Digesta* (*Dig.*)

Mommsen, Theodorus, ed. *Corpus Iuris Civilis. Volumen primum. Institutiones recognovit Paulus Krueger, Digesta recognovit Theodorus Mommsen*. Berlin, 1872.

2.16. Diomedes (Diom.)

Keil, Henricus, ed. *Grammatici Latini. Vol. I. Flavii Sosipatri Charisii Artis grammaticae libri V, Diomedis Artis grammaticae libri III, ex Charisii arte grammatica excerpta*. Leipzig, 1857.

2.17. Dionysius Halicarnaseus (Dion. Hal.)

Jacoby, Carolus, ed. *Dionysi Halicarnasensis Antiquitatum Romanarum quae supersunt. Volumen primum*. Leipzig, 1885.

———, ed. *Dionysii Halicarnasei Antiquitatum Romanarum quae supersunt. Vol. II. Editio stereotypa editionis primae (MDCCCLXXXVIII)*. Stuttgart / Leipzig, 1997.

2.18. Aelius Donatus (Don.)

Wessner, Paulus, ed. *Aeli Donati quod fertur Commentum Terenti, accedunt Eugraphi commentum et Scholia Bembina. Vol. II*. Leipzig, 1905.

2.19. *Excerpta rhetorica*

Halm, Carolus, ed. *Rhetores Latini minores. Ex codicibus maximam partem primum adhibitis emendabat*. Leipzig, 1863.

2.20. Q. Fabius Laurentius Victorinus (Fab. Laur. Vict.)

Halm, Carolus, ed. *Rhetores Latini minores. Ex codicibus maximam partem primum adhibitis emendabat*. Leipzig, 1863.

2.21. Sex. Pompeius Festus (Fest.) et Paulus (Paul. *Fest.*)

Lindsay, Wallace M., ed. *Sexti Pompei Festi De verborum significatu quae supersunt cum Pauli Epitome*. Leipzig, 1913. Reprint, Hildesheim / New York, 1965.

2.22. Consultus Fortunatianus (Cons. Fortun.)

Calboli Montefusco, Lucia, ed. *Consulti Fortunatiani Ars rhetorica. Introduzione, edizione critica, traduzione italiana e commento*. Edizioni e saggi universitari di filologica classica 24. Bologna, 1979.

Halm, Carolus, ed. *Rhetores Latini minores. Ex codicibus maximam partem primum adhibitis emendabat*. Leipzig, 1863.

2.23. Frontinus (Frontin.)

Ireland, Robert I., ed. *Iulii Frontini Strategemata recensuit*. Leipzig, 1990.

2.24. M. Cornelius Fronto (Fronto)

van den Hout, Michael J. P., ed. *M. Cornelii Frontonis epistulae schedis tam editis quam ineditis Emundi Hauleri usus iterum edidit*. Leipzig, 1988.

2.25. Q. Gargilius Martialis

Maire, Brigitte, ed. *Gargilius Martialis. Les remèdes tirés des légumes et des fruits. Texte établi, traduit et commenté*. CUF. Paris, 2002.

2.26. Aulus Gellius (Gell.)

Holford-Strevens, Leofranc, ed. *Auli Gelli Noctes Atticae, recognitae brevique adnotatione critica instructae*. 2 vols. Oxford, 2020.

2.27. Hieronymus / Jerome (Hieron.)

Hilberg, Isidorus, ed. *Sancti Eusebii Hieronymi Epistulae. Pars I: Epistulae I–LXX*. CSEL LIV; S. Eusebii Hieronymi opera I.I. Wien / Leipzig, 1910. Reprint, New York / London, 1961; ed. altera suppl. aucta.

2.28. Q. Horatius Flaccus (Hor.)

Shackleton Bailey, D. R., ed., *Q. Horati Flacci opera*. Stuttgart, 1985.

2.29. Hyginus (Hyg.)

Marshall, Peter K., ed. *Hygini Fabulae*. Stuttgart / Leipzig, 1993.

2.30. Isidorus (Isid.)

Codoñer, Carmen, ed. *Isidoro de Sevilla. Diferencias. Libro I. Introducción, Edición crítica, traducción y notas*. Collection Auteurs latin du moyen âge 8. Paris, 1992.

Lindsay, Wallace M., ed. *Isidori Hispalensis Episcopi Ety-*

mologiarum sive originum libri XX. Recognovit brevique adnotatione critica instruxit. 2 vols. Oxford, 1911.

2.31. Iulius Rufinianus (Iul. Rufin.)

Halm, Carolus, ed. *Rhetores Latini minores. Ex codicibus maximam partem primum adhibitis emendabat*. Leipzig, 1863.

2.32. Iulius Victor (Iul. Vict.)

Giomini, Remo, and Maria Silvana Celentano, eds. *C. Iulii Victoris Ars rhetorica*. Leipzig, 1980.

Halm, Carolus, ed. *Rhetores Latini minores. Ex codicibus maximam partem primum adhibitis emendabat*. Leipzig, 1863.

2.33. M. Iunianus Iustinus (Iust.)

Seel, Otto, ed. *M. Iuniani Iustini Epitoma Historiarum Philippicarum Pompei Trogi. Accedunt prologi in Pompeium Trogum. Post Franciscum Ruehl iterum edidit*. Stuttgart, 1972.

2.34. T. Livius (Liv.)

Briscoe, John, ed. *Titi Livi ab urbe condita. Libri XXXI–XL. Tomus I. Libri XXXI–XXXV*. Stuttgart, 1991.

———, ed. *Titi Livi ab urbe condita. Libri XXXI–XL. Tomus II. Libri XXXVI–XL*. Stuttgart, 1991.

———, ed. *Titi Livi ab urbe condita. Libri XLI–XLV*. Stuttgart, 1986.

Rossbach, Otto, ed. *T. Livi Periochae omnium librorum, fragmenta Oxyrhynchi reperta, Iulii Obsequentis prodigiorum liber*. Leipzig, 1910.

Walsh, Patrick G. *Titi Livi ab urbe condita. Libri XXVIII–XXX*. Stuttgart, 1986.

2.35. Ioannes Lydus (Lydus)

Bandy, Anastasius C., ed. *Ioannes Lydus, on Powers or the Magistracies of the Roman State. Introduction, Critical Text, Translation, Commentary, and Indices*. Memoirs of the American Philosophical Society 149. Philadelphia, 1983.

Wuensch, Ricardus, ed. *Ioannis Laurentii Lydi Liber de mensibus*. Leipzig, 1898.

2.36. Ambrosius Theodosius Macrobius (Macrob.)

Kaster, R. A., ed. *Ambrosii Theodosii Macrobii Saturnalia. Recognovit brevique adnotatione critica instruxit*. Oxford, 2011.

2.37. Marius Victorinus

Keil, Henricus, ed. *Grammatici Latini. Vol. VI. Scriptores artis metricae. Marius Victorinus, Maximus Victorinus, Caesius Bassus, Atilius Fortunatianus, Terentianus Maurus, Marius Plotius Sacerdos, Rufinus, Mallius Theodorus, Fragmenta et excerpta metrica*. Leipzig, 1874.

2.38. Mythographus Vaticanus Primus (Myth. Vat. Prim.)

Zorzetti, Nevio, and Jacques Berlioz, eds. *Le premier mythographe du Vatican. Texte établie par N. Z. et traduit per J. B.* CUF Lat. 328. Paris, 1995.

2.39. Cornelius Nepos (Nep.)

Marshall, Peter K., ed. *Cornelii Nepotis vitae cum fragmentis*. Leipzig, 1977.

2.40. Nonius Marcellus (Non.)

Lindsay, Wallace M., ed. *Nonii Marcelli De compendiosa doctrina libros XX, Onionsianis copiis usus edidit*. 3 vols. Leipzig, 1903. Reprint, Hildesheim, 1964.

2.41. *Origo gentis Romanae* (*Orig. gent. Rom.*)

Pichlmayr, Franciscus, and R. Gruendel, eds. *Sexti Aurelii Victoris Liber de Caesaribus. Praecedunt Origo gentis Romanae et Liber de viris illustribus urbis Romae. Subsequitur Epitome de Caesaribus. Recensuit F. P. Editio stereotypa correctior editionis primae, addenda et corrigenda iterum collegit et adiecit R. G.* Leipzig, 1966.

2.42. Osbern

Bertini, Ferruccio, and Vincenzo Ussani, Jr., eds. *Osberno, Derivazioni. A cura di Paola Busdraghi, Maria Chiabó, Andrea Dessì Fulgheri, Paolo Gatti, Rosanna Mazzacane, Luciana Roberti sotto la direzione di Ferruccio Bertini e Vincenzo Ussani jr.* 2 vols. Biblioteca di Medioevo Latino 16. Spoleto, 1996.

2.43. Panegyrici Latini (Pan. Lat.)

Mynors, R. A. B., ed. *XII Panegyrici Latini. Recognovit brevique adnotatione critica instruxit.* Oxford, 1964.

2.44. Paradoxographus Palatinus

Giannini, Alexander, ed. *Paradoxographorum Graecorum reliquiae. Recognovit, brevi adnotatione critica instruxit, latine reddidit*. Classici greci e latini, Sezione testi e commenti 3. Milano, 1966.

2.45. C. Plinius Secundus maior (Plin.)

Mayhoff, Carolus, ed. *C. Plini Secundi Naturalis Historiae libri XXXVII. Post Ludovici Iani obitum recognovit et scripturae discrepantia adiecta edidit*. 6 vols. Leipzig, 1892–1906.

2.46. C. Plinius Caecilius Secundus minor (Plin.)

Mynors, R. A. B., ed. *C. Plini Caecili Secundi Epistularum libri decem. Recognovit brevique adnotatione critica instruxit*. Oxford, 1963.

2.47. Plutarch (Plut.)

Hubert, Kurt, Max Pohlenz, and Hans Drexler, eds. *Plutarchi Moralia. Vol. V, Fasc. I. Recensuit et emendavit C. H., Praefationem scripsit M. P. Editio altera correctior, addenda adiecit H. D. Editio stereotypa editionis secundae (MCMLX)*. München / Leipzig, 2001.

Nachstädt, Wilhelm, Wilhelm Sieveking, and J. B. Titchener, eds. *Plutarchi Moralia. Vol. II. Recensuerunt et emendaverunt*. Leipzig, 1971.

Ziegler, Konrat, and Hans Gärtner, eds. *Plutarchi Vitae parallelae. Vol. I, Fasc. I. Quartum recensuit K. Z.*

Editionem quintam curavit H. G. München / Leipzig, 2000.

———, eds. *Plutarchi Vitae parallelae. Vol. II, Fasc. II. Iterum recensuit K. Z. Editionem correctiorem cum addendis curavit H. G.* Stuttgart / Leipzig, 1994.

2.48. Pompeius (Pomp.)

Keil, Henricus, ed. *Grammatici Latini. Vol. V. Artium scriptores minores. Cledonius, Pompeius, Iulianus, Excerpta ex commentariis in Donatum, Consentius, Phocas, Eutyches, Augustinus, Palaemon, Asper, De nomine et pronomine, De dubiis nominibus.* Leipzig, 1868.

2.49. Porphyrios (Porph.)

Schrader, Hermannus, ed. *Porphyrii Quaestionum Homericarum ad Iliadem pertinentium reliquias collegit, disposuit, edidit. Fasc. 1.* Leipzig, 1880.

2.50. Priscianus (Prisc.)

Hertz, Martinus, ed. *Grammatici Latini. Vol. II / III. Prisciani grammatici Caesariensis Institutionum grammaticarum libri XVIII.* Leipzig, 1855 / 1859.

Keil, Henricus, ed. *Grammatici Latini. Vol. III. Prisciani grammatici Caesariensis De figuris numerorum, De metris Terentii, De praeexercitamentis rhetoricis libri, Institutio de nomine et pronomine et verbo, Partitiones duodecim versuum Aeneidos principalium. Accedit Prisciani qui dicitur liber de accentibus.* Leipzig, 1859.

2.51. M. Fabius Quintilianus (Quint.)

Winterbottom, Michael, ed. *M. Fabi Quintiliani Institutionis oratoriae libri duodecim. Recognovit brevique adnotatione critica instruxit*. 2 vols. Oxford, 1970.

2.52. *Rhetorica ad Herennium* (*Rhet. Her.*)

Calboli, Gualtiero, ed. *Cornifici seu Incerti Auctoris Rhetorica ad C. Herennium. Vol. I: Prolegomena, testo e traduzione*. Sammlung wissenschaftlicher Kommentare. Berlin / Boston, 2020.

2.53. Sallust (Sall.)

Reynolds, L. D., ed. *C. Sallusti Crispi Catilina, Iugurtha, Historiarum fragmenta selecta, Appendix Sallustiana. Recognovit brevique adnotatione critica instruxit.* Oxford, 1991.

2.54. Iosephus Iustus Scaliger

Iosephi Scaligeri Iulii Caesaris filii *Coniectanea in M. Terentium Varronem De lingua Latina ad nobiliss. & eruditiss. iuvenem Ludovicum Castanaeum Rupipozaeum*. Paris, 1565.

2.55. Scholia Vallicelliana ad Isidori *Origines* (Schol. ad Isid. *Orig.*)

Lindsay, W. M., and J. W. Pirie, eds. *Glossaria Latina IV: Placidus, Festus*. Paris, 1930 (repr.).

2.56. Scholiastae et Commentatores Ciceronis (Schol. Bob.; Ps.-Asc.; Grillius)

Jakobi, Rainer, ed. *Commentum in Ciceronis Rhetorica.* Leipzig, 2011.

Stangl, Thomas, ed. *Ciceronis Orationum Scholiastae. Asconius. Scholia Bobiensia. Scholia Pseudasconii Sangallensia. Scholia Cluniacensia et recentiora Ambrosiana ac Vaticana. Scholia Lugdunensia sive Gronoviana et eorum excerpta Lugdunensia. Volumen II: Commentarios continens.* Wien / Leipzig, 1912.

2.57. Scholiastae et Commentatores Horatii (Ps.-Acr.)

Keller, Otto, ed. *Pseudacronis scholia in Horatium vetustiora.* 2 vols. Leipzig, 1902 / 1904.

2.58. Scholiastae et Commentatores Vergili (Schol. Veron.; Probus; Philargyrius)

Baschera, Claudio, ed. *Gli scholii veronesi a Virgilio. Introduzione, edizione critica e indici.* Verona, 1999.

Hagen, Hermannus, ed. *Servii Grammatici qui feruntur in Vergilii carmina commentarii. Vol. III. Fasc. II. Appendix Serviana. Ceteros praeter Servium et Scholia Bernensia Vergilii commentatores continens. Recensuit.* Leipzig, 1902. Reprint, Leipzig, 1927.

2.59. Scriptores Historiae Augustae (SHA)

Hohl, Ernst, Christa Samberger, and Wolfgang Seyfarth, eds. *Scriptores Historiae Augustae. Ed. E. H. Addenda*

et corrigenda adiecerunt C. S. et W. S. 2 vols. Leipzig, [5/3]1971. Reprint, 1997.

2.60. L. Annaeus Seneca maior (Sen.)

Håkanson, Lennart, ed. *L. Annaeus Seneca maior. Oratorum et rhetorum sententiae, divisiones, colores. Recensuit.* Leipzig, 1989.

2.61. L. Annaeus Seneca minor (Sen.)

Hosius, Carolus, ed. *L. Annaei Senecae opera quae supersunt. Vol. 1. Fasc. 2. L. Annaei Senecae De beneficiis libri VII*. Leipzig, 1900.

Reynolds, L. D., ed., *L. Annaei Seneca ad Lucilium Epistulae morales. Recognovit et adnotatione critica instruxit*. 2 vols. Oxford, 1965.

———, ed. *L. Annaei Seneca Dialogorum libri duodecim. Recognovit brevique adnotatione critica instruxit*. Oxford, 1977.

2.62. [Sergius]

Keil, Henricus, and Theodorus Mommsen, eds. *Grammatici Latini. Vol. IV. Probi Donati Servii qui feruntur De arte grammatica libri ex recensione H. K. Notarum laterculi ex recensione T. M.* Leipzig, 1864.

2.63. Servius (Serv. et Serv. auct.)

Keil, Henricus, and Theodorus Mommsen, eds. *Grammatici Latini. Vol. IV. Probi Donati Servii qui feruntur De arte grammatica libri ex recensione H. K. Notarum laterculi ex recensione T. M.* Leipzig, 1864.

Thilo, Georgius, ed. *Servii grammatici qui feruntur in Vergilii carmina commentarii. Vol. I. Aeneidos librorum I–V commentarii*. Leipzig / Berlin, 1881. Reprint, Leipzig / Berlin, 1923.

———, ed. *Servii grammatici qui feruntur in Vergilii carmina commentarii. Vol. II. Aeneidos librorum VI–XII commentarii*. Leipzig / Berlin, 1884. Reprint, Leipzig / Berlin, 1923.

———, ed. *Servii Grammatici qui feruntur in Vergilii carmina commentarii. Vol. III, Fasc. 1. In Bucolica et Georgica commentarii*. Leipzig, 1887. Reprint, Leipzig, 1927; Hildesheim, 1961.

2.64. C. Iulius Solinus (Solin.)

Mommsen, Theodorus, ed. *C. Iulii Solini Collectanea reum memorabilium. Iterum recensuit*. Berlin, 1895.

2.65. C. Suetonius Tranquillus (Suet.)

Kaster, R. A., ed. *C. Suetoni Tranquilli De vita Caesarum libros VIII et De grammaticis et rhetoribus librum. Recognovit brevique adnotatione critica instruxit*. Oxford, 2016.

2.66. Sulpicius Victor (Sulp. Vict.)

Halm, Carolus, ed. *Rhetores Latini minores. Ex codicibus maximam partem primum adhibitis emendabat*. Leipzig, 1863.

2.67. Symmachus (Symm.)

Seeck, Otto, ed. *Q. Aurelii Symmachi quae supersunt*. MGH, AA VI 1. Berlin, 1883.

2.68. P. Cornelius Tacitus (Tac.)

Heubner, Henricus, ed. *P. Cornelii Taciti libri qui supersunt. Tom. II, Fasc. 4. Dialogus de oratoribus*. Stuttgart, 1983.

2.69. Ioannes Tzetzes (Tzetz.)

Gaisford, Thomas, ed. *Poetae minores Graeci. Praecipua lectionis varietate et indicibus locupletissimis instruxit. Vol. III*. Oxford, 1820.

2.70. Valerius Maximus (Val. Max.)

Briscoe, John, ed. *Valeri Maximi Facta ed dicta memorabilia*. 2 vols. Stuttgart, 1998.

2.71. M. Terentius Varro (Varro)

Flach, Dieter, ed. and trans. *Marcus Terentius Varro. Gespräche über die Landwirtschaft. Herausgegeben, übersetzt und erläutert*. 3 vols. Texte zur Forschung 65–67. Darmstadt, 1996–2002.

De Melo, Wolfgang, ed. and trans. *Varro De Lingua Latina*. 2 vols. Oxford, 2019.

2.72. P. Flavius Vegetius Renatus (Veg.)

Reeve, Michael D., ed. *Vegetius, Epitoma rei militaris. Recognovit brevique adnotatione critica instruxit*. Oxford, 2004.

2.73. Velleius Paterculus (Vell. Pat.)

Watt, W. S., ed. *Velleii Paterculi Historiarum ad M. Vinicium consulem libri duo. Recognovit. Editio correctior editionis primae (MCMLXXXVIII)*. Stuttgart / Leipzig, 1998.

2.74. *Liber de viris illustribus urbis Romae* ([Aurel. Vict.] *Vir. ill.*)

Pichlmayr, Franciscus, and R. Gruendel, eds. *Sexti Aurelii Victoris Liber de Caesaribus. Praecedunt Origo gentis Romanae et Liber de viris illustribus urbis Romae. Subsequitur Epitome de Caesaribus. Recensuit F. P. Editio stereotypa correctior editionis primae, addenda et corrigenda iterum collegit et adiecit R. G.* Leipzig, 1966.

3. SECONDARY LITERATURE AND EDITIONS OF OTHER AUTHORS

Agache, Sylvie. "Caton le Censeur, les fortunes d'une légende." In *Colloque histoire et historiographie. Clio*, edited by R. Chevallier, 71–107. *Caesarodunum* XV bis. Paris, 1980.

Agnew, Malcom E. "A Numbered Legion in a Fragment of the Elder Cato." *AJPh* 60 (1939): 214–19.

von Albrecht, Michael. *Meister römischer Prosa von Cato bis Apuleius*. Darmstadt, [4]2012.

Alfonsi, Luigi. "Discussioni su letteratura storiografica 'inconnue.'" *Studi Urbinati* 49 B 1 (Atti del convegno: Gli

storiografi latini tramandati in frammenti [Urbino, 9–11 maggio 1974]) (1975): 39–47.

Astin, Alan E. *Cato the Censor*. Oxford, 1978.

Badian, E. "The Early Historians." In *Latin Historians*, edited by T. A. Dorey, 1–38. Studies in Latin Literature and Its Influence. London, 1966.

Baltrusch, Ernst. *Regimen morum. Die Reglementierung des Privatlebnes der Senatoren und Ritter in der römischen Republick und frühen Kaiserzeit.* Vestigia 41. München, 1989.

Barwick, Karl. "Zu den Schriften des Cornelius Celsus und des alten Cato." *WJA* 3 (1948): 117–32.

Barzanò, Alberto. "Catone il Vecchio e il processo contro Manio Acilio Glabrione candidato alla censura (189 a.C.)." In *Processi e politica nel mondo antico*, edited by Marta Sordi, 129–44. Contributi dell'Istituto di storia antica 22. Milano, 1996.

Baumgart, Max Oskar. *Untersuchungen zu den Reden des M. Porcius Cato Censorius. I. Teil. Litterar-historische Untersuchungen zu den Reden Catos des Älteren*. Diss., Breslau, 1905.

Boas, Marcus. "Die Epistola Catonis." *Verhandelingen der Koninklijke Akademie van Wetenschappen te Amsterdam, Afdeeling Letterkunde, Nieuwe Reeks. Deel XXXIII. No.* 1. Amsterdam, 1934.

———, ed. *Disticha Catonis. Recensuit et apparatu critico instruxit Marcus Boas. Opus post Marci Boas mortem edendum curavit Henricus Johannes Botschuyver*. Amsterdam, 1952.

Bömer, Franz. "Thematik und Krise der römischen Geschichtsschreibung im 2. Jahrhundert v. Chr." *Historia* 2 (1953): 189–209.

Bond, R. P. "Anti-feminism in Juvenal and Cato." In *Studies in Latin Literature and Roman History I*, edited by Carl Deroux, 418–47. Collection Latomus 164. Bruxelles, 1979.

Bremmer, J. N., and N. M. Horsfall. "Caeculus and the Foundation of Praeneste." In Bremmer and Horsfall, *Roman Myth and Mythography*, 49–62. BICS Suppl. 52. London, 1987.

Briscoe, John. "The Fragments of Cato's *Origines*." In *Colloquial and Literary Latin*, edited by Eleanor Dickey and Anna Chahoud, 154–60. Cambridge, 2010.

Brouwers, J. H. "Cato Maior, Romes eerste belangrijke redenaar." *Lampas* 34 (2001): 148–60.

Bruneau, Philippe. "*Pavimenta Poenica*." *Mélanges d'École Française de Rome (Antiquité)* 94 (1982): 639–55.

Burkard, Thorsten. "Schrieb Cato *dicae* und *faciae* oder *dice* und *facie*? Zu Quintilian, *Institutio oratoria* 1,7,23 und 9,4,39." *Hermes* 146 (2018): 208–18.

Calboli, Gualtiero. "La retorica preciceroniana e la politica a Roma." In *Éloquence et rhétorique chez Cicéron. Sept exposés suivis de discussions*, edited by Walther Ludwig, 41–99 (discussion at 100–108). Entretiens sur l'antiquité Classique XXVIII. Vandœuvres-Genève, 1982.

———. "I modelli dell'arcaismo: M. Porcio Catone." *Aion* 8 (1986): 37–69.

———. "Die Episode des Tribunen Q. Caedicius (Cato, *Orig.* frg. 7–43 Peter)." *Maia* 48 (1996): 1–32.

Carawan, Edwin M. "Cato's Speech against L. Flamininus: Liv. 39.42–3." *CJ* 85 (1990): 316–29.

Cardinali, Luca. "Le *Origines* di Catone iniziavano con un esametro?" *SCO* 37 (1988): 205–15.

Carsana, Chiara. "Il Catone di Plutarco: da modello ad an-

timodello." In *L'idéalisation de l'autre. Faire un modèle d'un anti-modèle. Actes du 2e colloque SoPHiA—Société Politique, Histoire de l'Antiquité tenu à Besançon les 26–28 novembre 2012*, edited by Antonio Gonzales and Maria Teresa Schettino, 243–66. Besançon, 2014.

Catalano, Pierangelo. "La divisone del potere in Roma (a proposito di Polibio e di Catone)." In *Studi in onore di Giuseppe Grosso VI*, 665–91. Torino, 1974.

Chassignet, Martine. "Caton et l'impérialisme romain au IIe siècle av. J.-C. d'après les *Origines*." *Latomus* 46 (1987): 285–300.

———. "Rhétorique et histoire dans les *Origines* de Caton." *Cahiers des études anciennes* 42 (2005 [2006]): 195–224.

Churchill, Bradford J. "On the Content and Structure of the Prologue to Cato's *Origines*." *ICS* 20 (1995): 91–106.

———. "*Dice* and *facie*: Quintilian, *Institutio oratoria* 1.7.23 and 9.4.39." *AJPh* 121 (2000a): 279–89.

———. "Cato *Orationes* 66 and the Case against M'. Acilius Glabrio in 189 B.C.E." *AJPh* 121 (2000b): 549–57.

Coletti, Maria Laetitia. "Tre modi di rievocare una prepotenza: Cato, fr. 58 Malc.—C. Sempronius Gracchus, fr. 48 Malc.—Cicero, *In Verrem* II 5,158–169." *Studi latini e italiani* 4 (1990): 83–92.

Cornell, Tim. "Cato the Elder and the Origins of Roman Autobiography." In *The Lost Memoirs of Augustus and the Development of Roman Autobiography*, edited by Christopher Smith and Anton Powell, 15–40. Swansea, 2009.

Crook, John. "*Sponsione Provocare*: Its Place in Roman Litigation." *JRS* 66 (1976): 132–38.

Crouzet, Sandrine. "De la bouillie punique à la destruction de Carthage: Caton, Carthage et l'hellénisme." *Pallas* 70: *L'Héllenisation en Méditerranée Occidentale au temps des guerres puniques (260–180 av. J. C.). Actes du Colloque international de Toulouse, 31 mars–2 avril 2005* (2006): 147–62.

Cugusi, Paolo. "Le epistole di Varrone." *RCCM* 9 (1967): 78–85.

———. "Studi sull'epistolografia latina. I: L'età preciceroniana." *Annali delle Facoltà di Lettere, Filosofia e Magistero dell'Università di Cagliari* 33.1 (1970a): 5–112.

———. "Catone oratore e Cicerone oratore." *Maia* 38 (1986): 207–16.

———. "Il proemio delle *Origines* di Catone." *Maia* 46 (1994): 263–72.

Cumont, Franz. "Lydus et Anastase le Sinaïte." *Byzantinische Zeitschrift* 30 (1929): 31–35.

———. "Un fragment de Caton ou Capiton." *Mélanges Paul Thomas. Recueil de mémoires concernant la philologie classique dédié à Paul Thomas*, 152–59. Bruges, 1930.

Damsté, P. H. "Ad S. Aurelium Victorem." *Mnemosyne* 45 (1917): 367–82.

Della Corte, Francesco. *Catone Censore. La vita e la fortuna*. 2nd ed. Florence, 1969.

———. "Catone Maggiore e i 'Libri ad Marcum filium.'" *RFIC* 69 (n.s. 19) (1942): 81–96. Reprinted in Francesco Della Corte, *Opuscula* II, 33–48. Pubblicazi-

oni dell'Istituto di Filologia Classica dell'Università di Genova 33. Genova, 1972.

Dench, Emma. *From Barbarians to New Men. Greek, Roman, and Modern Perceptions of Peoples of the Central Apennines*. Oxford Classical Monographs. Oxford, 1995.

Desideri, Paolo. "Catone e le donne (Il dibatitto liviano sull'abrogazione della *Lex Oppia*)." *Opus* 3 (1984): 63–74.

Desmouliez, André. "À propos du jugement de Cicéron sur Caton l'Ancien (*Brutus* XVI–XVIII 63–69 et LXXV–LXXXVII 292–300)." *Philologus* 126 (1982): 70–89.

Dubuisson, Michel. "Les *opici*: Osques, Occidentaux ou Barbares?" *Latomus* 42 (1983): 522–45.

———. "Caton et les Ligures: l'origine d'un stéréotype." *RBPh* 68 (1990): 74–83.

Ducos, Michèle. "Caton l'Ancien: un exemple de l'identité romaine." In *Figures de l'identité. Naissance et destin des modèles communautaires dans le monde romaine*, edited by Maëlys Blandenet, Clément Chillet, and Cyril Courrir, 87–101. Collection Sociétés, Espaces, Temps. Lyon, 2010.

Elliott, Jackie. "Reading Ennius' *Annals* and Cato's *Origins* at Rome." In *Ennius' Annals. Poetry and History*, edited by Cynthia Damon and Joseph Farrell, 107–24. Cambridge, 2020.

Elster, Marianne. *Die Gesetze der mittleren römischen Republik. Text und Kommentar*. Darmstadt, 2003.

———. *Die Gesetze der späten römischen Republik von den Gracchen bis Sulla (133–80 v. Chr.)*. Studien zur Alten Geschichte 28. Göttingen, 2020.

Ferrary, Jean-Louis. "À propos du fragment 90 Peter (IV, 15 Chassignet) des *Origines* de Caton et de la tradition varronienne sur les origines du *macellum*." *RPh* 75 (2001): 317–27.

Fiaccadori, Gianfranco. "Intorno all'anonimo Vaticano 'Περὶ πολιτικῆς ἐπιστήμης.'" *La Parola del Passato* 34 (1979): 127–47.

Flach, Dieter. *Die Gesetze der frühen römischen Republik. Text und Kommentar* (in Zusammenarbeit mit Stefan von der Lahr). Darmstadt, 1994.

———. *Römische Geschichtsschreibung*. Darmstadt, [3]1998.

Fo, Alessandro. "L'*argute loqui* dei Galli in un frammento di Catone." *Romanobarbarica* 4 (1979): 13–30.

Forde, Nels. W. *Cato the Censor*. Twayne's World Leaders Series 49. Boston, 1975.

Fotiou, A. S. "A New Fragment of Cato the Elder." *C&M* 23 (1981–1982): 125–33.

Fraccaro, Plinio. "Sulla biografia di Catone Maggiore sino al consolato e le sue fonti." *Atti e memorie della Accademia Virgiliana di Mantova*, n.s. 3 (1910a): 99–135. Reprinted in Plinio Fraccaro, *Opuscula I. Scritti di carattere generale, Studi catoniani, I processi degli Scipioni*, 139–76. Pavia, 1956.

———. "Le fonti per il consolato di M. Porcio Catone." *Studi storici per l'antichità classica* 3 (1910b): 120–202. Reprinted in Plinio Fraccaro, *Opuscula I. Scritti di carattere generale, Studi catoniani, I processi degli Scipioni*, 177–226. Pavia, 1956.

———. "Catoniana." *Studi storici per l'antichità classica* 3 (1910c): 241–85. Reprinted in Plinio Fraccaro, *Opus-*

cula I. Scritti di carattere generale, Studi catoniani, I processi degli Scipioni, 227–56. Pavia, 1956.

———. "L'orazione di Catone 'De sumtu suo.'" *Studi storici per l'antichità classica* 3 (1910d): 378–86. Reprinted in Plinio Fraccaro, *Opuscula I. Scritti di carattere generale, Studi catoniani, I processi degli Scipioni*, 257–62. Pavia, 1956.

———. "Ricerche storiche e letterarie sulla censura del 184/183 (M. Porcio Catone L. Valerio Flacco)." *Studi storici per l'antichità classica* 4 (1911): 1–137. Reprinted in Plinio Fraccaro, *Opuscula I. Scritti di carattere generale, Studi catoniani, I processi degli Scipioni*, 417–508. Pavia, 1956.

———. "Catone il censore in Tito Livio." In *Studi Liviani.* Scritti di Gaetano Mario Columba et al., 209–36. Roma, 1934. Reprinted in Plinio Fraccaro, *Opuscula I. Scritti di carattere generale, Studi catoniani, I processi degli Scipioni*, 115–37. Pavia, 1956.

Fraenkel, Eduard. *Leseproben aus Reden Ciceros and Catos*. Sussidi Eruditi 22. Roma, 1968.

Fuhrmann, Manfred. "Cato—Die altrömische Tradition im Kampf gegen die griechische Aufklärung." In *Aufklärung und Gegenaufklärung in der europäischen Literatur, Philosophie und Politik von der Antike bis zur Gegenwart*, edited by Jochen Schmidt, 72–92. Darmstadt, 1988.

Gabba, Emilio. "Studi su Dionigi da Alicarnasso. II. Il regno di Servio Tullio." *Athenaeum* 39 (1961): 98–121.

Gaggiotti, Marcello. "*Pavimenta Poenica marmore Numidico constrata.*" In *L'Africa romana. Atti del V convegno di studio, Sassari, 11–13 dicembre 1987*, edited by Attilio Mastino, 215–21. Pubblicazioni del Diparti-

mento di Storia dell'Università degli Studi di Sassari 9. Sassari, 1988.

Gamberale, Leopoldo. *La traduzione in Gellio*. Richerche di storia della lingua latina 3. Roma, 1969.

García, Julio Feo. "Turiam, conjetura a Catón (Jordán, 35) y a Livio (XXXIII, 44, 4)." *Saitabi* 9.39–42 (1952–1953): 11–21.

Gehrke, Hans-Joachim. "Römischer *mos* und griechische Ethik. Überlegungen zum Zusammenhang von Akkulturation und politischer Ordnung im Hellenismus." *HZ* 258 (1994): 593–622.

———. "Marcus Porcius Cato Censorius—ein Bild von einem Römer." In *Von Romulus zu Augustus. Große Gestalten der römischen Republik*, edited by Karl-Joachim Hölkeskamp and Elke Stein-Hölkeskamp, 147–58. München, 2000.

Gelzer, Matthias. "Nasicas Widerspruch gegen die Zerstörung Karthagos." *Philologus* 86 (1931), 261–99. Reprinted in Matthias Gelzer, *Vom Römischen Staat. Zur Politik und Gesellschaftsgeschichte der römischen Republik. I*, 78–124. Leipzig, 1944; and in Matthias Gelzer, *Kleine Schriften. Anlässlich des fünfundsiebzigsgen Geburstages von Matthias Gelzer hg. v. Hermann Strasburger und Christian Meier. Band* 2, 39–72. Wiesbaden, 1963.

Gelzer, Matthias, and Rudolf Helm. "Porcius (9)." *RE* XXII 1 (1953): 108–65.

Geus, Klaus. *Prosopographie der literarisch bezeugten Karthager*. Orientalia Lovaniensia Analecta 59 / Studia Phoenica 13. Leuven, 1994.

Gnauk, Rudolf. *Die Bedeutung des Marius und Cato Maior für Cicero*. Historische Abhandlungen 6. Berlin, 1936.

Goette, Hans Rupprecht. "Mulleus—Embas—Calceus. Ikonographische Studien zu römischem Schuhwerk." *JDAI* 103 (1988): 401–64.

Goldberg, Sander M. "Terence, Cato, and the Rhetorical Prologue." *CPh* 78 (1983): 198–222.

Gotter, Ulrich. "Die Vergangenheit als Kampfplatz der Gegenwart. Catos (konter)revolutionäre Konstruktion des republikanischen Erinnerungsraums." In *Formen römischer Geschichtsschreibung von den Anfängen bis Livius. Gattungen—Autoren—Kontexte*, edited by Ulrich Eigler, Ulrich Gotter, Nino Luraghi, and Uwe Walter, 115–34. Darmstadt, 2003.

———. "Cato's *Origines*: The Historian and His Enemies." In *The Cambridge Companion to the Roman Historians*, edited by Andrew Feldherr, 108–22. Cambridge, 2009.

Grilli, Alberto. "Un orazione di Catone Censore del 161 a.C.?" *Athenaeum* 85 (1997): 265–66.

Gruen, Erich S. *Culture and National Identity in Republican Rome*. Cornell Studies in Classical Philology LII / Townsend Lectures. Ithaca, NY, 1992.

Günther, Linda-Marie. "Ein Stephanus-Wunder im Weinkeller." *Münstersche Beiträge zur antiken Handelsgeschichte* 15 (1996): 19–29.

———. "Catos Feigen aus Karthago: Zur Interpretation einer Anekdote (Plutarch, *Cato maior*, 27, 1)." In *L'Africa romana. Le ricchezze dell'Africa. Risorse, produzioni, scambi. Atti del XVII convegno di studio, Sevilla, 14–17 dicembre 2006*, edited by Julián González, Paola Ruggeri, Cinzia Vismara, and Raimondo Zucca, 151–56. Collana del Dipartimento di Storia dell'Università degli Studi di Sassari, Nuova serie 35. Roma, 2008.

Habinek, Thomas N. *The Colometry of Latin Prose.* University of California Publications: Classical Studies 25. Berkeley / Los Angeles / London, 1985.

Haffter, Heinz. "Politisches Denken im alten Rom." *SIFC* 17 (1940): 97–121.

———. "Cato der Ältere in Politik und Kultur seiner Zeit. Interpretationen zum Catobild der Antike und dem unserer Gegenwart." In Heinz Haffter, *Römische Politik und römische Politiker. Aufsätze und Vorträge*, 159–92. Heidelberg, 1967.

Hafner, German. "Cato Censorius." In *Antike Porträts. Zum Gedächtnis von Helga von Heintze*, edited by Hans von Steuben, 107–12. Möhnesee 1999.

Hantos, Theodora. "Cato Censorius. Die Grundgedanken seiner Politik." In *Imperium Romanum. Studien zu Geschichte und Rezeption. Festschrift für Karl Christ zum 75. Geburtstag*, edited by Peter Kneissl and Volker Losemann, 317–33. Stuttgart, 1998.

Heichelheim, F. M. "Pap. Oxy. 2088. A Fragment from Cato's Origines I.?" *Aegyptus* 37 (1957): 250–58.

Hermand, Laure. "Entre figure historique et construction littéraire: Caton l'Ancien chez Cicéron." In *Figures de l'identité. Naissance et destin des modèles communautaires dans le monde romaine*, edited by Maëlys Blandenet, Clément Chillet, and Cyril Courrir, 103–15. Collection Sociétés, Espaces, Temps. Lyon, 2010.

Heurgon, Jacques. "Caton e la Gaule cisalpine." In *Mélanges d'histoire ancienne offerts à William Seston*, 231–47. Publications de la Sorbonne, Série "Études" 9. Paris, 1974.

Hoyos, B. D. "Cato's Punic Perfidies." *Ancient History Bulletin* 1 (1987): 112–21.

———. *Unplanned Wars. The Origins of the First and Second Punic Wars*. UaLG 50. Berlin / New York, 1998.

Janzer, Benno. *Historische Untersuchungen zu den Redefragmenten des M. Porcius Cato. Beiträge zur Lebensgeschichte und Politik Catos*. Würzburg, 1937.

Jefferson, Eleanor. "Problems and Audience in Cato's *Origines*." In *Process of Integration and Identity Formation in the Roman Republic*, edited by S. T. Roselaar, 311–26. Mnemosyne Suppl. 342. Leiden / Boston, 2012.

Jehne, Martin. "Cato und die Bewahrung der traditionellen *res publica*. Zum Spannungsverhältnis zwischen *mos maiorum* und griechischer Kultur im zweiten Jahrhundert v. Chr." In *Rezeption und Identität. Die kulturelle Auseinandersezung Roms mit Griechenland als europäisches Paradeigma*, edited by Gregor Vogt-Spira, Bettina Rommel, and Immanuel Musäus, 115–34. Stuttgart, 1999.

Kienast, Dietmar. *Cato der Zensor. Seine Persönlichkeit und seine Zeit. Mit einem Abdruck einiger Redefragmente Catos als Anhang*. Darmstadt, 1979 [corr. reprint with bibliographical add.; orig.: Heidelberg, 1954].

Kierdorf, Wilhelm. "Catos <Origines> und die Anfänge der römischen Geschichtsschreibung." *Chiron* 10 (1980): 205–24.

Klingner, Friedrich. "Cato Censorius und die Krisis Roms." *Die Antike* 10 (1934): 239–63. Reprinted in Friedrich Klingner, *Römische Geisteswelt*, 34–65. München, ^{4}1961.

Klussmann, Ernestus. "Additamentum ad M. Porcii Catonis Reliquias." *Philologus* 16 (1860): 150.

Knapp, R. C. "Cato in Spain, 195/194 B.C.: Chronology

and Geography." In *Studies in Latin Literature and Roman History II*, edited by Carl Deroux, 21–56. Collection Latomus 168. Bruxelles, 1980.

Krebs, Christopher B. "*Leonides Laco quidem simile apud Thermopylas fecit*: Cato and Herodotus." *BICS* 49 (2006): 93–103.

Lebek, Wolfgang Dieter. "*Pluria* und *compluria* in lateinischer Sprache und römischer Grammatik." *RhM* 114 (1971): 340–48.

Leeman, A. D. *Orationis ratio. The Stylistic Theories and Practice of the Roman Orators, Historians and Philosophers*. Amsterdam, 1963.

LeMoine, Fannie J. "Parental Gifts. Father-Son Dedications and Dialogues in Roman Didactic Literature." *ICS* 16 (1991): 337–66.

Lentano, Mario. "Una *crux* catoniana (*Carmen de moribus*, fr. 1 Jordan)." *Bollettino di studi latini* 29 (1999): 11–20.

Letta, Cesare. "L' 'Italia dei *mores Romani*' nelle *Origines* di Catone." *Athenaeum* 62 (1984): 3–30, 416–39.

———. "I *mores* dei Romani e l'origine dei Sabini in Catone." In *Convegno di studio: Preistoria, storia e civiltà dei Sabini. Rieti, ottobre 1982*, 15–34. Rieti, 1985.

Linderski, Jerzy. "Cato Maior in Aetolia." In *Transitions to Empire. Essays in Greco-Roman History, 360–146 B.C., in honor of E. Badian*, edited by Robert W. Wallace and Edward M. Harris, 376–408. Oklahoma Series in Classicual Culture. Norman, OK / London, 1996.

Lindsay, W. M. "Notes on Festus." *CQ* 7 (1913): 115–19.

Lippi, Donatella. "*Magalia, magaria, mapalia* (Verg., *Aen.* IV 259)." *Prometheus* 10 (1984): 241–42.

Malcovati, Enrica. "Sull'orazione di Catone *De bello Carthaginiensi*." *Athenaeum* 53 (1975): 205–11. Reprinted in E. Malcovati, *Florilegio*, 129–34.

———. "L'orazione di Catone *Pro Rhodiensibus*." *Athenaeum* 56 (1978): 378–81.

———. "Su un frammento di Catone: *ORF*[4] 8,207." *Athenaeum* 59 (1981): 466–68; Reprinted in E. Malcovati, *Florilegio*, 155–58.

———. *Florilegio critico di filologia e storia*. Bibliotheca di Athenaeum 14. Como, 1990.

Mariotti, Italo. "Verruca 'locus editus.'" In *Studi di filologia classica in onore di Giusto Monaco. II*, 581–85. Palermo, 1991.

Marmorale, Enzo V. *Cato Maior. Seconda Edizione*. Biblioteca di Cultura Moderna 459. Bari, 1949.

Mastrorosa, Ida. "Speeches *pro* and *contra* Women in Livy 34, 1–7: Catonian Legalism and Gendered Debates." *Latomus* 65 (2006): 590–611.

Mazzarino, Antonio. "I Feaci nell'*Odusia* di Livio Andronico." *Helikon* 18–19 (1978–1979): 387–90.

———. "Charisiana." *Nuovi Annali della Facoltà di Magistero dell'Università di Messina* 1 (1983): 395–99.

———. "Un frammento ignorato di Catone." *Nuovi Annali della Facoltà di Magistero dell'Università di Messina* 4 (1986): 543–48.

———. "Ancora un altro frammento ignorato di Catone." *Helikon* 22–27 (1982–1987): 457–66.

Mehl, Andreas. *Roman Historiography. An Introduction to Its Basic Aspects and Development*. Translated by Hans-Friedrich Mueller. Chichester, 2011. [German orig.: *Römische Geschichtsschreibung*. Stuttgart, 2001.]

Meijer, F J. "Cato's African Figs." *Mnemosyne* 37 (1984): 117–24.

Meister, Richard. "Zu römischen Historikern. 1. Der Titel von Catos Geschichtswerk." *AAWW* 101 (1964): 1–8.

Mensching, Eckart. "Tullus Hostilius, Alba Longa und Cluilius. Zu Livus I 22 f. und anderen." *Philologus* 110 (1966): 102–18.

Moretti, Luigi. "Le *Origines* di Catone, Timeo ed Eratostene." *RFIC* 80 (1952): 289–302.

Müller, Lucian. "Ein neues Fragment des Cato." *RhM* 23 (1868): 541–43, 704.

———. "Ein neues Fragment des Cato." *RhM* 24 (1869): 331–32.

Munk Olsen, B. *L'étude des auteurs classiques latins aux XIe et XIIe siècles. Tome I: Catalogue des manuscrits classiques latins copies du IXe au XIIe siècle. Apicius–Juvénal.* Documents, Études et Répertoires. Paris, 1982.

Nap, J. M. "Ad Catonis librum de re militari." *Mnemosyne* 55 (1927): 79–87.

Negri, Angela Maria. "La fortuna letteraria dell'*inertia* (Hor. *epist.* 1,11,28; Sen. *tranq.* 12,3)." *Paideia* 43 (1988): 177–88.

Nenci, Giuseppe. "La *De bello Carthaginiensi* di Catone Censore." *Critica storica* 1 (1962): 363–68.

———. "La testimonianza di Catone sulla 'decessio de foedere' saguntina (Fr. 84 Peter^2)." *Studi Annibalici. Atti del Convegno svoltosi a Cortona-Tuoro sul Trasimeno-Perugia, ottobre 1961*, 71–81. Cortona, 1964.

Neuhauser, Walter. *Patronus oder orator. Eine Geschichte der Begriffe von ihren Anfängen bis in die augusteische*

Zeit. Commentationes Aenipontanae XIV. Innsbruck, 1958.

O'Gorman, Ellen. "Cato the Elder and the Destruction of Carthage." *Helios* 31 (2004): 99–125.

Ortoleva, Vincentius, ed. *Maximus Planudes. Disticha Catonis in Graecum translata*. Roma, 1992.

Otto, A. *Die Sprichwörter und sprichwörtlichen Redensarten der Römer. Gesammelt und erklärt*. Leipzig, 1890.

Pasco-Pranger, Molly. "Naming Cato(s)." *CJ* 108 (2012): 1–35.

———. "Finding Examples at Home: Cato, Curius Dentatus, and the Origins of Roman Literary Exemplarity." *Classical Antiquity* 34 (2015): 296–321.

Perini, Giorgio Bernardi. "Un frammento fantasma di Catone (*inc. lib.* 51 Jordan = Gell. 10, 21, 2)." *Atti e Memorie dell'Accademia Patavina di Scienze, Lettere ed Arti* 91.3 (1978–1979): 5–13.

———. "Gelliana." *Museum Patavinum* 3 (1985): 131–42.

———. "Postilla Catoniana." *Museum Patavinum* 4 (1986): 185.

Perl, Gerhard, and Iradj El-Qalqili. "Zur Problematik der *Lex Oppia* (215 / 195 v. Chr.)." *Klio* 84 (2002): 414–39.

Pianezzola, Emilio. "Le ferite di Quinto Cedicio (Cato 'Orig.' IV 7 Jordan = fr. 83 P. [2] ap. Gell. III 7)." *Studi Urbinati* 49 B 1 (Atti del convegno: Gli storiografi latini tramandati in frammenti, Urbino, 9–11 maggio 1974) (1975): 73–80.

Pighi, Io. B. "Catonis carmen de moribus." *Latinitas* 14 (1966): 31–34.

Préaux, Jean. "Caton et l'*ars poetica*." *Latomus* 25 (1966): 710–25.

Primmer, Adolf. "Der Prosarhythmus in Catos Reden." In *Festschrift für Karl Vretska. Zum 70. Geburtstag am 18. Oktober 1970 überreicht von seinen Freunden und Schülern. Hg. v. Doris Ableitinger und Helmut Gugel*, 174–80. Heidelberg, 1970.

Reay, Brendon. "Agriculture, Writing, and Cato's Aristocratic Self-Fashioning." *CA* 24 (2005): 331–61.

Richard, Jean-Claude. "Ennemies ou alliés? Les Troyens et les Aborigènes dans les *Origines* de Caton." In *Hommages à Robert Schilling*, edited by Hubert Zehnacker and Gustave Hentz, 403–12. Collection d'Études Latines, Série Scientifique, Fascicule XXXVII. Paris, 1983a.

———. "Sur une triple étiologie du nom Iulus, II." *REL* 61 (1983b): 108–21.

Robert, Jean-Noël. "Remarques sur la légendaire misogynie de Caton l'Ancien." In *Hommages à Carl Deroux. III—Histoire et épigraphie, Droit*, edited by Pol Defosse, 376–83. Collection Latomus 270. Bruxelles, 2003.

Roos, Paolo. *Sentenza e proverbio nell'antichità e i 'Distici di Catone'. Il testo latino e i volgarizzamenti italiani. Con una scelta e traduzione delle massime e delle frasi proverbiali latine classiche più importanti o ancora vive oggi nel mondo neolatino*. Brescia, 1984.

Ruebel, James S. *The Political Development of Cato Censorius: The Man and the Image*. PhD diss., Cincinnati, 1972.

Ryan, Francis X. *Rank and Participation in the Republican Senate*. Stuttgart, 1998.

Sbardella, Marcus. "De compositione Originum Catonis." *Latinitas* 49 (2001a): 172–74.

Sbardella, Marco. "L'incipit esametrico delle *Origines* catoniane come cifra stilistica e programmatica del genere storico." *Aufidus* 45 (2001b): 33–36.

———. "Su due frammenti delle *Origines* catoniane attestati da Servio." *Aufidus* 48 (2002): 59–64.

———. "Le *Origines* catoniane: ipotesi di datazione, intitolazione, struttura." *Studi Romani* 51 (2003): 3–14.

Sblendorio, Maria Teresa. "Note sullo stile dell'oratoria catoniana." *Annali delle Facoltà di Lettere, Filosofia e Magistero dell'Università di Cagliari* 34 (1971): 5–32.

Sblendorio Cugusi, Maria Teresa. "Sulla struttura dell' orazione catoniana *Dierum dictarum de consulatu suo*." *Atti della Accademia delle Scienze di Torino, Classe di Scienze Morali, Storiche e Filologiche* 114 (1980): 247–58.

———. "Un nuovo frammento dell'orazione catoniana *De innocentia sua*." *Bollettino dei Classici* s. 3, fasc. 5 (1984): 178–82.

———. "Oratoria e retorica in Catone." *Atti della Accademia delle Scienze di Torino, Classe di Scienze Morali, Storiche e Filologiche* 121 (1987): 23–61.

———. "Catone, *ORF* 235 Malc.[4] e lat. (*de*)*torqueo*." *RFIC* 124 (1996a): 435–39.

———. "Per la storia di *nothus* e di *nugator* (e un frammento catoniano conservato *ad verbum*)." *Eikasmos* 7 (1996b): 219–41.

Sblendorio Cugusi, Maria Teresa, and Paolo Cugusi. "Problematica catoniana. Rassegna di studi 1978–1993 e contributi critici." *BSL* 26 (1996): 82–218.

Scardigli, Barbara. *Die Römerbiographien Plutarchs*. München, 1979.

Schmal, Stephan. "Cato, Sallust und Tacitus. Politik und Geschichtsschreibung im republikanischen und kaiserzeitlichen Rom." In *Gelehrte in der Antike. Alexander Demandt zum 65. Geburtstag*, edited by Andreas Goltz, Andreas Luther, and Heinrich Schlange-Schöningen, 87–103. Köln / Weimar / Wien, 2002.

Schmidt, Peter Lebrecht. "Catos Epistula ad M. filium und die Anfänge der römischen Briefliteratur." *Hermes* 100 (1972): 568–76.

Schmitt, Hatto H. *Rom und Rhodos. Geschichte ihrer politischen Beziehungen seit der ersten Berührung bis zum Aufgehen des Inselstaates im römischen Weltreich*. Münchener Beiträge zur Papryrusforschung und antiken Rechtsgeschichte 40. München, 1957.

Scholz, Udo W. "Zu Catos Origines I." *WJA* 4 (1978): 99–106.

———. "*M. Porcius Cato, Das erste Buch der Origines.* Ausgabe und Erklärung der Fragmente von Wilt Aden Schröder. Meisenheim am Glan: Hain 1971. 216 S. (Beiträge zur Klassischen Philologie. 41.)." *Gnomon* 51 (1979): 240–44.

———. "Catos Rede de Indigetibus." *RhM* 132 (1989): 149–54.

Schönberger, O. "Versuch der Gewinnung eines Cato-Fragments." *Philologus* 113 (1969): 283–87.

Schröder, Wilt Aden. "Caton, *Les origines (fragments)*. Texte ét., trad. et commenté par Martine Chassignet. Paris: Belles lettres 1986. LXVII, 123 z. T. Doppels. (Coll. des universités de France.) 180 F." *Gnomon* 62 (1990): 582–92.

Sciarrino, Enrica. "Putting Cato the Censor's *Origines* in Its Place." *Classical Antiquity* 23 (2004): 323–57.

———. "Roman Oratory Before Cicero: The Elder Cato and Gaius Gracchus." In *A Companion to Roman Rhetoric*, edited by William Dominik and Jon Hall, 54–66. Blackwell Companions to the Ancient World. Malden / Oxford, 2007.

———. *Cato the Censor and the Beginnings of Latin Prose. From Poetic Translation to Elite Transcription*. Columbus, 2011.

Scivoletto, Nino. "L'*Oratio contra Galbam* e le *Origines* di Catone." *GIF* 14 (1961): 63–68.

Scullard, H. H. *Roman Politics 220–150 B.C.*, Oxford, [1]1951, [2]1973.

———. "Ennius, Cato, and Surus." *CR* 3 (1953): 140–42.

Sierra de Cózar, Ángel. "*Rem tene, uerba sequentur*: notas para la historia de un tópico." In *Actes del IXè Simposi de la Secció Catalana de la SEEC. St. Feliu de Guíxols, 13–16 d'abril de 1988. Treballs en honor de Vergilio Bejarano*, edited by L. Ferreres, 1:459–66. Barcelona, 1991.

Solodow, J. B. "Cato, *Orationes*, frag. 75." *AJPh* 98 (1977): 359–61.

Stark, Rudolf. "Catos Rede De lustri sui felicitate." *RhM* 96 (1953): 184–87.

Stok, Fabio. "Catone e la *Lex Fannia*." *Maia* 37 (1985): 237–44.

———. "Gargilio Marziale: un epigono dell'enciclopedismo." In *Lingue tecniche del greco e del latino. Atti del I° Seminario internazionale sulla letteratura scientifica e tecnica greca e latina*, edited by Sergio Sconocchia and Lucio Toneatto, in collaboration with Daria Crismani and Piero Tassinari, 220–34. Università degli Studi di Trieste, 1993.

Suerbaum, Werner. "Sex and Crime im alten Rom: Von der humanistischen Zensur zu Cato dem Censor." *WJA* 19 (1993): 85–109.

———. "Vorliterarische römische Redner (bis zum Beginn des 2. Jhs. v. Chr.) in Ciceros 'Brutus' und in der historischen Überlieferung." *WJA* 21 (1996/1997): 169–98.

———, ed. *Handbuch der lateinischen Literatur der Antike. Erster Band. Die archaische Literatur. Von den Anfängen bis Sullas Tod. Die vorliterarische Periode und die Zeit von 240–78 v. Chr.* (*HLL 1*). HbdA VIII.1. München, 2002.

———. *Cato Censorius in der Forschung des 20. Jahrhunderts. Eine kommentierte chronologische Bibliographie für 1900–1999 nebst systematischen Hinweisen und einer Darstellung des Schriftstellers M. Porcius Cato (234–149 v. Chr.).* Bibliographien zur Klassischen Philologie 2. Hildesheim / Zürich / New York, 2004.

Thürlemann, Silvia. "Ceterum censeo Carthaginem esse delendam." *Gymnasium* 81 (1974): 465–75.

Till, Rudolf. *Die Sprache Catos*. Philologus Suppl. XXVIII 2. Leipzig, 1935; Italian translation: *Lingua di Catone. Traduzione e note supplementari di C. De Meo*. Ricerche di storia della lingua latina 5. Roma, 1968.

———. *Catonis orationum fragmenta interpretatus est*. Marburg, 1937.

———. "Zu Plutarchs Biographie des älteren Cato." *Hermes* 81 (1953): 438–46.

Timpe, Dieter. "Le "Origine" di Catone e la storiografia latina." *Atti e Memorie dell'Accademia Patavina di Scienze, Lettere ed Arti* 83.3 (1970–1971): 1–33.

Torres, Salvador Mas. "Catón el Censor y la invención de Grecia." In *La construcción ideológica de la ciudadanía.*

Identidades culturales y sociedad en el mundo griego antiguo, edited by Domingo Plácido, Miriam Valdés, Fernando Echeverría, and M.ª Yolanda Montes, 407–21. Madrid, 2006.

Traglia, Antonio. "Osservazioni su Catone prosatore." In *Hommages à Henry Bardon*, edited by Marcel Renard and Pierre Laurens, 344–59. Collecion Latomus 187. Bruxelles, 1985.

Tränkle, Hermann. "Catos Origines im Geschichtswerk des Livius." In *Forschungen zur römischen Literatur. Festschrift zum 60. Geburtstag von Karl Büchner*, edited by Walter Wimmel, 274–85. Wiesbaden, 1970.

———. *Cato in der vierten und fünften Dekade des Livius*. AAWM 4. Wiesbaden, 1971.

van der Blom, Henriette. *Cicero's Role Models. The Political Strategy of a Newcomer*. Oxford Classical Monographs. Oxford, 2010.

Vestergaard, Torben. "The Final -m Written or Omitted: A Question of Morphology, Phonology and Orthography in Inscriptions from Pompeii and Herculaneum." *Analecta Romana Instituti Danici* 26 (1999): 57–68.

Viré, Ghislaine. "À propos du fragment 2 de *l'Oratio pro Rhodiensibus* de Caton." *Antiquité Classique* 48 (1979): 549–58.

Vitale, Maria Teresa. "Cesellio Vindice." *Studi e ricerche dell'Istituto di Latino, Università degli Studi di Genova* 1 (1977): 221–58.

Vogt-Spira, Gregor. "'The Pervasive Inconsequence of All Morality': The Example of Cato the Elder." In *Double Standards in the Ancient and Medieval World*, edited by Karla Pollmann, 107–19. GfA Beihefte 1. Göttingen, 2000.

Waldherr, Gerhard H. "'Punica fides'—Das Bild der Karthager in Rom." *Gymnasium* 107 (2000): 193–222.

Watt, W. S. "Two Fragments of the Elder Cato." *Glotta* 52 (1984): 248–50.

———. "Gelliana." *Prometheus* 20 (1994): 278–82.

Weishaupt, Arnd. *Die lex Voconia*. Forschungen zum Römischen Recht 45. Köln / Weimar / Wien, 1999.

Wieacker, Franz. *Römische Rechtsgeschichte. Quellenkunde, Rechtsbildung, Jurisprudenz und Rechtsliteratur. Erster Abschnitt: Einleitung, Quellenkunde, Frühzeit und Republik*. HbdA X.III.1.1. Munich, 1988.

Williams, J. H. C. *Beyond the Rubicon. Romans and Gauls in Republican Italy*. Oxford Classical Monographs. Oxford, 2001.

Wiseman, T. P. "Rome on the Balance: Varro and the Foundation Legend." In *Varro varius. The Polymath of the Roman World*, edited by D. J. Butterfield, 93–122. Cambridge Classical Journal Supplement 39. Cambridge, 2015.

Wöhrle, Georg. "Cato und die griechischen Ärzte." *Eranos* 90 (1992): 112–25.

Wójcik, Andrzej. "Virtus Catonis. Legenda i autolegenda Katona Starszego." *Eos* 55 (1965): 296–309 [with summary in Latin].

Wulfram, Hartmut. *Ex uno plures. Drei Studien zum postumen Persönlichkeitsbild des Alten Cato*. Berlin, 2009.

Zanda, Emanuela. *Fighting Hydra-Like Luxury. Sumptuary Regulation in the Roman Republic*. London, 2011.

Zetzel, J. E. G. "Statilius Maximus and Ciceronian Studies in the Antonine Age." *BICS* 21 (1974): 107–23.

Zuccarelli, Ugo. "Rassegna bibliografica di studi e pubblicazioni su Catone (1940–1950)." *Paideia* 7 (1952): 213–17.

M. PORCIUS CATO

TESTIMONIA (T 1–99)

This section offers the testimonia providing information on Cato's life and literary works. They include the testimonia given in FRHist *and* ORF[4] *on Cato's life and the works covered by these editions as well as additional relevant texts, i.e., those providing meaningful details rather than all of the numerous passages in Roman literature that*

T 1 *Rhet. Her.* 4.7

. . . , nec mirum, cum ipse praeceptor artis omnia penes unum reperire non potuerit. allatis igitur exemplis a Catone, a Graccis, a Laelio, a Scipione, Galba, Porcina, Crasso, Antonio, ceteris, item sumptis aliis a poetis et historiarum scriptoribus necesse erit eum, qui discet, putare ab omnibus omnia, ab uno pauca vix potuisse sumi.

TESTIMONIA (T 1–99)

characterize Cato as "ex-censor" or mention him with honorific attributes without any further substantial information. (On the order and numbering of the testimonia, see General Introduction: Organization of This Edition; on what can be inferred from these texts, see General Introduction: Cato's Biography.)

T 1 *Rhetorica ad Herennium*

. . . , nor [is it] surprising, since the teacher of the art himself has been unable to find everything in a single author. Thus, when examples have been drawn from Cato, from the Gracchi [Ti. Sempronius Gracchus (*ORF*^{4} 34) + C. Sempronius Gracchus (*ORF*^{4} 48)], from Laelius [C. Laelius Sapiens (*ORF*^{4} 20)], from Scipio [P. Cornelius Scipio Aemilianus Africanus minor (*ORF*^{4} 21)], Galba [Ser. Sulpicius Galba (*ORF*^{4} 19)], Porcina [M. Aemilius Lepidus Porcina (*ORF*^{4} 25)], Crassus [L. Licinius Crassus (*ORF*^{4} 66)], Antonius [M. Antonius (*ORF*^{4} 65)], and others, when further [examples] have likewise been taken from poets and writers of histories, the learner will necessarily believe that all these could have been taken from them all, but scarcely a few from a single one.

T 2 Cic. *Inv. rhet.* 1.5

quod nostrum illum non fugit Catonem neque Laelium neque eorum, ut vere dicam, discipulum Africanum neque Gracchos,[1] Africani nepotes: quibus in hominibus erat summa virtus et summa virtute amplificata auctoritas et, quae et his rebus ornamento et rei publicae praesidio esset, eloquentia.

[1] Catonem, Caelium, Africanum et Gracchos *Grillius*: Laelium neque Africanum neque eorum, ut vere dicam, discipulos Gracchos *Martha* africanum. Neque *codd.*: neque . . . nepotes *om. Marius Victorinus* Gracchos *del. Ammon* Africani nepotes *del. Stroebel*

T 3 Cic. *Div. Caec.* 66

M. Catonem illum Sapientem, clarissimum virum et prudentissimum, cum multis gravis inimicitias gessisse accepimus propter Hispanorum, apud quos consul fuerat, iniurias.

T 4 Cic. *De or.* 1.171

[CRASSUS:] quid vero ille M.[1] Cato? nonne[2] et eloquentia tanta fuit, quantam illa tempora atque illa aetas in hac civitate efferre[3] maximam[4] potuit, et iuris civilis omnium peritissimus?

[1] M. *vel om. codd.* [2] nonne *codd.*: ratione *unus cod.*
[3] efferre *vel* ecferre *vel* et ferre *codd.* [4] maximam *vel* maxime *codd.*

T 2 Cicero, *On Invention*

This [i.e., the need to oppose demagogues] did not escape the notice of our Cato, or Laelius [C. Laelius Sapiens (*ORF*^{4} 20)], or their (to speak the truth) disciple Africanus [P. Cornelius Scipio Aemilianus Africanus minor (*ORF*^{4} 21)], or the Gracchi [Ti. Sempronius Gracchus (*ORF*^{4} 34) + C. Sempronius Gracchus (*ORF*^{4} 48)], grandsons of Africanus [P. Cornelius Scipio Africanus maior (*ORF*^{4} 4)]: these individuals possessed the highest virtue, and an authority strengthened by the highest virtue, and eloquence, which was both an adornment to these qualities and a fortification to the *res publica*.

T 3 Cicero, *Against Q. Caecilius*

We have learned that the famous M. Cato, the "Wise" [cf. *Orat.* F 154, 199A], a very distinguished and very sagacious man, sustained bitter hostilities with many because of the injustices done to the Iberians, among whom he had served as consul [195 BC].

T 4 Cicero, *On the Orator*

[Crassus:] And what of the famous M. Cato? Did he not possess eloquence as great as those times and that epoch could possibly produce in this community, and was he not the most expert of all in civil law?

T 5 Cic. *De or.* 1.215

[ANTONIUS:] neque vero, si quis utrumque potest, aut ille consilii publici auctor ac senator bonus ob eam ipsam causam orator est, aut hic disertus atque eloquens, si est idem in procuratione civitatis egregius, aliquam[1] scientiam dicendi copia est consecutus. multum inter se distant istae facultates longeque sunt diversae atque seiunctae, neque eadem ratione ac via M. Cato, P. Africanus, Q. Metellus, C. Laelius, qui omnes eloquentes fuerunt, orationem suam et rei publicae dignitatem exornabant.

[1] aliquam *codd.*: illam *Manutius*: eam ipsam *Klotz*: civilem aliquam *Muther*: reliquam *Gesner*: aliam *Stroebel*: aliam quoque *Cima*: alteram *Reid*

T 6 Cic. *De or.* 2.51–54

"age vero" inquit ANTONIUS "qualis oratoris et quanti hominis in dicendo putas esse historiam scribere?" "si, ut Graeci scripserunt, summi" inquit CATULUS; "si, ut nostri, nihil opus est oratore; satis est non esse mendacem." "atqui ne nostros contemnas" inquit ANTONIUS, "Graeci quoque sic initio scriptitarunt, ut noster Cato, ut Pictor, ut Piso. [52] erat enim historia nihil aliud nisi annalium confectio, cuius rei memoriaeque publicae retinendae causa, ab initio rerum Romanarum usque ad P. Mucium ponti-

T 5 Cicero, *On the Orator*

[ANTONIUS:] But then, if someone is able [to do] both [i.e., be a leading figure in public life and a good orator], neither is that originator of public policy and good senator, for that very reason, an orator, nor has this eloquent and skilled speaker, if the same person is outstanding in public administration, attained any knowledge [of it] through fluency in speaking. There is a vast distance between these accomplishments, and they are far separated and distinct from each other; nor was it by the same principle and method that M. Cato, P. Africanus [P. Cornelius Scipio Aemilianus Africanus minor (*ORF*[4] 21)], Q. Metellus [Q. Caecilius Metellus Macedonicus (*ORF*[4] 18)], and C. Laelius [C. Laelius Sapiens (*ORF*[4] 20)], who were all eloquent, gave brilliance to their speaking and to the reputation of the *res publica*.

T 6 Cicero, *On the Orator*

"Now, further," said ANTONIUS, "what kind of orator and how great a master of speaking is qualified, in your opinion, to write history?" "If [they are to write] as the Greeks have written, a supreme [orator]," said CATULUS; "if as our countrymen, there is no need of an orator; it is sufficient that the person is not a liar." "But, so that you do not look down upon our own people," said ANTONIUS, "the Greeks too habitually wrote, in the beginning, like our Cato, like Pictor [Q. Fabius Pictor (*FRHist* 1)], like Piso [L. Calpurnius Piso Frugi (*FRHist* 9)]. [52] For historical writing was nothing other than a compilation of annals, for the sake of which, and in order to preserve public memory, from the beginning of Rome's affairs up to P. Mucius' [P.

ficem maximum res omnes singulorum annorum mandabat litteris pontifex maximus efferebatque[1] in album et proponebat tabulam domi, potestas ut esset populo cognoscendi: ii qui etiam nunc annales maximi nominantur. [53] hanc similitudinem scribendi multi secuti sunt, qui sine ullis ornamentis monumenta solum temporum hominum locorum gestarumque rerum reliquerunt. itaque qualis apud Graecos Pherecydes, Hellanicus, Acusilas fuit aliique permulti, talis noster Cato et Pictor et Piso, qui neque tenent quibus rebus ornetur oratio—modo enim huc ista sunt importata—et, dum intellegatur quid dicant, unam dicendi laudem putant esse brevitatem. [54] paulum se erexit, et addidit maiorem historiae sonum vocis[2] vir optimus, Crassi familiaris, Antipater, ceteri non exornatores rerum, sed tantummodo narratores fuerunt."

[1] referebatque *Lambinus* [2] vocis *del. Schuetz, Ellendt*

T 7a Cic. *De or.* 3.56

[CRASSUS:] hanc, inquam, cogitandi pronuntiandique rationem vimque dicendi veteres Graeci sapientiam nominabant. hinc illi Lycurgi, hinc Pittaci, hinc Solones, atque ab hac similitudine Coruncanii nostri, Fabricii, Catones, Scipiones fuerunt, non tam fortasse docti, sed impetu mentis simili et voluntate.

Mucius Scaevola, cos. 133 BC] term as chief pontiff, the chief pontiff used to commit to writing all the events of the individual years, and record them on a white surface, and set up the tablet at his house, so that it was possible for the People to find out about them: those records that are even now called *annales maximi* ['pontifical chronicles']. [53] A similar kind of writing has been adopted by many who, without any rhetorical ornament, have left records only of dates, individuals, places, and events. Thus, what, among the Greeks, Pherecydes, Hellanicus, Acusilaus [Greek historiographers], and very many others were like, such are our Cato, and Pictor, and Piso, who do not have at their disposal the means by which discourse is adorned—for only recently have such things been brought over here—and who, so long as what they say is understood, regard conciseness as the single merit of expression. [54] Someone who raised himself a little further and imparted to history a higher tone of speaking was Antipater [L. Coelius Antipater (*FRHist* 15)], an excellent man and a friend of Crassus [L. Licinius Crassus (*ORF*[4] 66)]; others were not embellishers of events, but merely chroniclers."

T 7a Cicero, *On the Orator*

[Crassus:] This ability to think and to state one's opinions and this power of speech, was, I say, called wisdom by the ancient Greeks. Hence there were those men like Lycurgus, like Pittacus, like Solon [Greek statesmen], and, on the basis of similarity with these, men like our Coruncanius, Fabricius, Cato, and Scipio [Roman statesmen], not so much perhaps as a result of having been taught, but from a similar mental impulse and will.

T 7b Cic. *Sen.* 5

["CATO":] quocirca si sapientiam meam admirari soletis (quae utinam digna esset opinione vestra nostroque cognomine!), in hoc sumus sapientes, quod naturam, optimam ducem, tamquam deum sequimur eique paremus; . . .

T 7c Cic. *Amic.* 6–10

[FANNIUS:] sed existimare debes omnium oculos in te esse coniectos: unum te[1] sapientem et appellant et existimant. tribuebatur hoc modo M. Catoni, scimus L. Acilium apud patres nostros appellatum esse sapientem, sed uterque alio quodam modo: Acilius quia prudens esse in iure civili putabatur, Cato quia multarum rerum usum habebat. multa eius et in senatu et in foro vel provisa prudenter vel acta constanter vel responsa acute ferebantur; propterea quasi cognomen iam habebat in senectute sapientis. [7] te autem alio quodam modo, non solum natura et moribus, verum etiam studio et doctrina esse sapientem: nec sicut vulgus, sed ut eruditi solent appellare sapientem, . . . [8] . . .

[LAELIUS:] . . . [9] tu autem, Fanni, quod mihi tantum tribui dicis quantum ego nec agnosco nec postulo, facis amice, sed ut mihi videris, non recte iudicas de Catone. aut enim nemo, quod quidem magis credo, aut, si quis-

[1] esse coniectos. unum te *sic dist. codd. praeter unum, ubi dist. ante* coniectos, *et alterum, in quo distinctio post* coniectos *fort. erasa est*

T 7b Cicero, *On Old Age*

["CATO":] Therefore, if you are accustomed to marvel at my wisdom (and would that it were worthy of your judgment and of our cognomen!), it is in this that we are wise, that we follow nature, the best guide, as if she were a god, and we obey her; . . .

T 7c Cicero, *On Friendship*

[FANNIUS:] But you must consider that the eyes of all are fixed on you [Laelius]: it is you alone whom they both call "wise" and believe to be so. Recently this [description] was assigned to M. Cato; we know that L. Acilius [jurist; cf. Cic. *Leg.* 2.59] was called "wise" among our fathers, but each of the two in a certain and different way: Acilius because he was believed to be an expert in civil law, Cato because he had experience of many matters. Many of his actions both in the Senate and in the Forum were said to have displayed shrewdness of foresight, resolution of conduct, or sagacity in reply; for that reason, in old age he then had, as it were, the cognomen of "Wise." [7] But as to yourself, [people call] you "wise" in some other way, not only because of your natural endowments and character, but also because of your devotion to study and your learning, and they use the appellation of "wise," not as the ignorant do, but as the learned are accustomed to do, . . . [8] . . .
[LAELIUS:] . . . [9] Now you are very kind, Fannius, in saying that so much merit is ascribed to me, as much as I neither recognize nor claim; but, as it seems to me, you are not making the right assessment of Cato. For either no one was wise, which I indeed believe more, or, if anyone,

quam, ille sapiens fuit. quomodo, ut alia omittam, mortem fili tulit! memineram Paulum, videram Galum; sed hi in pueris, Cato in perfecto et spectato viro. [10] quamobrem cave Catoni anteponas ne istum quidem ipsum quem Apollo, ut ais, sapientissimum iudicavit: huius enim facta, illius dicta laudantur.

T 7d Cic. *Off.* 3.16

nec vero, cum duo Decii aut duo Scipiones fortes viri commemorantur aut cum Fabricius aut Aristides[1] iustus nominatur, aut ab illis fortitudinis aut ab his iustitiae tamquam a sapiente petitur exemplum; nemo enim horum sic sapiens ut sapientem volumus intellegi, nec ii qui sapientes habiti et nominati, M. Cato et C. Laelius, sapientes fuerunt, ne illi quidem septem, sed ex mediorum officiorum frequentia similitudinem quandam gerebant speciemque sapientium.

[1] aut Aristides *del. Heusinger* (*recepto ex Lact.* hoc *pro* his *infra*)

T 8 Cic. *De or.* 3.135

[Crassus:] quid enim M. Catoni praeter hanc politissimam doctrinam transmarinam atque adventiciam defuit? num quia ius civile didicerat causas non dicebat? aut quia

it was that man. Putting aside other things, how did he bear the death of his son [cf. T 62]! I remembered Paulus [L. Aemilius Paullus, cos. 182, 168 BC (*ORF*^{4} 12)], I had seen Galus [C. Sulpicius Galus, cos. 166 BC (*ORF*^{4} 14)], but these men [experienced such losses] in relation to children, Cato in relation to a grown-up and well-respected man. [10] For this reason, take care not to give the precedence over Cato even to that man, whom, as you say, Apollo judged to be the wisest [Socrates]: for, of the former the deeds are praised, of the latter the words.

T 7d Cicero, *On Duties*

And to be sure, when the two Decii or the two Scipios [famous Roman consuls and generals] are recalled as "brave men," or when Fabricius or Aristides [Athenian statesman, fl. ca. 500 BC] is called "just," it is not that from the former a model of courage or from the latter a model of justice is sought, as if from a wise individual. For no one of these was wise in the sense in which we would like "a wise person" to be understood, neither were wise those who were considered and called "wise," M. Cato and C. Laelius [C. Laelius Sapiens, cos. 140 BC (*ORF*^{4} 20)], not even the famous Seven [Sages of Greece], but as a result of their constant observance of middle duties [i.e., according to Stoic doctrine] they exhibited a certain semblance to and appearance of wise men.

T 8 Cicero, *On the Orator*

[Crassus:] For what did M. Cato lack except this extremely refined learning imported from across the seas and from foreign places? Do you think, just because he

poterat dicere, iuris scientiam neglegebat? at utroque in genere et elaboravit[1] et praestitit. num propter hanc ex privatorum negotiis collectam gratiam tardior in re publica capessenda fuit? nemo apud populum fortior, nemo melior senator, idem facile optimus imperator; denique nihil in hac civitate temporibus illis sciri discive potuit, quod ille non cum investigarit et scierit tum etiam conscripserit.

1 elaboravit *vel* et laboravit *vel* et elaboravit *codd.*

T 9 Cic. *Rep.* 1.1

Marco vero Catoni, homini ignoto et novo (quo omnes qui isdem rebus studemus, quasi exemplari ad industriam virtutemque ducimur), certe licuit Tusculi[1] se in otio delectare salubri et propinquo loco; sed homo demens, ut isti putant, cum cogeret eum necessitas nulla, in his undis et tempestatibus ad summam senectutem maluit iactari, quam in illa tranquillitate atque otio iucundissime vivere.

1 licuit Tusculi *Mai, cod.*[2] *(ap. Ziegler)*: licuitusculi *cod. (corr. sub textu Augustini latet)*

T 10 Cic. *Rep.* 2.1–3

hic[1] <. . . cupidi>tate audiendi, ingressus est sic loqui SCIPIO: "Catonis hoc senis est, quem ut scitis unice dilexi

1 *huius vocabuli in principio libri vestigia dispexisse Powellio videtur, cetera usque ad* -tate (*id est tres versus codicis) evanuerunt*: ut omnis igitur vidit incensos cupiditate *Mai*: cum omnes flagrarent cupiditate *Heinrich*

had studied civil law, he refrained from pleading cases? Or, because he was able to speak, he neglected the science of jurisprudence? Instead, in both fields he both exerted himself and excelled. Surely, he was not, on account of this influence acquired from doing the business of private clients, slower in engaging in political matters? No one [was] more vigorous in front of the People, no one [was] a better senator, he [was] easily the best general too; in short, nothing in this community in those times could be known or learned that he had not merely studied and come to know, but had even brought together in writing.

T 9 Cicero, *On the Republic*

For Marcus Cato again, an unknown and "new" man (by whom, like a model, all of us who are devoted to the same pursuits are drawn to diligence and moral excellence), it would surely have been possible to enjoy a leisurely life at Tusculum, a healthy and nearby place [i.e., close to Rome]. But he, a mad person, as those people [i.e., those disapproving of political activity] believe, preferred, although no necessity forced him, to be tossed by waves and storms here into extreme old age, rather than to live most pleasantly in tranquility and leisure there.

T 10 Cicero, *On the Republic*

Then, [when he saw the interlocutors full of] eagerness to hear [?], Scipio [P. Cornelius Scipio Aemilianus Africanus minor (*ORF*[4] 21)] began to speak as follows: "This is a statement by Cato of old, whom, as you know, I loved es-

maximeque sum admiratus, cuique vel patris utriusque iudicio vel etiam meo studio me totum ab adulescentia dedidi; cuius me numquam satiare potuit oratio, tantus erat in homine usus rei publicae, quam et domi et militiae cum optime tum etiam diutissime gesserat, et modus in dicendo et gravitate mixtus lepos, et summum vel discendi[2] studium vel docendi, et orationi vita admodum congruens. [2] . . . [*Orig.* F 131] . . . [3] quamobrem, ut ille solebat, ita nunc mea repetet oratio populi Romani originem (libenter enim etiam verbo utor Catonis); . . ."

[2] discendi *Mai*: dicendi *cod.*

Cf. Cic. *Rep.* 2.37.

T 11 Cic. *Leg.* 1.6

[A.:] nam post annalis pontificum maximorum, quibus nihil potest esse ieiunius,[1] si aut ad Fabium aut ad eum qui tibi semper in ore est, Catonem, aut ad Pisonem aut ad Fannium aut ad Vennonium venias, quamquam ex his alius alio plus habet virium, tamen quid tam exile quam isti omnes?

[1] ieiunius *Ursinus*: iucundius *codd.*: nudius *R. Stephanus*: *alii alia*

T 12 Cic. *Leg.* 2.5

[A.:] sed illud tamen quale est quod paulo ante dixisti, hunc locum (id est, <ut>[1] ego te accipio dicere, Arpinum)

[1] id est <ut> *Vahlen*: idem *codd.*: item *Zumpt*

pecially and admired greatly; and, on the advice of both my fathers [i.e., the biological and the adoptive father] and also my own inclination, I devoted myself fully to him from my youth onward. Of his speaking I could never have enough: so great was the man's experience of public affairs, with which he had dealt both in peace and in war, not only very well, but also for a very long period, his moderation in speaking, his charm combined with dignity, his utmost zeal for learning or teaching, and his life entirely consonant with his discourse. [2] . . . [*Orig*. F 131] . . . [3] For that reason, as he [Cato] was accustomed to do, so my discourse will now trace 'the origin' of the Roman People (for I gladly use also an expression of Cato's); . . ."

T 11 Cicero *On the Laws*

[A.:] For after the annals of the chief pontiffs, which are dryer than anything else, if you come to Fabius [Q. Fabius Pictor (*FRHist* 1)], or to him, whose name is always on your lips, Cato, or to Piso [L. Calpurnius Piso Frugi (*FRHist* 9)], or to Fannius [C. Fannius (*FRHist* 12)], or to Vennonius [*FRHist* 13], although, among these, one may display more vigor than another, yet, what is so plain as all of them?

T 12 Cicero *On the Laws*

[A.:] But what is this that you were saying a little earlier, that this place (that is, <as> I take it you mean, Arpinum)

germanam patriam esse vestram? quid? vos duas habetis[2] patrias? an est una illa patria communis? nisi forte sapienti illi Catoni fuit patria non Roma, sed Tusculum.
[M.:] ego mehercule et illi et omnibus municipibus duas esse censeo patrias, unam naturae, alteram[3] civitatis; ut ille Cato, cum esset Tusculi natus, in populi Romani civitatem susceptus est. ita cum ortu Tusculanus esset, civitate Romanus, habuit alteram loci patriam, alteram iuris.

[2] quid vos duas habetis *vel* quid vasis habitis *vel* numquid duas habetis *vel* mi(hi) qui duas habetis *vel* quid duasne habetis *codd.*
[3] naturae, alteram *codd. rec.*: naturam (-a) *codd.*

T 13 Cic. *Brut.* 60–69

[CICERO:] at hic Cethegus consul cum P. Tuditano fuit bello Punico secundo quaestorque his consulibus M. Cato modo plane annis CXL ante me consulem; . . . [61] hunc igitur Cethegum consecutus est aetate Cato, qui annis IX post eum fuit consul. eum nos ut perveterem habemus, qui L. Marcio M'. Manilio consulibus mortuus est, annis LXXXVI ipsis ante me consulem. nec vero habeo quemquam antiquiorem, cuius quidem scripta proferenda putem, nisi quem Appi Caeci oratio haec ipsa de Pyrrho et nonnullae mortuorum laudationes forte delectant. [62] et hercules eae quidem exstant: ipsae enim familiae sua quasi ornamenta ac monumenta servabant et ad usum, si quis

is your true fatherland? What? Do you have two fatherlands? Or is that single fatherland covering both? Unless perhaps that famous Cato, the "Wise," had as his fatherland not Rome, but Tusculum.
[M.:] By Hercules, I believe that both he and all those from Italian towns have two fatherlands, one by nature and the other by citizenship; just as that Cato, although he was born in Tusculum, was received into the citizenship of the Roman People. Thus, as he was a Tusculan by birth and a Roman by citizenship, he had one fatherland from the place of his birth, another by law.

T 13 Cicero, *Brutus*

[CICERO:] And this Cethegus [M. Cornelius Cethegus (*ORF*[4] 7)] was consul [204 BC] with P. Tuditanus [P. Sempronius Tuditanus] in the Second Punic War [218–201 BC], and M. Cato was quaestor under these consuls, only 140 years, to be exact, before my consulship [63 BC]; . . . [61] This Cethegus, then, was followed next in point of time by Cato, who was consul nine years after him [195 BC]. Him we regard as very early, he who died in the consulship of L. Marcius and M'. Manilius [L. Marcius Censorinus and M'. Manilius, cos. 149 BC], exactly 86 years before my consulship [63 BC]. Still, I do not have anyone earlier whose writings I believe should be adduced, unless perchance the very speech of Appius Caecus concerning Pyrrhus [App. Claudius Caecus (*ORF*[4] 1 F 4–11)] or some eulogies of the dead delight anyone. [62] And, by Hercules, those are extant: for the families themselves have preserved them as ornaments and monuments of themselves, for use, if anyone of the same family should

eiusdem generis occidisset, et ad memoriam laudum domesticarum et ad illustrandam nobilitatem suam. . . . [63] Catonis autem orationes non minus multae fere sunt quam Attici Lysiae, cuius arbitror plurimas esse . . . et quodam modo est nonnulla in iis etiam inter ipsos similitudo: acuti sunt, elegantes faceti breves; sed ille Graecus ab omni laude felicior. [64] habet enim certos sui studiosos, qui non tam habitus corporis opimos quam gracilitates consectentur; quos, valetudo modo bona sit, tenuitas ipsa delectat—quamquam in Lysia sunt saepe etiam lacerti, sic ut {et}[1] fieri nihil possit valentius; verum est certe genere toto strigosior—, sed habet tamen suos laudatores, qui hac ipsa eius subtilitate admodum gaudeant. [65] Catonem vero quis nostrorum oratorum, qui quidem nunc sunt, legit? aut quis novit omnino? at quem virum, di boni! mitto civem aut senatorem aut imperatorem; oratorem enim hoc loco quaerimus: quis illo gravior in laudando, acerbior in vituperando, in sententiis argutior, in docendo edisserendoque subtilior? refertae sunt orationes amplius centum quinquaginta, quas quidem adhuc invenerim et legerim, et verbis et rebus inlustribus. licet ex his eligant ea quae notatione et laude digna sint: omnes oratoriae virtutes in eis reperientur. [66] iam vero Origines eius quem florem aut quod lumen eloquentiae non habent? amatores huic desunt, sicuti multis iam ante saeclis et Philisto Syracusio et ipsi Thucydidi. nam ut horum concisis sententiis, interdum etiam[2] non satis apertis {autem}[3] cum brevitate tum

[1] *del. edd.*: ut et *codd.*: ut eo *Manutius*: uti *Stangl*

[2] etiam *codd.*: autem *Martha*

[3] *del. edd.*

have died, and for remembering the glories of their houses, and for illustrating their nobility. . . . [63] But Cato's orations are virtually no less numerous than those of the Athenian Lysias, of whom there are very many I believe . . . , and in some way concerning those [speeches] there is also some similarity between these men: they are acute, refined, clever, brief. But in respect of fame that Greek man has been altogether more fortunate. [64] He has certain devotees of his who cultivate not so much a full habit of body as leanness, whom, if only health is fine, sparseness itself delights—while in Lysias there is often a muscular vigor so that {and} there could be nothing stronger; still, in his style as a whole he is certainly of the more meager type—, yet, he has his admirers who enjoy this very slightness of his to a great extent. [65] But as for Cato, who of our orators, at least of those who are around at present, reads him? Or who has any familiarity with him at all? And yet, what a man, good heavens! I pass over the citizen, the senator, or the general; for at this point we seek the orator: who is weightier in commendation than him, sharper in censure, shrewder in aphorisms, more subtle in presentation and proof? His orations, more than one hundred and fifty, at least that I have yet found and read, are packed with brilliant diction and matter. Let them select from these those passages that are worthy of note and praise: all the virtues of oratory will be found in those. [66] Further, his *Origines*, what flower or what luster of eloquence do they not have? Ardent admirers he lacks, just as many centuries earlier already Philistus the Syracusan [Greek historian, fl. ca. 400 BC] and even Thucydides. For just as the path of their concise statements, sometimes also not sufficiently clear {but} due to brevity or too much

nimio acumine, officit Theopompus elatione atque altitudine orationis suae—quod idem Lysiae Demosthenes—, sic Catonis luminibus obstruxit haec posteriorum quasi exaggerata altius oratio. [67] sed ea[4] in nostris inscitia est, quod hi ipsi, qui in Graecis antiquitate delectantur eaque subtilitate, quam Atticam appellant, hanc in Catone ne[5] noverunt quidem. Hyperidae volunt esse et Lysiae. laudo: sed cur nolunt Catones?[6] [68] Attico genere dicendi se gaudere dicunt. sapienter id quidem; atque utinam imitarentur nec ossa solum sed etiam sanguinem! gratum est tamen, quod volunt. cur igitur Lysias et Hyperides amatur, cum penitus ignoretur Cato? antiquior est huius sermo et quaedam horridiora verba. ita enim tum loquebantur. id muta, quod tum ille non potuit, et adde numeros et, ‹ut›[7] aptior sit oratio, ipsa verba compone et quasi coagmenta, quod ne Graeci quidem veteres factitaverunt: iam neminem antepones Catoni. [69] ornari orationem Graeci putant, si verborum immutationibus utantur, quos appellant *τρόπους*, et sententiarum orationisque formis, quae vocant *σχήματα*: non veri simile est quam sit in utroque genere et creber et distinctus Cato. nec vero ignoro nondum esse satis politum hunc oratorem et quaerendum esse aliquid perfectius; quippe cum ita sit ad nostrorum temporum rationem vetus, ut nullius scriptum exstet dignum quidem lectione, quod sit antiquius. sed maiore honore in omnibus artibus quam in hac una arte[8] dicendi versatur antiquitas.

4 ea *Bake*: et *codd.*
5 ne *edd.*: non *codd.*
6 Catones *edd.*: Catonis *codd.*
7 ut *add. edd.*
8 arte *del. edd.*

shrewdness, is blocked by Theopompus [Greek historian, 4th cent. BC] with the high-flown loftiness of his prose—what Demosthenes also [did] to Lysias—, so this prose of later [writers], as if piled up to greater heights, has obstructed the light of Cato. [67] But such is the ignorance among our people that the very individuals who, concerning the Greeks, find pleasure in the early period and in that fineness that they call Attic, have not even realized this [quality] in Cato. They would like to be a Hyperides and a Lysias [Attic orators, 4th cent. BC]. I praise that: but why do they not want to be a Cato? [68] They say that they enjoy the Attic style of speaking. This at any rate is sensible; and if they only imitated not just its bones, but also its blood! Still, it is welcome what they wish. But why then are Lysias and Hyperides loved, while Cato is wholly unknown? His language is rather archaic, and some of his words are quite uncouth. For they spoke in this way then. Change that which he could not at that time, and add rhythm, and, ‹to› fit the utterance together more smoothly, rearrange the words themselves, cement them as it were together, what even the early Greeks did not do: you will then not place anyone before Cato. [69] The Greeks consider that an utterance is embellished if they employ such interchanges in the use of words as they call *tropoi*, and such figures of thought and language as they term *schemata*; it is incredible how rich and marked out Cato is in both these features. And I am certainly not unaware that this orator is not yet sufficiently polished and that something more finished is to be sought, obviously, since in relation to our times he is so ancient that there exists no piece of writing by anyone, at least none worth reading, that is older. But antiquity is held in greater honor with respect to all other arts than to this one art of speaking.

T 14 Cic. *Brut.* 80

[CICERO:] et[1] vero etiam tum Catone vivo, qui annos quinque et octoginta natus excessit e vita, cum quidem eo ipso anno contra Ser. Galbam ad populum summa contentione dixisset, quam etiam orationem scriptam reliquit—sed vivo Catone minores natu multi uno tempore oratores floruerunt.

[1] et *Lambinus*: at *codd.*

T 15 Cic. *Brut.* 293–94

"quia primum," inquit [ATTICUS], "ita laudavisti quosdam oratores ut imperitos posses in errorem inducere. equidem in quibusdam risum vix tenebam, cum Attico Lysiae Catonem nostrum comparabas, magnum mercule hominem vel potius summum et singularem virum—nemo dicet secus—, sed oratorem? sed etiam Lysiae similem? quo nihil potest esse pictius. bella ironia, si iocaremur; sin adseveramus, vide ne religio nobis tam adhibenda sit quam si testimonium diceremus. [294] ego enim Catonem tuum ut civem, ut senatorem, ut imperatorem, ut virum denique cum prudentia et diligentia tum omni virtute excellentem probo; orationes autem eius ut illis temporibus valde laudo—significant enim formam quandam ingeni, sed admodum impolitam et plane rudem—, Origines vero cum omnibus oratoris[1] laudibus refertas diceres et Catonem cum Philisto et Thucydide comparares, Brutone te id censebas an mihi probaturum? quos enim ne e Graecis quidem quisquam imitari potest, his tu comparas

[1] oratoris *codd.*: oratoriis *Manutius*

T 14 Cicero, *Brutus*

[CICERO:] And to be sure even still in the lifetime of Cato, who passed away after a life of eighty-five years, when in that very year [of his death] he had spoken against Ser. Galba before the People with the greatest intensity [*Orat.* F 196–99A], a speech that he also left in written form—yet in the lifetime of Cato there flourished many younger orators at a single point in time.

T 15 Cicero, *Brutus*

"Because, first of all," he [ATTICUS] said, "you have praised certain orators in such a manner that you could mislead the uninitiated. In fact, in some instances I could scarcely refrain from laughter, when you compared with the Athenian Lysias our Cato [T 13], a great man, by Hercules, or rather first-rate and unique—no one will say otherwise—, but an orator? But even like Lysias? Nothing can be more carefully finished than him. Pleasant irony, if we are jesting; but if we are making a serious statement, consider that we should employ the same scrupulousness as if we were giving testimony on oath. [294] For I esteem your Cato as a citizen, as a senator, as a general, in short, as a man preeminent in sagacity and conscientiousness, and also in every virtue. His speeches too for their time I praise strongly—for they reveal a certain outline of talent, but rather unpolished and quite rough. But when you described the *Origines* as packed with all the qualities of an orator and compared Cato with Philistus and Thucydides [T 13], did you believe that you could demonstrate that to Brutus or me? For no one even among the Greeks can imitate them, and you compare with these men a person

hominem Tusculanum nondum suspicantem quale esset copiose et ornate dicere. . . ."

T 16 Cic. *Brut.* 298

["CICERO":] volvendi enim sunt libri cum aliorum tum in primis Catonis. intelleges nihil illius liniamentis nisi eorum pigmentorum, quae inventa nondum erant, florem et colorem defuisse.

T 17 Cic. *Orat.* 152

sed Graeci viderint; nobis ne si cupiamus quidem distrahere voces conceditur. indicant orationes illae ipsae horridulae Catonis, indicant omnes poetae praeter eos qui ut versum facerent saepe hiabant, ut . . .

T 18 Cic. *Sen.* 3

. . . : hunc librum ad te de senectute misimus. omnem autem sermonem tribuimus non Tithono, ut Aristo Ceus—parum enim esset auctoritatis in fabula—, sed M. Catoni seni, quo maiorem auctoritatem haberet oratio; apud quem Laelium et Scipionem facimus admirantes quod is tam facile senectutem ferat, eisque eum respondentem. qui si eruditius videbitur disputare quam consuevit ipse in suis libris, attribuito litteris Graecis, quarum constat eum perstudiosum fuisse in senectute.

from Tusculum who had not yet the faintest notion of what speaking with oratorical fullness and elaboration is. . . ."

T 16 Cicero, *Brutus*

["Cicero":] For [to answer this question] one has to unroll books by others and especially by Cato. You will see that his drawing lacked nothing other than the flower and color of those ornaments that had not yet been discovered.

T 17 Cicero, *Orator*

But let the Greeks see [to their own practice]; to us [Romans], even if we should desire it, it is not permitted to separate vowels. This is shown by those very orations, famous though slightly rough, of Cato; this is shown by all the poets except those who, so as to create a verse, often used hiatus, like . . .

T 18 Cicero, *On Old Age*

. . . : this book that we are sending to you is on old age. But the entire discourse we have attributed, not to Tithonus, like Aristo of Ceos [Peripatetic philosopher]—for there would be too little authority in a myth—, but to the elderly M. Cato, so that thereby the discourse might have greater authority; and we portray Laelius [C. Laelius Sapiens (*ORF*^{4} 20)] and Scipio [P. Cornelius Scipio Aemilianus Africanus minor (*ORF*^{4} 21)] in his presence, expressing admiration that he bears old age so easily, and him replying to them. If he will appear to argue more learnedly than he himself generally did in his own books, you may give the credit for that to Greek literature, which, as is well known, he studied eagerly in old age [cf. Cic. *Arch.* 16].

T 19 Cic. *Sen.* 10

["Cato":] ego Quintum Maximum, eum qui Tarentum recepit, senem adulescens ita dilexi ut aequalem; erat enim in illo viro comitate condita gravitas, nec senectus mores mutaverat; quamquam eum colere coepi non admodum grandem natu, sed tamen iam aetate provectum. anno enim post consul primum fuerat quam ego natus sum; cumque eo quartum consule adulescentulus miles ad Capuam profectus sum, quintoque anno post ad Tarentum. quaestor deinde quadriennio post factus sum, quem[1] magistratum gessi consulibus Tuditano et Cethego, cum quidem ille admodum senex suasor legis Cinciae de donis et muneribus fuit.

[1] quaestor . . . quem *Pighius*: quaestor. deinde aedilis. quadriennio post factus sum praetor. quem a: quaestor. quem (quaestor. quõ *vel* quaestor.) *codd.* quaestorque *Mommsen*

T 20a Cic. *Sen.* 26

["Cato":] sed videtis ut senectus non modo languida atque iners non sit, verum etiam sit operosa et semper agens aliquid et moliens, tale scilicet quale cuiusque studium in superiore vita fuit. quid qui etiam addiscunt aliquid, ut et Solonem versibus gloriantem videmus, qui se cotidie aliquid addiscentem dicit senem fieri, et ego feci, qui litteras Graecas senex didici? quas quidem sic avide adripui, quasi diuturnam sitim explere cupiens, ut ea ipsa mihi nota

T 19 Cicero, *On Old Age*

["CATO":] I loved Quintus Maximus [Q. Fabius Maximus Verrucosus Cunctator, cos. 233, 228, 215, 214, 209 BC (*ORF*[4] 3)], the man who recaptured Tarentum [209 BC], as a contemporary, though he was an old man and I was a young man; for there was in that man a dignity seasoned with courtesy, and age had not altered his habits; yet, when I began to regard him highly, he was not extremely old, though he was well advanced in age. For he had been consul for the first time in the year after I was born [234 BC]; and when he was consul for the fourth time, I was a very young man setting out as a soldier with him for Capua [214 BC], and five years later for Tarentum [209 BC]. Then, four years after that, I was appointed quaestor, which office I held in the consulship of Tuditanus and Cethegus [P. Sempronius Tuditanus and M. Cornelius Cethegus (*ORF*[4] 7), 204 BC], while that man, far advanced in age, was a supporter of the Cincian Law on gifts and donations [*LPPR*, pp. 261–62; Elster 2003, 255–61; *ORF*[4] 3 F 6].

T 20a Cicero, *On Old Age*

["CATO":] But you see that not only is old age not feeble and inactive, but that it is even busy and always doing and working at something, that is to say, something of the kind that was each person's pursuit earlier in life. And what of those who even learn something in addition? For instance, we see Solon boasting in verses, saying that he grows old learning something in addition every day [Plut. *Sol.* 2.2, 31.3]; and I have done it, as I have studied Greek literature as an old man. I seized upon that as ardently as if I had been eager to satisfy a long-lasting thirst, so that those very

essent quibus me nunc exemplis uti videtis. quod cum fecisse Socraten in fidibus audirem, vellem equidem etiam illud (discebant enim fidibus antiqui), sed in litteris certe elaboravi.

T 20b Quint. *Inst.* 12.11.23

M. igitur Cato, idem summus imperator, idem sapiens, idem orator, idem historiae conditor, idem iuris, idem rerum rusticarum peritissimus fuit; inter tot operas militiae, tantas domi contentiones rudi saeculo litteras ‹Graecas›[1] aetate iam declinata didicit, ut esset hominibus documento ea quoque percipi posse quae senes concupissent.

[1] gr(a)ecas *unus cod. rec.*: *om. cod. mai.*

T 21 Cic. *Sen.* 32

["Cato":] sed redeo ad me: quartum ago annum et octogesimum. vellem equidem idem possem gloriari quod Cyrus; sed tamen hoc queo dicere, non me quidem eis esse viribus quibus aut miles bello Punico aut quaestor eodem bello aut consul in Hispania fuerim, aut quadriennio post cum tribunus militaris depugnavi apud Thermopylas Manio Acilio Glabrione consule; sed tamen ut vos videtis, non plane me enervavit, non adflixit senectus; non curia vires meas desiderat, non rostra, non amici, non clientes, non hospites. nec enim umquam sum adsensus veteri illi laudatoque proverbio, quod monet mature fieri

things have become known to me that you now see me using as examples. When I heard what Socrates had done in the case of the lyre, I should have liked to do that too (for the ancients were accustomed to learn to play the lyre), but in literature I have certainly labored hard.

T 20b Quintilian, *The Orator's Education*

M. Cato, then, was at the same time an outstanding general, a wise man, an orator, the founder of historiography, a great expert in law and in agriculture; among so many labors in war and such great political struggles at home, in an uncultivated era, he studied <Greek> literature when his age was already declining, so as to be an example to people that those things too that old men have set their hearts on can be grasped.

T 21 Cicero, *On Old Age*

["Cato":] But I return to myself: I am in my eighty-fourth year. If only I could boast in the same way as Cyrus [king of Persia] did; but still I can say this: that, indeed, I do not have that physical strength that I had as a private soldier in the Punic War [217 BC; cf. T 26, 55], or as quaestor in the same war [204 BC], or as consul in the Iberian peninsula [195 BC], or when, four years later [191 BC], as military tribune, I fought the war out at Thermopylae under the consul Manius Acilius Glabrio; but still, as you see, old age has not completely weakened, not crushed me. The Senate does not find my strength wanting, nor does the speaker's platform, nor my friends, nor my dependents, nor my guests. For I have never assented to that ancient and much quoted proverb that advises becoming old early

senem si diu velis senex esse; ego vero me minus diu senem esse mallem, quam esse senem antequam essem. itaque nemo adhuc convenire me voluit cui fuerim occupatus.

T 22 Cic. *Sen.* 38–41

["Cato":] septimus mihi liber Originum est in manibus; omnia antiquitatis monumenta colligo; causarum illustrium quascumque defendi nunc cum maxime conficio orationes; ius augurium pontificium civile tracto; multumque etiam Graecis litteris utor; Pythagoreorumque more, exercendae memoriae gratia, quid quoque die dixerim audierim egerim commemoro vesperi. hae sunt exercitationes ingeni, haec curricula mentis; in his desudans atque elaborans corporis vires non magnopere desidero. adsum amicis, venio in senatum frequens; utroque[1] adfero res multum et diu cogitatas, easque tueor animi, non corporis viribus. quae[2] si exsequi nequirem, tamen me lectulus meus oblectaret, ea ipsa cogitantem quae iam agere non possem. sed ut possim facit acta vita; semper enim in his studiis laboribusque viventi non intellegitur quando obrepat senectus: ita sensim sine sensu aetas senescit, nec subito frangitur, sed diuturnitate exstinguitur. [39] . . . accipite enim, optimi adulescentes, veterem orationem Archytae Tarentini, magni in primis et praeclari viri, quae

[1] utroque *vel* ultroque *codd.*
[2] quae *vel* quas *codd.*

if you would like to be old for a long time. For my part I would prefer to be old less long than be old before my time. Accordingly, no one so far has wished to consult me for whom I was busy.

T 22 Cicero, *On Old Age*

["CATO":] I am working on the seventh book of the *Origines*; I am collecting all the records of the past; I am finishing off now particularly the speeches from all the famous cases that I defended; I am examining augural, pontifical, and civil law; and I am also dealing a lot with Greek literature; and, in the manner of the Pythagoreans, in order to exercise my memory, I run over in my mind in the evening all that I have said, heard, or done each day. These are the exercises of my intellect, these the circuits of my mind; and while I sweat and toil at them, I do not greatly feel the absence of bodily strength. I am there for my friends, I frequently attend the Senate; in both cases I bring up matters after having pondered over them a great deal and for a long time, and I look at those matters with the strength of the mind, not of the body. If I could not carry out these things, nevertheless, my couch would afford me delight, as I would reflect on those very things that I was no longer able to do. But that I could [do that] is the result of the life that I have led; for someone who lives always amid such studies and tasks does not notice when old age stealthily approaches: thus life gradually and imperceptibly glides into old age, and it is not broken suddenly, but extinguished by long duration. [39] . . . Now listen, most noble young men, to an ancient speech of Archytas of Tarentum [Greek philosopher, early 4th cent. BC], an especially great and very distinguished man,

mihi tradita est cum essem adulescens Tarenti cum Quinto Maximo. . . . [41] . . . haec cum Gaio Pontio Samnite, patre eius a quo Caudino proelio Sp. Postumius T. Veturius consules superati sunt, locutum Archytam, Nearchus Tarentinus hospes noster, qui in amicitia populi Romani permanserat, se a maioribus natu accepisse dicebat; cum quidem ei sermoni interfuisset Plato Atheniensis, quem Tarentum venisse L. Camillo Ap. Claudio consulibus reperio.

T 23 Cic. *Sen.* 53–54

["CATO":] quid ego irrigationes, quid fossiones agri repastinationesque proferam, quibus fit multo terra fecundior? quid de utilitate loquar stercorandi? [54] dixi in eo libro, quem de rebus rusticis scripsi; . . .

T 24 Cic. *Amic.* 4–5

sed ut in Catone Maiore,[1] qui est scriptus ad te de senectute, Catonem induxi senem disputantem, quia nulla videbatur aptior persona quae de illa aetate loqueretur quam eius qui et diutissime senex fuerit et in ipsa senectute

[1] feci *post* Catone Maiore *codd., del. unus cod.*[2]

which was passed on to me when, as a young man, I was at Tarentum [209 BC] with Quintus Maximus [Q. Fabius Maximus Verrucosus Cunctator, cos. 233, 228, 215, 214, 209 BC (*ORF*[4] 3)]. . . . [41] . . . Nearchus of Tarentum, my host, who had remained steadfast in his friendship to the Roman People, said that he had heard from older men that Archytas had said this in conversation with Gaius Pontius the Samnite, father of the man by whom the consuls Sp. Postumius and T. Veturius [Sp. Postumius Albinus and T. Veturius Calvinus, cos. 334, 321 BC] were defeated in the battle of the Caudine Forks [in the Second Samnite War]; and that Plato the Athenian had been present at this conversation, and I find that he [Plato] came to Tarentum in the consulship of L. Camillus and Ap. Claudius [L. Furius Camillus and App. Claudius Crassus Inregillensis, cos. 349 BC].

T 23 Cicero, *On Old Age*

["Cato":] Why should I mention the irrigation, the digging of the field, and the frequent turning over, whereby the soil becomes far more fertile? Why should I talk about the benefits of manuring? [54] I discussed this in that book that I have written on agricultural matters; . . .

T 24 Cicero, *On Friendship*

But, as in *Cato the Elder*, which has been written to you [Cicero's friend T. Pomponius Atticus] on the subject of old age, I introduced the elderly Cato as the principal speaker, because no figure seemed more suitable to talk about that period of life than that of an individual who both had been an old man a very long time and, in old age

praeter ceteros floruisset; sic cum accepissemus a patribus maxime memorabilem Gai Laeli et Publi Scipionis familiaritatem fuisse, idonea mihi Laeli persona visa est quae de amicitia ea ipsa dissereret quae disputata ab eo meminisset Scaevola. genus autem hoc sermonum positum in hominum veterum auctoritate et eorum illustrium, plus nescioquo pacto videtur habere gravitatis; itaque ipse mea legens sic afficior interdum, ut Catonem, non me, loqui existimem. [5] sed ut tum ad senem senex de senectute, sic hoc libro ad amicum amicissimus scripsi de amicitia; tum est Cato locutus quo erat nemo fere senior temporibus illis, nemo prudentior; nunc Laelius et sapiens (sic enim est habitus) et amicitiae gloria excellens de amicitia loquetur.

T 25 Varro, *Rust.* 1.2.28

"quasi vero," inquam ["Varro"], "non apud ceteros quoque scriptores talia reperiantur. an non in magni illius Catonis libro, qui de agri cultura est editus, scripta sunt permulta similia, ut haec, quem ad modum placentam facere oporteat, quo pacto libum, qua ratione pernas sallere?" "illud non dicis," inquit Agrius, "quod scribit: 'si velis in convivio multum bibere cenareque libenter, ante

itself, had flourished beyond others; so, since we had learned from our forefathers that the close friendship of Gaius Laelius [C. Laelius Sapiens, cos. 140 BC (*ORF*[4] 20)] and Publius Scipio [P. Cornelius Scipio Aemilianus Africanus minor, cos. 147, 134, censor 142 BC (*ORF*[4] 21)] was most noteworthy, the figure of Laelius seemed to me fit to expound those very points on friendship that Scaevola [Q. Mucius Scaevola augur, cos. 117 BC (*ORF*[4] 50)] remembered to have been discussed by him. Besides, this kind of discourse, founded on the influence of individuals of ancient times, especially of those who are renowned, seems in some way to have greater dignity; hence, reading my own work, I am at times so affected that I believe Cato is speaking and not myself. [5] But as I wrote then as one old man to another old man about old age, so in this book I have written as a most affectionate friend to a friend about friendship. Then the speaker was Cato, whom scarcely anyone in those times exceeded in age and none in wisdom; now, about friendship, the speaker will be Laelius, a man both wise (for he was regarded as such) and outstanding by the renown of his friendship.

T 25 Varro, *On Agriculture*

"Just as if indeed," I ["Varro"] said, "such things are not also to be found in other writers. Are there not very many similar items written in the book of that great Cato, which was published on agriculture, such as how one should make a cake [*Agr.* 76], in what way a pancake [*Agr.* 75], and in what manner salt hams" [*Agr.* 162]? "You do not mention that famous one that he writes," said Agrius: "'If you wish to drink a lot at a feast and to eat cheerfully, you

esse oportet brassicam crudam ex aceto aliqua folia quinque.'"

T 26 Nep. *Cat.* 1.1–3.5

[1.1] M. Cato, ortus municipio Tusculo, adulescentulus, priusquam honoribus operam daret, versatus est in Sabinis, quod ibi heredium a patre relictum habebat. inde hortatu L. Valerii Flacci, quem in consulatu censuraque habuit collegam, ut M. Perpenna censorius narrare solitus est, Romam demigravit in foroque esse coepit. [2] primum stipendium meruit annorum decem septemque. Q. Fabio M. Claudio consulibus tribunus militum in Sicilia fuit. inde ut rediit, castra secutus est C.[1] Claudii Neronis, magnique opera eius existimata est in proelio apud Senam, quo cecidit Hasdrubal, frater Hannibalis. [3] quaestor obtigit P. Africano consuli, cum quo non pro sortis necessitudine vixit: namque ab eo perpetua dissensit vita. aedilis plebi factus est cum C. Helvio. [4] praetor provinciam obtinuit Sardiniam, ex qua quaestor superiore tempore ex

[1] C. *Lambinus*: P. *codd.*

should eat about five leaves of raw cabbage with vinegar beforehand'" [*Agr.* 156].

T 26 Cornelius Nepos, *Life of Cato*

[1.1] M. Cato, born in the town of Tusculum, as a very young man, before he applied himself to a political career, spent time among the Sabines, since he had a hereditary property there, left by his father. Then, with the encouragement of L. Valerius Flaccus, whom he had as colleague in the consulship [195 BC] and the censorship [184 BC], as M. Perpenna, the ex-censor [M. Perperna, cos. 92, censor 86 BC], frequently related, he moved to Rome and began to be active in the Forum. [2] He first served in a military campaign at the age of seventeen [217 BC; cf. T 55]. In the consulship of Q. Fabius and M. Claudius [Q. Fabius Maximus Verrucosus Cunctator, cos. 233, 228, 215, 214, 209 BC (*ORF*[4] 3), and M. Claudius Marcellus, cos. 222, 215, 214, 210, 208 BC] he was tribune of the soldiers in Sicily [214 BC]. Once he had returned from there, he joined the military campaign of C. Claudius Nero [cos. 207 BC], and his achievements in the battle at Sena [Sena Gallica, modern Senigallia near Ancona; now called Battle of the Metaurus], in which Hasdrubal, the brother of Hannibal, fell, were regarded highly. [3] As quaestor [204 BC] he was allotted to the consul P. Africanus [P. Cornelius Scipio Africanus maior, cos. 205, 194, censor 199 BC (*ORF*[4] 4)], with whom he did not live according to the close association resulting from the lot: for with him he disagreed throughout his whole life. He was made plebeian aedile with C. Helvius [199 BC]. [4] As praetor [198 BC] he obtained the province of Sardinia, from which at

Africa decedens Q. Ennium poetam deduxerat, quod non minoris aestimamus quam quemlibet amplissimum Sardiniensem triumphum. [2.1] consulatum gessit cum L. Valerio Flacco, sorte provinciam nactus Hispaniam citeriorem, exque ea triumphum deportavit. [2] ibi cum diutius moraretur, P. Scipio Africanus consul iterum, cuius in priore consulatu quaestor fuerat, voluit eum de provincia depellere et ipse ei succedere, neque hoc per senatum efficere potuit, cum quidem Scipio principatum in civitate obtineret, quod tum non potentia, sed iure res publica administrabatur. qua ex re iratus senatui ‹consulatu›[2] peracto privatus in urbe mansit. [3] at Cato, censor cum eodem Flacco factus, severe praefuit ei potestati. nam et in complures nobiles animadvertit et multas res novas in edictum addidit, qua re luxuria reprimeretur, quae iam tum incipiebat pullulare. [4] circiter annos octoginta, usque ad extremam aetatem ab adulescentia, rei publicae causa suscipere inimicitias non destitit. a multis tentatus non modo nullum detrimentum existimationis fecit, sed, quoad vixit, virtutum laude crevit. [3.1] in omnibus rebus singulari fuit industria: nam et agricola sollers et {rei p.} peritus[3] iuris consultus et magnus imperator et probabilis orator et cupidissimus litterarum fuit. [2] quarum studium etsi[4] senior arripuerat, tamen tantum progressum fecit, ut

[2] *add. Bosius*

[3] peritus *Klotz*: rei p. peritus *codd.*: rei p. peritus, ‹bonus› *Guillemin*

[4] etsi *vel* et *codd.*

an earlier time, as quaestor [204 BC], when leaving Africa, he had brought Q. Ennius, the poet, to Rome [cf. T 82], an act that we do not regard as less glorious than the greatest possible triumph concerning Sardinia. [2.1] He held the consulship with L. Valerius Flaccus [195 BC]; by lot he received the province of Hither Iberia, and from there he brought home a triumph [194 BC]. [2] When he lingered there somewhat too long, P. Scipio Africanus, consul for the second time, in whose earlier consulship he had been quaestor, wished to drive him out of the province and himself to succeed him. But he was not able to achieve this through the Senate, although Scipio held the leading position in the community, because in those days the state was administered, not according to personal influence, but according to the law. Therefore, angry with the Senate, after the completion of ‹his consulship›, he remained in the city [of Rome] as a private citizen. [3] But Cato, having been made censor, once again with Flaccus [184 BC], conducted that office with severity. For he took punitive action against several noblemen, and he added to the edict many new provisions by which to restrain extravagance, which was then already beginning to spring up [cf. T 39]. [4] For about eighty years, until the very end of his life from his youth onward, he did not cease to take up hostilities for the sake of the *res publica*. Although attacked by many, he not only suffered no loss of reputation, but, as long as he lived, he advanced in the fame of his virtues. [3.1] In all matters he was a man of extraordinary assiduousness: for he was a skilled farmer, a skillful legal expert, a great general, a commendable orator, and the most eager for literature. [2] Although he had taken up its study as an older man, nevertheless he made such progress that one

non facile reperiri possit neque de Graecis neque de Italicis rebus quod ei fuerit incognitum. ab adulescentia confecit orationes. [3] senex historias scribere instituit. earum sunt libri septem. primus continet res gestas regum populi Romani, secundus et tertius unde quaeque civitas orta sit Italica, ob quam rem omnes Origines videtur appellasse. in quarto autem bellum Poenicum est primum, in quinto secundum. [4] atque haec omnia capitulatim sunt dicta. reliquaque bella pari modo persecutus est usque ad praeturam Servii Galbae, qui diripuit Lusitanos: atque horum bellorum duces non nominavit, sed sine nominibus res notavit. in eisdem exposuit, quae in Italia Hispaniisque aut fierent aut viderentur admiranda: in quibus multa industria et diligentia comparet, nulla doctrina. [5] huius de vita et moribus plura in eo libro persecuti sumus quem separatim de eo fecimus rogatu T. Pomponii Attici. quare studiosos Catonis ad illud volumen delegamus.

T 27 Hor. *Ars P.* 55–58

ego cur, acquirere pauca / si possum, invideor, cum lingua Catonis et Enni / sermonem patrium ditaverit et nova rerum / nomina protulerit?

cannot easily find anything concerning Greek or Italic matters that was unknown to him. From early manhood he composed speeches. [3] As an old man he began to write histories. Of these there are seven books. The first contains the deeds of the kings of the Roman People; the second and the third the origins of each community in Italy: for that reason he seems to have called the entire work *Origines*. Then in the fourth there is the First Punic War, in the fifth the Second. [4] And all this is told in summary fashion. And he went through the other wars in the same manner down to the praetorship of Servius Galba [Ser. Sulpicius Galba, praet. 151 BC (*ORF*^{4} 19)], who plundered the Lusitanians: and he did not name the leaders of these wars, but noted down the facts without names. In the same [books] he set out remarkable features that occurred or were seen in Italy and the provinces of the Iberian peninsula: in those [books] much diligence and care is in evidence, but no erudition. [5] Concerning this man's life and character we have gone over fuller details in that book that we wrote separately about him at the request of T. Pomponius Atticus. Therefore, we may refer those who are interested in Cato to that volume.

T 27 Horace, *The Art of Poetry*

Why, if I am able to add a few items, am I regarded with ill will, when the language of Cato and of Ennius has enriched the speech of our fathers and brought forth new terms for things?

T 28 Dion. Hal. *Ant. Rom.* 1.7.3

καὶ τὰ μὲν παρὰ τῶν λογιωτάτων ἀνδρῶν, οἷς εἰς ὁμιλίαν ἦλθον, διδαχῇ παραλαβών, τὰ δ' ἐκ τῶν ἱστοριῶν ἀναλεξάμενος, ἃς οἱ πρὸς αὐτῶν ἐπαινούμενοι Ῥωμαίων συνέγραψαν Πόρκιός *τε* Κάτων *καὶ* Φάβιος Μάξιμος *καὶ* Οὐαλέριος <ὁ>[1] Ἀντιεὺς *καὶ* Λικίνιος Μάκερ Αἴλιοί *τε καὶ* Γέλλιοι *καὶ* Καλπούρνιοι *καὶ ἕτεροι συχνοὶ πρὸς τούτοις ἄνδρες οὐκ ἀφανεῖς, ἀπ' ἐκείνων ὁρμώμενος τῶν πραγματειῶν (εἰσὶ δὲ ταῖς* Ἑλληνικαῖς *χρονογραφίαις ἐοικυῖαι), τότε ἐπεχείρησα τῇ γραφῇ.*

[1] *add.* Bücheler

T 29 Dion. Hal. *Ant. Rom.* 1.11.1

οἱ δὲ λογιώτατοι τῶν Ῥωμαϊκῶν *συγγραφέων, ἐν οἷς ἐστι* Πόρκιός *τε* Κάτων *ὁ τὰς γενεαλογίας τῶν ἐν* Ἰταλίᾳ *πόλεων ἐπιμελέστατα συναγαγὼν* . . . [*Orig.* F 49a].

T 30 Liv. 29.25.10

cum viginti rostratis se ac L. Scipionem ab dextro cornu, ab laevo totidem rostratas et C. Laelium praefectum classis cum M. Porcio Catone—quaestor is tum erat—onerariis futurum praesidio.

T 28 Dionysius of Halicarnassus, *Roman Antiquities*

And some details I received from men of the greatest learning, with whom I associated, through their teaching; others I gathered from histories that had been written by authors respected among the Romans themselves, Porcius Cato, Fabius Maximus [Q. Fabius Maximus Servilianus (*FRHist* 8)], Valerius Antias [*FRHist* 25], Licinius Macer [C. Licinius Macer (*FRHist* 27)], people like Aelius [L. and Q. Aelius Tubero (*FRHist* 38)], like Gellius [Cn. Gellius (*FRHist* 14)], and like Calpurnius [L. Calpurnius Piso Frugi (*FRHist* 9)], and many other men not without fame in addition; starting out from those works (they are like the Greek annalistic accounts), I then put my hand to writing.

T 29 Dionysius of Halicarnassus, *Roman Antiquities*

But the most learned of the Roman historians, among whom is Porcius Cato, who compiled the pedigrees of the cities in Italy with the greatest care . . . [*Orig.* F 49a].

T 30 Livy, *History of Rome*

That with twenty warships he [M. Pomponius Matho, praet. 204 BC] and L. Scipio [L. Cornelius Scipio Asiaticus, cos. 190, leg. 204 BC] would protect the transports on the right wing, while the same number of warships and C. Laelius [cos. 190, pref. 204 BC], admiral of the fleet, with M. Porcius Cato, who was at that time quaestor [204 BC], would do so on the left wing.

T 31 Liv. 34.5.6–7

["L. Valerius Tappo":] ". . . verba magna quae rei augendae causa conquirantur et haec et alia esse scio, et M. Catonem oratorem non solum gravem sed interdum etiam trucem esse scimus omnes, cum ingenio sit mitis. [7] nam quid tandem novi matronae fecerunt, quod frequentes in causa ad se pertinente in publicum processerunt? nunquam ante hoc tempus in publico apparuerunt? tuas adversus te Origines revolvam. . . ."

T 32a Liv. 34.17.7–18.5

quod ubi consuli renuntiatum est, senatores omnium civitatium ad se vocari iussit, atque iis "non nostra" inquit "magis quam vestra refert vos non rebellare, [8] siquidem id maiore Hispanorum malo quam exercitus Romani labore semper adhuc factum est. id ut ne fiat, uno modo arbitror caveri posse, si effectum erit ne possitis rebellare. [9] volo id quam mollissima via consequi. vos quoque in ea re consilio me adiuvate: nullum libentius sequar quam quod vosmet ipsi attuleritis." [10] tacentibus spatium se ad deliberandum dierum paucorum dare dixit. [11] cum

T 31 Livy, *History of Rome*

["L. Valerius Tappo":] ". . . I know that there are forceful words that are hunted out to exaggerate a case, both those he has used and others, and we all know M. Cato to be not only a stern, but sometimes even a savage orator, though he is by nature mild. [7] For, what novel thing actually did the matrons do when they came forward into public space in large numbers in a matter concerning them? Have they never appeared in public before this time? I shall unroll your *Origines* against you. . . ."[1]

[1] This excerpt from a "speech" put into the mouth of L. Valerius Tappo comes from the discussion about the repeal of *Lex Oppia* in 195 BC (*Orat*. F 17A). It is generally thought that Cato's *Origines* had not been written by that time and the reference is included anachronistically (see Introduction to *Origines*).

T 32a Livy, *History of Rome*

When this [that Iberians had taken their own lives in the face of Cato's measures] was reported to the consul [Cato in 195 BC], he had the elders of all the communities summoned to him and said to them: "That you do not rebel is not more in our interest than in yours, [8] if at any rate that [course] has always up to now proved more of a disaster for the Iberians than a hardship for the Roman army. That this cannot happen can be secured, I think, in one way only, if it is achieved that you cannot rebel. [9] I want to attain this in the smoothest possible way. You, too, please help me in that matter with advice: I will follow nothing more willingly than what you have brought yourselves." [10] When they remained silent, he said that he was giving them a period of a few days to think it over. [11]

revocati secundo quoque consilio tacuissent, uno die muris omnium dirutis, ad eos qui nondum parebant profectus, ut in quamque regionem venerat, omnes qui circa incolebant populos in dicionem accepit. [12] Segesticam tantum, gravem atque opulentam civitatem, vineis et pluteis cepit. [18.1] . . . [3] sed in consule ea vis animi atque ingenii fuit ut omnia maxima minimaque per se adiret atque ageret, nec cogitaret modo imperaretque quae in rem essent, [4] sed pleraque ipse per se transigeret, nec in quemquam omnium gravius severiusque quam in semet ipsum imperium exerceret, [5] parsimonia et vigiliis et labore cum ultimis militum certaret, nec quicquam in exercitu suo praecipui praeter honorem atque imperium haberet.

T 32b Liv. 39.40.3–12

sed omnes patricios plebeiosque nobilissimarum familiarum M. Porcius longe anteibat. [4] in hoc viro tanta vis animi ingeniique fuit ut quocumque loco natus esset, fortunam sibi ipse facturus fuisse videretur. nulla ars neque privatae neque publicae rei gerendae ei defuit; urbanas rusticasque res pariter callebat. [5] ad summos honores alios scientia iuris, alios eloquentia, alios gloria militaris

When they had been called back and had remained silent at the second meeting too, in a single day he tore down all their city walls, set out against those who still were not submitting, and, in each area to which he had come, he brought under his control all the peoples who lived in the neighborhood. [12] Only Segestica, an important and wealthy city, did he capture by siege sheds and mantlets. [18.1] . . . [3] But in the consul there was so much energy of mind and character that he personally embarked upon and undertook all [manner of operations], whether the greatest or the smallest; and that, instead of simply developing plans and giving orders appropriate to the situation, [4] for the most part he saw them through himself; and that he would not bring his authority to bear more rigorously and more severely on anyone among all than on himself; [5] and that, in frugal living, in watch duties, and in toil, he rivaled the lowest ranking of the soldiers; and that in his army he had no special privilege apart from his rank and command.

T 32b Livy, *History of Rome*

But all patricians and plebeians of the most noble families were far surpassed by M. Porcius [Cato]. [4] In this man there was such strength of intellect and character that it was obvious that he would have achieved success for himself to whatever status he had been born. He lacked none of the expertise needed for conducting private or public business; he was equally skilled in affairs of the city and of the farm. [5] Some have been advanced to the highest offices by legal expertise, others by rhetorical ability, others again by a distinguished military record: his versatile

provexit: huic versabile ingenium sic pariter ad omnia fuit ut natum ad id unum diceres quodcumque ageret: [6] in bello manu fortissimus multisque insignibus clarus pugnis, idem postquam ad magnos honores pervenit summus imperator, idem in pace, si ius consuleres, peritissimus, si causa oranda esset, eloquentissimus, [7] nec is tantum cuius lingua vivo eo viguerit, monumentum eloquentiae nullum exstet: vivit immo vigetque eloquentia eius sacrata scriptis omnis generis. [8] orationes et pro se multae et pro aliis et in alios: nam non solum accusando sed etiam causam dicendo fatigavit inimicos. [9] simultates nimio plures et exercuerunt eum et ipse exercuit eas; nec facile dixeris utrum magis presserit eum nobilitas an ille agitaverit nobilitatem. [10] asperi procul dubio animi et linguae acerbae et immodice liberae fuit, sed invicti a cupiditatibus animi, rigidae innocentiae, contemptor gratiae divitiarum. [11] in parsimonia in patientia laboris periculi ferrei prope corporis animique, quem ne senectus quidem, quae solvit omnia, fregerit, [12] qui sextum et octogesimum annum agens causam dixerit, ipse pro se oraverit scripseritque, nonagesimo anno Ser. Galbam ad populi adduxerit iudicium.

talent was so evenly suited to everything that one might have said that he was born for whatever single thing he was busy with: [6] in war he was a most valiant fighter and brilliant in many famous battles, likewise, after he reached higher offices, he was an outstanding general, likewise in peace, if you consulted him on the law, he was most expert, if there was a case to plead, he was most eloquent. [7] Nor was he the sort of man whose speaking ability bloomed only while he was alive, but for whom no record of the eloquence survives; in fact, his eloquence is alive and vigorous, enshrined in writings of every kind. [8] There are numerous speeches written in defense of himself and both in defense of and against others: for he exhausted his enemies not only by prosecuting them but also by pleading cases. [9] The enmities that harassed him and with which he harassed others were all too numerous; and you could not easily say whether the nobility applied more pressure to him or he attacked the nobility more. [10] He undoubtedly had a stern attitude and a sharp and unrestrainedly free tongue, but was of a character unconquered by desires, of unshakable integrity, and disdainful of influence of wealth. [11] In frugality and in the ability to face hardship and danger he was of an almost iron physique and mind, and even old age, which undoes everything, did not break him. [12] In his eighty-sixth year he pleaded a case, and he spoke on his own behalf and wrote the speech himself; in his ninetieth year he brought Ser. Galba to trial before the People [*Orat.* F 196–99A; incorrect age].

T 32c Liv. 42.34.6–7

["Sp. Ligustinus":] ". . . devicto Philippo Macedonibusque cum in Italiam <re>portati[1] ac dimissi essemus, continuo miles voluntarius cum M. Porcio consule in Hispaniam sum profectus. [7] neminem omnium imperatorum qui vivant acriorem virtutis spectatorem ac iudicem fuisse sciunt qui et illum et alios duces longa militia experti sunt. . . ."

[1] <re>portati *Perizonius*: portati *cod.*: <de>portati *Drakenborch*

T 33 Liv. 39.44.1–9

in equitatu recognoscendo L. Scipioni Asiageni[1] ademptus equus. in censibus quoque accipiendis tristis et aspera in omnes ordines censura fuit. [2] ornamenta et vestem muliebrem et vehicula, quae pluris quam quindecim milium aeris essent, <deciens tanto pluris quam quanti essent>[2] in censum referre iuratores[3] iussi; [3] item mancipia minora annis viginti quae post proximum lustrum decem milibus aeris aut pluris eo venissent, uti ea quoque deciens tanto pluris quam quanti essent aestimarentur, et his rebus omnibus terni in milia aeris attribuerentur. [4] aquam publicam omnem in privatum aedificium aut agrum fluentem ademerunt; et quae in loca publica inaedificata immolitave privati habebant, intra dies triginta demoliti

[1] Asiageni *vel* Asiatico *codd.* [2] <deciens . . . essent> *add. Wesenberg*: <deciens pluris> *hic add. Mommsen, post* referre *Huschke*: *om. codd. plur.* [3] iuratores *codd. plur.*: viatores *cod. unus*: iuratos *Gronovius*: curatores *Heusinger*

T 32c Livy, *History of Rome*

["SP. LIGUSTINUS":] ". . . After the defeat of Philip [Philip V, king of Macedonia] and the Macedonians [in 197 BC], when we had been brought <back> to Italy and discharged, I set out immediately for the Iberian peninsula as a volunteer soldier with M. Porcius [Cato] the consul [195 BC]. [7] No one, of all the generals now living, was a keener observer and judge of bravery, as those know who have had experience of both him and other leaders through long military service. . . ."

T 33 Livy, *History of Rome*

In the review of the equestrian class L. Scipio Asiagenes [L. Cornelius Scipio Asiaticus, cos. 190 BC] had his horse [i.e., equestrian status] taken away. In property assessments too the censorship [of Cato and L. Valerius Flaccus, 184 BC] was bitter and severe toward all classes [cf. T 26]. [2] The officers administering the census were instructed to assess decorative articles, women's dresses, and carriages that were worth more than 15,000 asses <at ten times more than they were worth> for the census; [3] likewise [it was ordered] as regards slaves less than twenty years of age who had been sold for 10,000 asses or more than that since the last lustrum, that they should also be assessed at ten times more than they were worth; and on all these items a tax of three asses per thousand was to be imposed [cf. Plut. *Cat. Mai.* 18.2–3]. [4] They shut off all public water flowing into a private building or land; and any structures that private individuals had had built or erected on public land were demolished within thirty

sunt. [5] opera deinde facienda ex decreta in eam rem pecunia, lacus sternendos lapide, detergendasque, qua opus esset, cloacas, in Aventino et in aliis partibus qua nondum erant faciendas locaverunt. [6] et separatim Flaccus molem ad Neptunias aquas, ut iter populo esset, et viam per Formianum montem, [7] Cato atria duo, Maenium et Titium, in lautumiis, et quattuor tabernas in publicum emit basilicamque ibi fecit, quae Porcia appellata est. et vectigalia summis pretiis, ultro tributa infimis locaverunt. [8] quas locationes cum senatus precibus et lacrimis victus publicanorum induci et de integro locari iussisset, censores, edicto submotis ab hasta qui ludificati priorem locationem erant, omnia eadem paulum imminutis pretiis locaverunt. [9] nobilis censura fuit simultatiumque plena, quae M. Porcium, cui acerbitas ea adsignabatur, per omnem vitam exercuerunt.

T 34 Liv. *Epit.* 49

tertii Punici belli initium altero et sescentesimo ab urbe condita anno, intra quintum annum quam, erat coeptum, consummati. inter M. Porcium Catonem et Scipionem

days. [5] They next contracted out works that were to be carried out with money designated for that purpose: paving of cisterns with stone, cleaning of sewers where necessary, and constructing them on the Aventine and in other areas where they did not yet exist. [6] And, individually, Flaccus built a causeway at the Neptunian waters [location uncertain], to provide a public footpath, and a road across the hill at Formiae [place in Latium]; [7] Cato purchased for public use two auction rooms, the Maenian and the Titian, in the area of the Lautumiae [on the northeastern slope of the Capitoline Hill], and four shops, and constructed there a basilica, which was called the Porcian [T 82; *Orat.* F 87]. Furthermore, they charged the highest rates in contracting out tax collection and themselves paid the lowest to contractors for commissioned works. [8] When the Senate, won over by the pleas and tears of the contractors, ordered that these contracts be canceled and new ones assigned, the censors removed by an edict from the bidding those who had made a mockery of the previous contracts and then let out all the same contracts at only slightly reduced rates. [9] It was a remarkable censorship and full of controversies, which exercised M. Porcius [Cato] throughout his entire life since that severity was attributed to him.

T 34 Livy, *Epitome*

The beginning of the Third Punic War fell in the six hundred and second year after the founding of the city [151 BC], a war concluded within the fifth year after it had been begun [here 151–146 BC]. There was a contest of opposing opinions between M. Porcius Cato and Scipio Nasica

Nasicam, quorum alter sapientissimus vir in civitate habebatur, alter optimus vir etiam iudicatus a senatu erat, diversis certatum sententiis est, Catone suadente bellum et ut tolleretur delereturque Carthago, Nasica dissuadente. . . . Catonis sententia evicit,[1] ut in decreto perstaretur et ut consules quam primum ad bellum proficiscerentur. . . . quam virtutem eius et Cato, vir promptioris ad vituperandum linguae, in senatu sic prosecutus est, ut diceret reliquos, qui in Africa militarent, umbras volitare,[2] Scipionem vigere, . . . cum L. Scribonius tr. pl. rogationem promulgasset, ut Lusitani, qui in fidem populo R. dediti ab Servio Galba in Galliam venissent, in libertatem restituerentur, M. Cato acerrime suasit. extat oratio in annalibus ipsius inclusa. Q. Fulvius Nobilior ei, saepe ab eo in senatu laceratus, respondit pro Galba; . . .

1 evicit *Halm*: devicit *codd.*: pervicit *ed. princ.*
2 volitare *Gronovius*: militare *codd.*, *ed. princ.*

Cf. Diod. Sic. 32.9a.2.

T 35 Vell. Pat. 1.17.2–3

historicos et‹iam›,[1] ut Livium quoque priorum aetati adstruas, praeter Catonem et quosdam veteres et obscuros minus LXXX annis circumdatum aevum tulit, ut nec poe-

1 et‹iam› *Vossius*: et *cod.*, *ed. pr.*

[P. Cornelius Scipio Nasica Corculum, cos. 162, 155, censor 159 BC], one of whom was considered the wisest man in the community and the other of whom had even been adjudged by the Senate to be a man of the greatest excellence: Cato argued for war and for the removal and destruction of Carthage, while Nasica argued against it. . . . Cato's position prevailed, namely that one should stand by the decree and that the consuls should set out to war as soon as possible. . . . That valor of that man [P. Cornelius Scipio Aemilianus Africanus minor (*ORF*[4] 21)] even Cato, a man with a tongue readier for insult, praised in the Senate so highly as to say that the others who were doing military service in Africa were shadows flitting around while Scipio was full of energy [cf. *Op. cet.* F 76], . . . When L. Scribonius, a Tribune of the People [L. Scribonius Libo, trib. pl. 149 BC (*ORF*[4] 29)], had proposed a bill that the Lusitanians, who had surrendered themselves to the protection of the Roman People and had then been sold to Gaul by Servius Galba [Ser. Sulpicius Galba, cos. 144 BC (*ORF*[4] 19 F 12–14)], should be restored to liberty, M. Cato most vigorously supported it [*Orat.* F 196–99A]. His speech is extant, included in his own *Annals* [*Orig.* F 104–7]. Q. Fulvius Nobilior [cos. 153, censor 136 BC (*ORF*[4] 19A F 2)], who had often been assailed by him in the Senate, answered him on behalf of Galba; . . .

T 35 Velleius Paterculus, *Compendium of Roman History*

The historians as well, inasmuch as you add Livy also to the period of the older [writers], with the exception of Cato and certain old and obscure ones, have emerged within an era comprised of less than eighty years, just as

tarum in antiquius citeriusve processit ubertas. [3] at oratio ac vis forensis perfectumque prosae eloquentiae decus, ut idem separetur Cato (pace P. Crassi Scipionisque et Laelii et Gracchorum et Fannii et Servii Galbae dixerim), ita universa sub principe operis sui erupit Tullio, ut delectari ante eum paucissimis, mirari vero neminem possis nisi aut ab illo visum aut qui illum viderit.

T 36 Val. Max. 3.4.6

M. vero Porci Catonis incrementa publicis votis expetenda fuerunt, qui nomen suum Tusculi ignobile Romae nobilissimum reddidit: ornata sunt enim ab eo litterarum Latinarum monumenta, adiuta disciplina militaris, aucta maiestas senatus, prorogata familia, in qua maximum decus posterior ortus est Cato.

T 37 Val. Max. 8.7.1

Cato sextum et octogesimum annum agens, dum in re publica tuenda iuvenili animo perstat, ab inimicis capitali crimine accusatus causam suam egit, neque aut memoriam eius quisquam tardiorem aut firmitatem lateris ulla

the copious flow of poets has not extended to an earlier or a later date. [3] But oratory and the forensic art, and the perfected splendor of eloquence in prose, with Cato again excepted (I say this with due respect to P. Crassus [P. Licinius Crassus Dives Mucianus (*ORF*^{4} 31)], Scipio [P. Cornelius Scipio Aemilianus Africanus minor (*ORF*^{4} 21)], Laelius [C. Laelius Sapiens (*ORF*^{4} 20)], the Gracchi [Ti. Sempronius Gracchus (*ORF*^{4} 34) + C. Sempronius Gracchus (*ORF*^{4} 48)], Fannius [C. Fannius (*ORF*^{4} 32)], and Servius Galba [Ser. Sulpicius Galba (*ORF*^{4} 19)]), burst forth fully formed under the chief exponent of this activity, Tullius [Cicero], in such a way that you can be pleased by very few before him and admire no one other than those whom he saw [during his lifetime] or who saw him [during their lifetimes].

T 36 Valerius Maximus, *Memorable Doings and Sayings*

M. Porcius Cato's rise without doubt deserved to be prayed for by public vows: he rendered his name, ignoble in Tusculum, most noble in Rome. For the memorials of Latin literature were adorned by him, military discipline enhanced, the majesty of the Senate increased, and his family extended, a family in which, as its greatest glory, the younger Cato [M. Porcius Cato Uticensis / Cato the Younger, 95–46 BC] was born.

T 37 Valerius Maximus, *Memorable Doings and Sayings*

In his eighty-sixth year Cato continued in public affairs with the spirit of a young man: prosecuted by his enemies on a capital charge, he pleaded his own case, nor did anyone observe his memory to be slower, or the strength of

ex parte quassatam aut os haesitatione impeditum animadvertit, quia omnia ista in suo statu aequali ac perpetua industria continebat. quin etiam in ipso diutissime actae vitae fine disertissimi oratoris Galbae accusationi defensionem[1] suam pro Hispania opposuit. idem Graecis litteris erudiri concupivit—quam sero inde aestimemus quod etiam Latinas paene iam senex didicit—, cumque eloquentia magnam gloriam partam haberet, id egit ut iuris civilis quoque esset peritissimus.

[1] accusationi defensionem *codd.*: defensioni accusationem *Gertz*

T 38 Columella, *Rust.* 1.1.12

et ut agricolationem Romana tandem civitate donemus (nam adhuc istis auctoribus Graecae gentis fuit), iam nunc M. Catonem Censorium illum memoremus, qui eam Latine loqui primus instituit, . . .

T 39 Sen. *Ep.* 87.9–10

M. Cato Censorius, quem tam e re publica fuit nasci quam Scipionem (alter enim cum hostibus nostris bellum, alter cum moribus gessit), cantherio vehebatur et hippoperis quidem inpositis, ut secum utilia portaret. o quam cuperem illi nunc occurrere aliquem ex his trossulis, in via divitibus, cursores et Numidas et multum ante se pulveris agentem! hic sine dubio cultior comitatiorque quam M. Cato videretur, hic qui inter illos apparatus delicatos cum

his lungs in any degree enfeebled, or his mouth impeded by hesitation, since he maintained all those things by steady and perpetual diligence in relation to his situation. Even at the very end of his extremely long life he countered the accusation of Galba, a most eloquent orator, with his defense on behalf of Iberia [*Orat.* F 196–99A]. He was also keen to be instructed in Greek literature—how late we may judge from the fact that he studied even Latin [literature] when already almost an old man—; and although he enjoyed great fame won for eloquence, he managed to be also most expert in civil law.

T 38 Columella, *On Agriculture*

And that we may endow agriculture at last with Roman citizenship (for it has belonged thus far to those writers of the Greek nation), let us now recall that famous M. Cato, the ex-censor, who first taught her to speak in Latin, . . .

T 39 Seneca, *Epistles*

M. Cato, the ex-censor, whose birth was as much a benefit to the *res publica* as that of Scipio [P. Cornelius Scipio Africanus maior, cos. 205, 194, censor 199 BC (*ORF*[4] 4)] (for one of them fought a war against our enemies, the other against our morals), used to ride a donkey, with saddlebags on top, so that he carried his necessaries with him. O how I would love him now to meet one of these dandies, plentiful on the road, driving before themselves forerunners and Numidians and a lot of dust! This person would no doubt seem more refined and well-attended than M. Cato, this person, who, in the midst of all those

maxime dubitat utrum se ad gladium locet an ad cultrum. [10] o quantum erat saeculi decus, imperatorem,[1] triumphalem, censorium, quod[2] super omnia haec est, Catonem uno caballo esse contentum et ne toto quidem; partem enim sarcinae ab utroque latere dependentes occupabant. ita non omnibus obesis mannis et asturconibus et tolutariis praeferres unicum illum equum ab ipso Catone defrictum?

[1] *post* imperatorem *dist. Axelson*
[2] <et> quod *correcturae vel coniecturae codd. rec.*

T 40 Plin. *HN* 1

Lib. III: ex auctoribus: . . . Catone censorio . . .

Cf. sim. ad Lib. IV, VII, VIII, XI, XIV, XV, XVII, XVIII, XIX, XX, XXI, XXVIII, XXXVI.

T 41a Plin. *HN* 7.61–62

nam <in>[1] viris Masinissam regem post LXXXVI annum generasse filium, quem Methimannum appellaverit, clarum est, Catonem censorium octogensimo exacto e filia Saloni clientis sui. [62] qua de causa aliorum eius liberum propago Liciniani sunt cognominati, hi Saloniani, ex quis Uticensis fuit.

[1] *add. edd.*

luxurious paraphernalia, chiefly considers whether he should turn to the sword or to the hunting knife. [10] O what a glory to those times, that a general, a former triumphator, an ex-censor, and, what goes beyond all this, a Cato is content with a single nag, and not even a whole one! For the baggage hanging down on either flank took up a part. Would you not therefore prefer that single horse rubbed down by Cato himself to all fat cobs, ambling horses, and trotters?

T 40 Pliny the Elder, *Natural History*

Book 3: from these authorities: . . . Cato, the ex-censor . . .

Cf. similar notices for Books 4, 7, 8, 11, 14, 15, 17, 18, 19, 20, 21, 28, 36.

T 41a Pliny the Elder, *Natural History*

And <as for> men, it is well known that king Masinissa [king of Numidia], when he was beyond his 86th year, fathered a son, whom he called Methimannus, and that Cato, the ex-censor, having completed his eightieth year, [had a son] by the daughter of Salonius, his client [T 62, 79, 82; *Op. cet.* F 75]. [62] For this reason the offspring of his other children have the cognomen Liciniani [from Cato's first wife, Licinia], these Saloniani [from his second wife, Salonia], of whom [Cato] Uticensis [M. Porcius Cato Uticensis / Cato the Younger, 95–46 BC] was one.

T 41b Solin. 1.59

post annum quinquagesimum fecunditas omnium conquiescit: nam in annum octogesimum viri generant, sicuti Masinissa rex Mathumannum filium septuagesimum et sextum annum agens genuit, Cato octogesimo exacto ex filia Salonis clientis sui avum Uticensis Catonis procreavit.

T 42 Plin. *HN* 7.100

Cato primus Porciae gentis tres summas in homine res praestitisse existimatur, ut esset optimus orator, optimus imperator, optimus senator, quae mihi omnia, etiamsi non prius, attamen clarius fulsisse in Scipione Aemiliano videntur, dempto praeterea plurimorum odio, quo Cato laboravit. itaque sit proprium Catonis quater et quadragiens causam dixisse, nec quemquam saepius postulatum et semper absolutum.

T 41b Solinus

After the fiftieth year of age the fertility of all [women] ceases; for men father into their eightieth year, as king Masinissa [king of Numidia] fathered his son Mathumannus [different spelling of name], when he was in his seventy-sixth year, and Cato, having completed his eightieth year, fathered, by the daughter of Salonius, his client, the grandfather of Cato Uticensis.

T 42 Pliny the Elder, *Natural History*

Cato, the first of that name in the *gens Porcia*, is deemed to have excelled in the three supreme human achievements, in that he was the greatest orator, the greatest general, and the greatest senator; all these distinctions seem to me to have shone, even though not earlier, yet with greater brilliance in Scipio Aemilianus [P. Cornelius Scipio Aemilianus Africanus minor (*ORF*[4] 21)], and also without the unpopularity among very many, under which Cato labored. Accordingly, it may be regarded as characteristic of Cato that he defended himself forty-four times and that nobody was sued more frequently and always acquitted [cf. T 60, 82].

T 43 Plin. *HN* 8.11

certe Cato, cum imperatorum nomina annalibus detraxerit, eum, qui fortissime proeliatus esset in Punica acie, Surum[1] tradidit vocatum altero dente mutilato.

[1] sutrum *unus cod., edd. vet.*

T 44 Plin. *HN* 14.44–47

Catonum ille primus, triumpho et censura super cetera insignis, magis tamen etiamnum claritate litterarum praeceptisque omnium rerum expetendarum datis generi Romano, inter prima vero agrum colendi, ille aevi confessione optimus ac sine aemulo agricola, pauca attigit vitium genera, quarundam ex iis iam etiam nominibus abolitis. [45] separatim toto tractatu sententia eius indicanda est, ut in omni genere noscamus quae fuerint celeberrima anno DC urbis, circa captas Carthaginem ac Corinthum, cum supremum is diem obiit, et quantum postea CCXXX annis vita profecerit. [46] ergo de vitibus uvisque ita prodidit: . . . [*Agr.* 6.4] . . . [47] nec sunt vetustiora de illa re Latinae linguae praecepta. tam prope ab origine rerum sumus.

T 43 Pliny the Elder, *Natural History*

In fact, although Cato removed the names of generals from the *Annals*, he recorded that the one [the elephant] who fought most bravely in the Punic battle line was called Surus, and that it had one of the tusks broken off.[1]

[1] While Cato is said not to have named the human leading fighters in the *Origines* (cf. T 26), Pliny notes that he named a Carthaginian war elephant. *Surus* (in Latin) means both "Syrian" (perhaps in the sense of "Indian elephant") and "stake" (implying a pun; see Scullard 1953).

T 44 Pliny the Elder, *Natural History*

That first of the Catos, celebrated for his triumph [194 BC] and his censorship [184 BC] beyond anything else, though yet more even now for the distinction in literature and the precepts given to the Roman nation on every matter to be sought after and certainly in particular on agriculture, that outstanding and unrivaled agriculturalist by the admission of his contemporaries, has touched upon a few varieties of vines, including some even the names of which are now extinct. [45] His opinion ought to be set out separately at full length, so that we learn which varieties were the most famous in the entire class in the 600th year of the city, about the time of the conquest of Carthage and Corinth [146 BC], when he passed away [149 BC], and how much life has progressed in the 230 years afterward. [46] This is therefore what he set down about vines and grapes: . . . [*Agr.* 6.4] . . . [47] Nor are there any older instructions on that matter in the Latin language. So near are we to the origin of things.

T 45 Plin. *HN* 19.147

nihil diligentius comprehendit Cato, novissimumque libri est, ut appareat ⟨rem⟩[1] repentem[2] ac noviciam fuisse.

1 ⟨rem⟩ *Mayhoff*: *om. codd., edd. vet.*
2 repentinam *edd. ante Salmasium*: recentem *Detlefsen*

T 46 Plin. *Ep.* 1.20.1–5

frequens mihi disputatio est cum quodam docto homine et perito, cui nihil aeque in causis agendis ut brevitas placet. [2] quam ego custodiendam esse confiteor, si causa permittat: alioqui praevaricatio est transire dicenda, praevaricatio etiam cursim et breviter attingere quae sint inculcanda infigenda repetenda. [3] nam plerisque longiore tractatu vis quaedam et pondus accedit, utque corpori ferrum, sic oratio animo non ictu magis quam mora imprimitur. [4] hic ille mecum auctoritatibus agit ac mihi ex Graecis orationes Lysiae ostentat, ex nostris Gracchorum Catonisque, quorum sane plurimae sunt circumcisae et breves: ego Lysiae Demosthenen Aeschinen Hyperiden multosque praeterea, Gracchis et Catoni Pollionem Caesarem Caelium, in primis M. Tullium oppono, cuius oratio optima fertur esse quae maxima. et hercule ut aliae bonae res, ita bonus liber melior est quisque quo maior. [5] vides ut statuas signa picturas, hominum denique multorumque

T 45 Pliny the Elder, *Natural History*

There is nothing that Cato describes more carefully [than asparagus], and it is the very last item of the book [*Agr.* 161], so that it is evident that it was a recent and novel <thing>.

T 46 Pliny the Younger, *Letters*

I have frequent arguments with a certain learned and experienced person, who likes nothing in pleading cases as much as brevity. [2] That this is to be maintained, I admit, if the case is such as to permit it; otherwise it is mismanagement to pass over points that should be mentioned, it is also mismanagement to touch upon points hurriedly and briefly if they should be driven home, impressed, and repeated. [3] For most points acquire a certain emphasis and weight by a fuller treatment, and, like a sword on the body, thus speech is impressed on the mind not more by the thrust than by the time to sink in. [4] At this point that man produces his authorities to me, and he shows me from the Greeks the speeches of Lysias, from our own those of the Gracchi [Ti. Sempronius Gracchus (*ORF*[4] 34) + C. Sempronius Gracchus (*ORF*[4] 48)] and of Cato; most of their speeches are indeed clipped and short. I counter Lysias with Demosthenes, Aeschines, Hyperides, and many besides, and the Gracchi and Cato with Pollio [C. Asinius Pollio (*ORF*[4] 174)], Caesar [C. Iulius Caesar (*ORF*[4] 121)], Caelius [M. Caelius Rufus (*ORF*[4] 162)], and, above all, M. Tullius [Cicero], whose longest speech is generally considered his best. And, by Hercules, like other good things, a good book is all the better the longer it is. [5] You see that statues, busts, paintings, and drawings of human beings,

animalium formas, arborum etiam, si modo sint decorae, nihil magis quam amplitudo commendet. idem orationibus evenit; quin etiam voluminibus ipsis auctoritatem quandam et pulchritudinem adicit magnitudo.

T 47 Quint. *Inst.* 2.5.21

duo autem genera maxime cavenda pueris puto: unum, ne quis eos antiquitatis nimius admirator in Gracchorum Catonisque et aliorum similium lectione durescere velit; fient enim horridi atque ieiuni: nam neque vim eorum adhuc intellectu consequentur et elocutione, quae tum sine dubio erat optima, sed nostris temporibus aliena est, contenti, quod est pessimum, similes sibi magnis viris videbuntur.

T 48 Quint. *Inst.* 3.1.19

Romanorum primus, quantum ego quidem sciam, condidit aliqua in hanc materiam M. Cato, . . .

and indeed of many animals, and also of trees, as long as they are fine in appearance, are made attractive by nothing more than large scale. The same applies to speeches; and even to published volumes size adds a certain authority and beauty.

T 47 Quintilian, *The Orator's Education*

And there are two types [of writing] which I think boys should be particularly kept away from: one, that no zealous admirer of antiquity wishes them to become stiff by reading the Gracchi [Ti. Sempronius Gracchus (*ORF*[4] 34) + C. Sempronius Gracchus (*ORF*[4] 48)], Cato, and other similar [writers]: for they will become uncouth and jejune, as they will not yet be able to grasp the force of these [writers] with their understanding; and if they content themselves with the style, which was doubtless excellent then, but is alien to our times, they will think themselves similar to these great men, which is the worst [result].

T 48 Quintilian, *The Orator's Education*

The first of the Romans, as far as I know at any rate, who wrote anything on this subject [rhetorical theory] was M. Cato,[1] . . .

1 This comment probably does not imply that Cato produced a full-scale rhetorical treatise of which no traces remain; instead, it refers to self-contained statements or comments on oratory in other contexts (see General Introduction).

T 49 Quint. *Inst.* 8.3.29

nec minus noto Sallustius epigrammate incessitur: "et verba antiqui multum furate Catonis, / Crispe, Iugurthinae conditor historiae."

T 50 Quint. *Inst.* 12.1.35

neque enim Academici, cum in utramque disserunt partem, non secundum alteram vivunt, nec Carneades ille, qui Romae audiente Censorio Catone non minoribus viribus contra iustitiam dicitur disseruisse quam pridie pro iustitia dixerat, iniustus ipse vir fuit.

T 51 Quint. *Inst.* 12.3.9–10

quod si plerique desperata facultate agendi ad discendum ius declinaverunt, quam id scire facile est oratori quod discunt qui sua quoque confessione oratores esse non possunt! verum et M. Cato cum in dicendo praestantissimus, tum iuris idem fuit peritissimus, et Scaevolae Servioque Sulpicio concessa est etiam facundiae virtus, [10] et M. Tullius non modo inter agendum numquam est destitutus scientia iuris, sed etiam componere aliqua de eo coeperat, ut appareat posse oratorem non discendo tantum iuri vacare sed etiam docendo.

T 49 Quintilian, *The Orator's Education*

And Sallust [C. Sallustius Crispus (*ORF*[4] 152)] is assailed by an equally well-known epigram [F *Inc.* 40 *FPL*[4]]: "And you, Crispus, a great plunderer of old Cato's words [cf. T 65, 66, 71], the author of the Jugurthine history."

T 50 Quintilian, *The Orator's Education*

After all, the Academics, although they argue both sides of a question, do not live according to the other [i.e., morally worse] side; and not even the famous Carneades [Greek Academic philosopher], who is said to have spoken at Rome [in 155 BC] in the hearing of the ex-censor Cato no less forcefully against justice than he had spoken in defense of justice the day before, was himself an unjust man.

T 51 Quintilian, *The Orator's Education*

And if very many, having despaired of acquiring the capacity to plead, have diverted to learning the law, how easy it is for an orator to know that matter that is learned by people who, on their own admission, cannot be orators! In fact, M. Cato was not only outstanding in oratory but also most expert in the law; and to [the well-known jurists] Scaevola [Q. Mucius Scaevola pontifex maximus (*ORF*[4] 67)] and Servius Sulpicius [Ser. Sulpicius Rufus (*ORF*[4] 118)] the mastery of eloquence is also conceded. [10] And not only did M. Tullius [Cicero] never find himself at a loss for legal knowledge when conducting a case, but he had also begun to write something on that subject, so that it is obvious that an orator can find time not only to learn the law but even to teach it.

T 52 Quint. *Inst.* 12.10.10

sed fuere quaedam genera dicendi condicione temporum horridiora, alioqui magnam iam ingenii vim prae se ferentia. hinc sint Laelii, Africani, Catones etiam Gracchique, quos tu licet Polygnotos vel Callonas appelles.

T 53 Quint. *Inst.* 12.10.39

an non in privatis et acutus et distinctus[1] et non supra modum elatus M. Tullius? non in M. Calidio insignis haec virtus? non Scipio, Laelius, Cato in loquendo[2] velut Attici Romanorum fuerunt? cui porro non satis est quo nihil esse melius potest?

[1] et distinctus *Becher*: et indistinctus *vel del. codd.*
[2] eloquendo *ed. Ald.*

T 54 Tac. *Dial.* 18.2–4

[Aper:] agere enim fortius iam et audentius volo, si illud ante praedixero, mutari cum temporibus formas quoque et genera dicendi. sic Catoni seni comparatus C. Gracchus plenior et uberior, sic Graccho politior et ornatior Crassus, sic utroque distinctior et urbanior et altior Cicero, Cicerone mitior Corvinus et dulcior et in verbis magis elabo-

T 52 Quintilian, *The Orator's Education*

But there were certain types of speaking [appearing] rather unpolished because of the conditions of the times, yet in other respects already displaying great force of talent. In this category there may be men like Laelius [C. Laelius Sapiens (*ORF*[4] 20)], Africanus [P. Cornelius Scipio Aemilianus Africanus minor (*ORF*[4] 21)], Cato, and also the Gracchi [Ti. Sempronius Gracchus (*ORF*[4] 34) + C. Sempronius Gracchus (*ORF*[4] 48)]; you could call them men like Polygnotus or Callon [early Greek artists].

T 53 Quintilian, *The Orator's Education*

Is not M. Tullius [Cicero] acute, precise, and not too lofty in private [cases]? Is not this quality a notable one in M. Calidius [M. Calidius (*ORF*[4] 140)]? Were not Scipio [P. Cornelius Scipio Aemilianus Africanus minor (*ORF*[4] 21)], Laelius [C. Laelius Sapiens (*ORF*[4] 20)], and Cato, as it were, like the Romans' Attic [orators] in their speaking? Moreover, who is not content with something that cannot be bettered?

T 54 Tacitus, *Dialogue on Oratory*

[APER:] For I now wish to argue more forcefully and boldly, if I have first said this, namely that the forms and types of oratory too change with the times. So, compared to Cato of old, C. Gracchus [C. Sempronius Gracchus (*ORF*[4] 48)] is fuller and richer; so, compared to Gracchus, Crassus [L. Licinius Crassus (*ORF*[4] 66)] is more finished and more ornate; so, compared to either of them, Cicero is more lucid, more refined, and more elevated; compared to Cicero, Corvinus [M. Valerius Messalla Corvinus (*ORF*[4] 176)] is mellower, sweeter, and more elaborate in the

ratus. [3] nec quaero quis disertissimus: hoc interim probasse contentus sum, non esse unum eloquentiae vultum, sed <in>[1] illis quoque quos vocatis antiquos plures species deprehendi, nec statim deterius esse quod diversum est, vitio autem malignitatis humanae vetera semper in laude, praesentia in fastidio esse. [4] num dubitamus inventos qui prae Catone Appium Caecum magis mirarentur?

[1] in *unus cod. s. lin.*

T 55 Plut. *Cat. Mai.* 1.1–8

Μάρκῳ δὲ Κάτωνί φασιν ἀπὸ Τούσκλου τὸ γένος εἶναι, δίαιταν δὲ καὶ βίον ἔχειν πρὸ τῶν στρατειῶν καὶ τῆς πολιτείας ἐν χωρίοις πατρῴοις περὶ Σαβίνους. τῶν δὲ προγόνων παντάπασιν ἀγνώστων γεγονέναι δοκούντων αὐτὸς ὁ Κάτων καὶ τὸν πατέρα Μᾶρκον ὡς ἀγαθὸν ἄνδρα καὶ στρατιωτικὸν ἐπαινεῖ, καὶ Κάτωνα τὸν πρόπαππον ἀριστείων πολλάκις τυχεῖν φησι καὶ πέντε πολεμιστὰς ἵππους ἐν μάχαις ἀποβαλόντα τὴν τιμὴν ἀπολαβεῖν ἐκ τοῦ δημοσίου δι' ἀνδραγαθίαν. [2] εἰωθότων δὲ τῶν Ῥωμαίων τοὺς ἀπὸ γένους μὲν δόξαν οὐκ ἔχοντας, ἀρχομένους δὲ γνωρίζεσθαι δι' αὑτῶν, καινοὺς προσαγορεύειν ἀνθρώπους, ὥσπερ καὶ τὸν Κάτωνα προσηγόρευον, αὐτὸς ἔλεγε καινὸς εἶναι πρὸς ἀρχὴν καὶ δόξαν, ἔργοις δὲ προγόνων καὶ ἀρεταῖς παμπάλαιος. [3] ἐκαλεῖτο δὲ τῷ τρίτῳ τῶν ὀνομάτων πρότερον οὐ Κάτων, ἀλλὰ Πρῖσκος, ὕστερον δὲ τὸν Κάτωνα τῆς δυνάμεως ἐπώνυμον ἔσχε· Ῥωμαῖοι γὰρ τὸν ἔμπειρον

choice of words. [3] And I am not asking who is the most eloquent: for now I am content with having demonstrated this, that there is not one single face of eloquence but that even <in> those whom you call "ancients" several types are found, that what is different is not automatically worse, but that it is through the fault of human meanness that what is old is always held in high esteem and what is contemporary is held in contempt. [4] We do not doubt surely that there have been people who admired Appius Caecus [App. Claudius Caecus (*ORF*[4] 1)] more than Cato?

T 55 Plutarch, *Life of Cato the Elder*

The family of Marcus Cato, they say, was from Tusculum, but he made his home and lived, before undertaking military campaigns and politics, on an ancestral estate in the country of the Sabines. While his ancestors appear to have been altogether unknown, Cato himself praises his father, Marcus, as a good man and soldier, and he says that Cato, his great-grandfather, often won prizes for soldierly valor and, having lost five war horses in battle, received their value from the treasury because of his bravery. [2] The Romans were accustomed to call men having no distinction from their family and coming into public notice through themselves "new men," as they also called Cato; he himself said that he was new as regards office and distinction, but with respect to deeds and valor of one's ancestors very old [*Op. cet.* F 59]. [3] He was called, for the third of his names, not Cato at first, but Priscus; later he received the cognomen Cato for his abilities: for the Romans call an astute man *catus* ["shrewd, prudent"].

κάτον[1] *ὀνομάζουσιν.* [4] *ἦν δὲ τὸ μὲν εἶδος ὑπόπυρρος καὶ γλαυκός, ὡς ὁ ποιήσας τὸ ἐπιγραμμάτιον οὐκ εὐμενῶς παρεμφαίνει· "πυρρόν, πανδακέτην, γλαυκόμματον, οὐδὲ θανόντα* / *Πόρκιον εἰς ἀΐδην Φερσεφόνη δέχεται."* [5] *τὴν δὲ τοῦ σώματος ἕξιν αὐτουργίᾳ καὶ διαίτῃ σώφρονι καὶ στρατείαις ἀπ' ἀρχῆς συντρόφου γεγονότος, πάνυ χρηστικὴν εἶχε καὶ πρὸς ἰσχὺν καὶ πρὸς ὑγίειαν ὁμαλῶς συνεστῶσαν. τὸν δὲ λόγον ὥσπερ δεύτερον σῶμα καὶ τῶν καλῶν μονονοὺκ*[2] *ἀναγκαῖον ὄργανον ἀνδρὶ μὴ ταπεινῶς βιωσομένῳ μηδ' ἀπράκτως ἐξηρτύετο καὶ παρεσκεύαζεν, ἐν ταῖς περιοικίσι κώμαις καὶ τοῖς πολιχνίοις ἑκάστοτε συνδικῶν τοῖς δεομένοις καὶ πρῶτον μὲν ἀγωνιστὴς εἶναι δοκῶν πρόθυμος, εἶτα καὶ ῥήτωρ ἱκανός.* [6] *ἐκ δὲ τούτου μᾶλλον τοῖς χρωμένοις κατεφαίνετο βάρος τι καὶ φρόνημα περὶ αὐτὸν ἤθους, πραγμάτων μεγάλων καὶ πολιτείας δεόμενον ἡγεμονικῆς.* [7] *οὐ γὰρ μόνον ὡς ἔοικε μισθαρνίας καθαρὸν αὑτὸν ἐπὶ τὰς δίκας καὶ τοὺς ἀγῶνας παρεῖχεν, ἀλλ' οὐδὲ τὴν δόξαν ὡς μέγιστον ἀγαπῶν ἐφαίνετο τὴν ἀπὸ τῶν τοιούτων ἀγώνων, πολὺ δὲ μᾶλλον ἐν ταῖς μάχαις ταῖς πρὸς τοὺς πολεμίους καὶ ταῖς στρατείαις βουλόμενος εὐδοκιμεῖν, ἔτι μειράκιον ὢν τραυμάτων τὸ σῶμα μεστὸν ἐναντίων εἶχε.* [8] *φησὶ γὰρ αὐτὸς ἑπτακαίδεκα γεγονὼς ἔτη τὴν πρώτην στρατεύσασθαι στρατείαν περὶ ὃν Ἀννίβας χρόνον εὐτυχῶν ἐπέφλεγε τὴν Ἰταλίαν* [*Orat.* F 188].

[1] *κάτον Anonymus*: *κάτωνα codd.*

[2] *μονονοὺκ Orelli, Naber*: *οὐ μόνον codd.*

[4] As for his outward appearance, he had reddish hair and gray eyes, as the author of that little epigram unkindly indicates: "The red-haired, biting all, gray-eyed Porcius Persephone does not accept into Hades, not even when he is dead." [5] The constitution of his body, which had become accustomed from the beginning to manual labor, to a temperate mode of life, and to military duties, was very serviceable, and disposed alike to vigor and health. His discourse, like a second body and almost a necessary instrument in noble services for a man aiming to live neither obscurely nor idly, he got ready and prepared, in the neighboring villages and small towns, serving on each occasion as an advocate for those who needed him, and he first gained a reputation for being a spirited contender and later for being a competent orator. [6] And from that time, to those who had more dealings with him, a certain weight and seriousness of purpose revealed themselves in relation to his character, suited to great affairs and political leadership. [7] For he not only gave his services in lawsuits and contests free of any fee, as is fitting, but he also appeared not to cherish either, as being the most important thing, even the repute won in such contests, but to be far more desirous to be of high repute in battles against the enemy and in military campaigns; while he was still a young man, he had his body covered with wounds from the oncoming enemy. [8] For he says himself that, when seventeen years old, he carried out his first military campaign [217 BC; cf. T 26], at the time when a successful Hannibal was consuming Italy with fire [*Orat.* F 188].

T 56 Plut. *Cat. Mai.* 2.3–6

Φαβίου δὲ Μαξίμου τὴν Ταραντίνων πόλιν ἑλόντος, ἔτυχε μὲν ὁ Κάτων στρατευόμενος ὑπ᾽ αὐτῷ κομιδῇ μειράκιον ὤν, Νεάρχῳ δέ τινι τῶν Πυθαγορικῶν ξένῳ χρησάμενος, ἐσπούδασε τῶν λόγων μεταλαβεῖν. [4] ἀκούσας δὲ ταῦτα διαλεγομένου τοῦ ἀνδρὸς οἷς καὶ Πλάτων κέχρηται, τὴν μὲν ἡδονὴν ἀποκαλῶν μέγιστον κακοῦ δέλεαρ, συμφορὰν δὲ τῇ ψυχῇ τὸ σῶμα πρώτην, λύσιν δὲ καὶ καθαρμὸν οἷς μάλιστα χωρίζει καὶ ἀφίστησιν αὑτὴν τῶν περὶ τὸ σῶμα παθημάτων λογισμοῖς, ἔτι μᾶλλον ἠγάπησε τὸ λιτὸν καὶ τὴν ἐγκράτειαν. [5] ἄλλως δὲ παιδείας Ἑλληνικῆς ὀψιμαθὴς λέγεται γενέσθαι, καὶ πόρρω παντάπασιν ἡλικίας ἐληλακὼς Ἑλληνικὰ βιβλία λαβὼν εἰς χεῖρας, βραχέα μὲν ἀπὸ Θουκυδίδου, πλείονα δ᾽ ἀπὸ Δημοσθένους εἰς τὸ ῥητορικὸν ὠφεληθῆναι. [6] τὰ μέντοι συγγράμματα καὶ δόγμασιν Ἑλληνικοῖς καὶ ἱστορίαις ἐπιεικῶς διαπεποίκιλται, καὶ μεθηρμηνευμένα πολλὰ κατὰ λέξιν ἐν τοῖς ἀποφθέγμασι καὶ ταῖς γνωμολογίαις τέτακται.

T 57 Plut. *Cat. Mai.* 4.1–3

τῷ δὲ Κάτωνι πολλὴ μὲν ἀπὸ τοῦ λόγου δύναμις ηὔξητο, καὶ Ῥωμαῖον αὐτὸν οἱ πολλοὶ Δημοσθένη προσηγόρευον, ὁ δὲ βίος μᾶλλον ὀνομαστὸς ἦν αὐτοῦ καὶ περιβόητος. [2] ἡ μὲν γὰρ ἐν τῷ λέγειν δεινότης προέκειτο τοῖς νέοις ἀγώνισμα κοινὸν ἤδη καὶ περι-

T 56 Plutarch, *Life of Cato the Elder*

When Fabius Maximus [Q. Fabius Maximus Verrucosus Cunctator, cos. 233, 228, 215, 214, 209 BC (*ORF*[4] 3)] took the city of Tarentum [209 BC], it chanced that Cato, serving under him and quite a young man, being lodged with a certain Nearchus [cf. T 22], one of the Pythagoreans, was eager to learn about these doctrines. [4] When he heard the man discussing these matters, with words that Plato also used [Pl. *Tim.* 69d], calling pleasure the greatest incentive to evil and the body the chief impediment to the soul, and release and purification the reasonings by which, above all, it separates and divorces itself from bodily sensations, he embraced simplicity and restraint all the more. [5] Otherwise he is said to have learned Greek culture at a late stage and to have been quite advanced in age when he took Greek books into his hands, then to have benefited, in relation to his oratory, from Thucydides to some small extent and to a greater extent from Demosthenes. [6] Nonetheless, his writings are moderately embellished with Greek sayings and stories, and many things translated literally have found a place among his sayings and maxims.

T 57 Plutarch, *Life of Cato the Elder*

Cato's influence had increased greatly as a result of his oratory, and the people called him a Roman Demosthenes; but his manner of life was even more talked about and noised abroad. [2] For his skill in speaking set before the young men a goal already commonly known and much

σπούδαστον, ὁ δὲ τὴν πάτριον αὐτουργίαν ὑπομένων καὶ δεῖπνον ἀφελὲς καὶ ἄριστον ἄπυρον καὶ λιτὴν ἐσθῆτα καὶ δημοτικὴν ἀσπαζόμενος οἴκησιν καὶ τὸ μὴ δεῖσθαι τῶν περιττῶν μᾶλλον ἢ τὸ κεκτῆσθαι θαυμάζων σπάνιος ἦν, ἤδη τότε τῆς πολιτείας τὸ καθαρὸν ὑπὸ μεγέθους οὐ φυλαττούσης, ἀλλὰ τῷ κρατεῖν πραγμάτων πολλῶν καὶ ἀνθρώπων πρὸς πολλὰ μειγνυμένης ἔθη καὶ βίων παραδείγματα παντοδαπῶν ὑποδεχομένης. [3] εἰκότως οὖν ἐθαύμαζον τὸν Κάτωνα, τοὺς μὲν ἄλλους ὑπὸ τῶν πόνων θραυομένους καὶ μαλασσομένους ὑπὸ τῶν ἡδονῶν ὁρῶντες, ἐκεῖνον δὲ ὑπ' ἀμφοῖν ἀήττητον, οὐ μόνον ἕως ἔτι νέος καὶ φιλότιμος ἦν, ἀλλὰ καὶ γέροντα καὶ πολιὸν ἤδη μεθ' ὑπατείαν καὶ θρίαμβον, ὥσπερ ἀθλητὴν νικηφόρον, ἐγκαρτεροῦντα τῇ τάξει τῆς ἀσκήσεως καὶ διομαλίζοντα μέχρι τῆς τελευτῆς.

T 58 Plut. *Cat. Mai.* 7.1–3

τοιαύτην δέ τινα φαίνεται καὶ ὁ λόγος τοῦ ἀνδρὸς ἰδέαν ἔχειν· εὔχαρις γὰρ ἅμα καὶ δεινὸς ἦν, ἡδὺς καὶ καταπληκτικός, φιλοσκώμμων καὶ αὐστηρός, ἀποφθεγματικὸς καὶ ἀγωνιστικός, ὥσπερ ὁ Πλάτων τὸν Σωκράτη φησὶν ἔξωθεν ἰδιώτην καὶ σατυρικὸν καὶ ὑβριστὴν τοῖς ἐντυγχάνουσι φαινόμενον, ἔνδοθεν σπουδῆς καὶ πραγμάτων μεστὸν εἶναι δάκρυα κινούντων τοῖς ἀκροωμένοις καὶ τὴν καρδίαν στρεφόντων. [2] ὅθεν οὐκ οἶδ' ὅτι πεπόνθασιν οἱ τῷ Λυσίου λόγῳ τὰ μάλιστα προσεοικέναι φάμενοι τὸν Κάτωνος. [3] οὐ

sought after; but a man who continued to do work with his own hands as his fathers, was content with a frugal meal, a cold breakfast, plain clothes, and a humble dwelling, and placed value on not wanting the superfluities of life rather than on possessing them was rare, while the state was by then already failing to safeguard its integrity because of its size, and, as a result of ruling over many realms and peoples, was already mingling with many customs and adopting patterns of modes of life of every sort. [3] Naturally, therefore, they admired Cato, when they saw others broken down by exertions and enervated by pleasures, but him unbeaten by either, and not only while he was still young and ambitious, but also as an old man with gray hair, even after a consulship [195 BC] and a triumph [194 BC]; like a victorious athlete, he persisted in the regimen of his training and remained consistent until the end [cf. *Orat.* F 175].

T 58 Plutarch, *Life of Cato the Elder*

Such a character the man's [Cato's] oratory seemed to have too: for it was at the same time graceful and powerful, pleasant and compelling, full of jests and severe, sententious and belligerent, just as Plato [Pl. *Symp.* 215] says that Socrates from the outside appeared as rude, uncouth, and arrogant to those who met him, but on the inside was full of earnestness and of matters that moved the listeners to tears and wrung their hearts. [2] Therefore I do not know what has befallen those who say that Cato's oratory most resembled that of Lysias [cf. T 13]. [3] But this should be

μὴν ἀλλὰ ταῦτα μὲν οἷς μᾶλλον ἰδέας λόγων Ῥωμαϊκῶν αἰσθάνεσθαι προσήκει διακρινοῦσιν, ἡμεῖς δὲ τῶν ἀπομνημονευομένων βραχέα γράψομεν, οἳ τῷ λόγῳ πολὺ μᾶλλον ἢ τῷ προσώπῳ, καθάπερ ἔνιοι νομίζουσι, τῶν ἀνθρώπων φαμὲν ἐμφαίνεσθαι τὸ ἦθος.

T 59 Plut. *Cat. Mai.* 14.2–4

ὁ δὲ Κάτων ἀεὶ μέν τις ἦν ὡς ἔοικε τῶν ἰδίων ἐγκωμίων ἀφειδὴς καὶ τὴν ἄντικρυς μεγαλαυχίαν ὡς ἐπακολούθημα τῆς μεγαλουργίας οὐκ ἔφευγε, πλεῖστον δὲ ταῖς πράξεσι ταύταις ὄγκον περιτέθεικε, καί φησι τοῖς ἰδοῦσιν αὐτὸν τότε διώκοντα καὶ παίοντα τοὺς πολεμίους παραστῆναι μηδὲν ὀφείλειν Κάτωνα τῷ δήμῳ τοσοῦτον ὅσον Κάτωνι τὸν δῆμον, αὐτόν τε Μάνιον τὸν ὕπατον θερμὸν ἀπὸ τῆς νίκης ἔτι θερμῷ περιπλακέντα πολὺν χρόνον ἀσπάζεσθαι καὶ βοᾶν ὑπὸ χαρᾶς, ὡς οὔτ᾽ ἂν αὐτὸς οὔθ᾽ ὁ σύμπας δῆμος ἐξισώσειε τὰς ἀμοιβὰς ταῖς Κάτωνος εὐεργεσίαις. [3] μετὰ δὲ τὴν μάχην εὐθὺς εἰς Ῥώμην ἐπέμπετο τῶν ἠγωνισμένων αὐτάγγελος, καὶ διέπλευσε μὲν εἰς Βρεντέσιον εὐτυχῶς, μιᾷ δ᾽ ἐκεῖθεν ἡμέρᾳ διελάσας εἰς Τάραντα καὶ τέσσαρας ἄλλας ὁδεύσας, πεμπταῖος εἰς Ῥώμην ἀπὸ θαλάσσης ἀφίκετο καὶ πρῶτος ἀπήγγειλε τὴν νίκην, [4] καὶ τὴν μὲν πόλιν ἐνέπλησεν εὐφροσύνης καὶ θυσιῶν, φρονήματος δὲ τὸν δῆμον, ὡς πάσης γῆς καὶ θαλάσσης κρατεῖν δυνάμενον.

decided by those who may more properly discern the characteristics of Roman oratory; we will record a few of his famous sayings, as we maintain that people's characters are revealed much more by their speech than, as some think, by their looks [cf. *Op. cet.* F 63].

T 59 Plutarch, *Life of Cato the Elder*

Cato, it seems, was always a person not sparing in his own praises, and he did not shy away from open boasting as a consequence of his great achievements; he conferred most of his bombastic effort upon these affairs [i.e., the Roman victory over Antiochus III the Great], and he says that those who saw him at that time pursuing and hewing down the enemy, confirmed that Cato did not owe as much to the People as the People to Cato, also that the consul Manius [M'. Acilius Glabrio, cos. 191 BC] himself, flushed with victory, put his arms around him, still flushed, and embraced him a long time, crying out with joy that neither he himself nor the whole Roman People could repay in equal measure Cato's benefactions. [3] Straight after the battle he [Cato] was sent to Rome as the messenger of his own achievements. And he sailed over to Brundisium [modern Brindisi] smoothly, went on from there to Tarentum in a single day, traveled another four days, and on the fifth day after landing arrived in Rome and was the first to announce the victory [cf. Liv. 36.21.4–8; *CCMR*, App. A: 144]. [4] And he filled the city with joy and sacrifices and the People with the proud feeling that it could master every land and sea.

T 60 Plut. *Cat. Mai.* 15.1–6

τῶν μὲν οὖν πολεμικῶν πράξεων τοῦ Κάτωνος αὗται σχεδόν εἰσιν ἐλλογιμώταται· τῆς δὲ πολιτείας φαίνεται τὸ[1] περὶ τὰς κατηγορίας καὶ τοὺς ἐλέγχους τῶν πονηρῶν μόριον οὐ μικρᾶς ἄξιον σπουδῆς ἡγησάμενος. αὐτός τε γὰρ ἐδίωξε πολλούς, καὶ διώκουσιν ἑτέροις συνηγωνίσατο καὶ παρεσκεύασεν ὅλως διώκοντας, ὡς ἐπὶ Σκηπίωνα τοὺς περὶ Πετίλιον. [2] τοῦτον μὲν οὖν ἀπ᾽ οἴκου τε μεγάλου καὶ φρονήματος ἀληθινοῦ ποιησάμενον ὑπὸ πόδας τὰς διαβολὰς μὴ † ἀποκτεῖναι[2] δυνηθεὶς ἀφῆκε, Λεύκιον δὲ τὸν ἀδελφὸν αὐτοῦ μετὰ τῶν κατηγόρων συστὰς καταδίκῃ περιέβαλε χρημάτων πολλῶν πρὸς τὸ δημόσιον, ἣν οὐκ ἔχων ἐκεῖνος ἀπολύσασθαι καὶ κινδυνεύων δεθῆναι, μόλις ἐπικλήσει τῶν δημάρχων ἀφείθη. [3] λέγεται δὲ καὶ νεανίσκῳ τινὶ τεθνηκότος πατρὸς ἐχθρὸν ἠτιμωκότι καὶ πορευομένῳ δι᾽ ἀγορᾶς μετὰ τὴν δίκην ἀπαντήσας ὁ Κάτων δεξιώσασθαι καὶ εἰπεῖν, ὅτι ταῦτα χρὴ τοῖς γονεῦσιν ἐναγίζειν, οὐκ ἄρνας οὐδ᾽ ἐρίφους, ἀλλ᾽ ἐχθρῶν δάκρυα καὶ καταδίκας. [4] οὐ μὴν οὐδ᾽ αὐτὸς ἐν τῇ πολιτείᾳ περιῆν ἀθῷος, ἀλλ᾽ ὅπου τινὰ λαβὴν τοῖς ἐχθροῖς παράσχοι, κρινόμενος καὶ κινδυνεύων διετέλει. λέγεται γὰρ ὀλίγον ἀπολιπούσας τῶν

[1] τὸ *Reiske*: τότε *codd.*

[2] ἀποκτεῖναι *def. Till*: ἀποκλῖναι *Madvig*: ἀποκναίειν *Kronenberg*: κατακρῖναι *Erbse*

T 60 Plutarch, *Life of Cato the Elder*

These, then, are perhaps the most highly valued of Cato's military activities [cf. T 59]. In political life he seems to have regarded the impeachment and conviction of malefactors as an area worthy of no small effort. For he prosecuted many himself, assisted others who were prosecuting and generally encouraged people to prosecute, as those around Petilius [Q. Petillius + Q. Petillius (Spurinus), trib. pl. 187 BC] to prosecute Scipio [P. Cornelius Scipio Africanus maior, cos. 205, 194, censor 199 BC (*ORF*[4] 4), F 3–5; on the trials of the Scipios, see Scullard 1973, 290–303]. [2] That man, then, on the basis of his great house and his true loftiness of spirit, trampled the charges under foot, and Cato, unable to secure a capital conviction [?], walked away. But, cooperating with the accusers, he had Lucius, his [Scipio's] brother, condemned to pay a substantial financial penalty to the public purse. That man [Lucius] did not have the means to pay the fine and was therefore at risk of being imprisoned; only by an appeal to the Tribunes was he set free. [3] When some young man had got a verdict of civil outlawry against an enemy of his dead father and was passing through the Forum on the conclusion of the case, Cato, encountering him, is said to have greeted him and to have said [*Op. cet.* F 68]: "This is the kind of sacrifice one must offer to one's dead parents, not lambs and kids, but tears and condemnations of their enemies." [4] He himself, however, did not go unscathed in his political career, but where he gave some lever to his enemies, he was constantly prosecuted and running the risk of condemnation. He is said to have been a defendant in almost fifty cases [cf. T 42, 82], the

πεντήκοντα φυγεῖν δίκας, μίαν δὲ τὴν τελευταίαν ἓξ ἔτη καὶ ὀγδοήκοντα γεγονώς· ἐν ᾗ καὶ τὸ μνημονευόμενον εἶπεν, ὡς χαλεπόν ἐστιν ἐν ἄλλοις βεβιωκότα ἀνθρώποις ἐν ἄλλοις ἀπολογεῖσθαι. [5] καὶ τοῦτο πέρας οὐκ ἐποιήσατο τῶν ἀγώνων, τεσσάρων δ' ἄλλων ἐνιαυτῶν διελθόντων Σερουίου Γάλβα κατηγόρησεν ἐνενήκοντα γεγονὼς ἔτη. κινδυνεύει γὰρ ὡς ὁ Νέστωρ εἰς τριγονίαν τῷ βίῳ καὶ ταῖς πράξεσι κατελθεῖν· [6] Σκιπίωνι γὰρ ὡς λέλεκται τῷ μεγάλῳ πολλὰ διερεισάμενος ἐν τῇ πολιτείᾳ διέτεινεν εἰς Σκιπίωνα τὸν νέον, ὃς ἦν ἐκείνου κατὰ ποίησιν υἱωνός, υἱὸς δὲ Παύλου τοῦ Περσέα καὶ Μακεδόνας καταπολεμήσαντος.

Cf. Plut. *Mor.* 784D (*An seni r. p. ger. sit*).

T 61 Plut. *Cat. Mai.* 20.11–12

ἐφ' ᾧ καὶ Παῦλος ὁ στρατηγὸς ἠγάσθη τὸ μειράκιον, καὶ Κάτωνος αὐτοῦ φέρεταί τις ἐπιστολὴ πρὸς τὸν υἱὸν ὑπερφυῶς ἐπαινοῦντος τὴν περὶ τὸ ξίφος φιλοτιμίαν αὐτοῦ καὶ σπουδήν. [12] ὕστερον δὲ καὶ Παύλου θυγατέρα Τερτίαν ἔγημεν ὁ νεανίας, ἀδελφὴν Σκηπίωνος, οὐχ ἧττον ἤδη δι' αὑτὸν ἢ τὸν πατέρα κατα-

last one at the age of eighty-six years. In the course of that he also uttered the memorable saying: "It is hard for one who has lived among people of one generation to make their defense before those of another." [5] And even this case he did not make the end to his forensic contests, but after another four years had passed, at the age of ninety [F 196–99A; incorrect age], he laid charges against Servius Galba [Ser. Sulpicius Galba (*ORF*[4] 19)]. Indeed, like Nestor, he seems to have lived through three generations in his life and activities [cf. Cic. *Sen.* 31]. [6] For after having contended a lot with Scipio the Elder [P. Cornelius Scipio Africanus maior, cos. 205, 194, censor 199 BC (*ORF*[4] 4)] in relation to political issues, as has been mentioned, he lived to be contemporary with Scipio the Younger [P. Cornelius Scipio Aemilianus Africanus minor, cos. 147, 134, censor 142 BC (*ORF*[4] 21)], who was that man's grandson by adoption and the son of that Paulus who subdued Perseus and the Macedonians [L. Aemilius Paulus, cos. 182, 168 BC (*ORF*[4] 12)].

T 61 Plutarch, *Life of Cato the Elder*

Because of this [heroic recovery of lost sword] Paulus, the commander [L. Aemilius Paullus, cos. 182, 168 BC (*ORF*[4] 12)], was delighted with the young man [Cato's elder son], and there is extant a letter from Cato himself to his son, in which he praises him extravagantly for this love of honor and zeal in relation to the sword [*Op. cet.* F 36]. [12] Later the young man married Paulus' daughter Tertia, a sister of Scipio [P. Cornelius Scipio Aemilianus Africanus minor, cos. 147, 134, censor 142 BC (*ORF*[4] 21)], and he was joined with so great a family no less through himself than

μιγνύμενος εἰς γένος τηλικοῦτον. ἡ μὲν οὖν περὶ τὸν υἱὸν ἐπιμέλεια τοῦ Κάτωνος ἄξιον ἔσχεν τέλος.

T 62 Plut. *Cat. Mai.* 24.1–2, 9–10

καὶ περί γε τοῦτο φαίνεται γεγονὼς οὐκ ἀνεμέσητος· καὶ γὰρ τὴν γυναῖκα καὶ τὸν υἱὸν ἀπέβαλεν. αὐτὸς δὲ τῷ σώματι πρὸς εὐεξίαν καὶ ῥώμην ἀσφαλῶς πεπηγὼς ἐπὶ πλεῖστον ἀντεῖχεν, ὥστε καὶ γυναικὶ πρεσβύτης ὢν σφόδρα πλησιάζειν, καὶ γῆμαι γάμον οὐ καθ' ἡλικίαν ἐκ τοιαύτης προφάσεως. [2] *ἀποβαλὼν τὴν γυναῖκα τῷ μὲν υἱῷ* Παύλου *θυγατέρα,* Σκηπίωνος *δὲ ἀδελφὴν, ἠγάγετο πρὸς γάμον, αὐτὸς δὲ χηρεύων ἐχρῆτο παιδίσκῃ, κρύφα φοιτώσῃ πρὸς αὐτόν.* . . . [*Op. cet.* F 75] . . . [9] *γήμαντι δὲ τῷ* Κάτωνι *γίνεται παῖς, ᾧ παρωνύμιον ἀπὸ τῆς μητρὸς ἔθετο* Σαλώνιον. *ὁ δὲ πρεσβύτερος υἱὸς ἐτελεύτησε στρατηγῶν, καὶ μέμνηται μὲν αὐτοῦ πολλάκις ἐν τοῖς βιβλίοις ὁ* Κάτων *ὡς ἀνδρὸς ἀγαθοῦ γεγονότος,* [10] *πρᾴως δὲ καὶ φιλοσόφως λέγεται τὴν συμφορὰν ἐνεγκεῖν καὶ μηδὲν ἀμβλύτερος δι' αὐτὴν εἰς τὰ πολιτικὰ γενέσθαι.*

through his father. Thus, Cato's careful attention to the education of his son had a worthy result.

T 62 Plutarch, *Life of Cato the Elder*

And as regards this [mistrust of foreign doctors and reliance on his own cures] he [Cato] seems not to have gone unpunished; for he lost both his wife and his [elder] son. He himself, being well-established in bodily health and vigor, held out against age to a very great extent, so that, even when an old man, he very much indulged in sexual intercourse with a woman and entered a marriage not in line with his age, for the following reason. [2] After losing his wife, he married his son to Paulus' [L. Aemilius Paullus, cos. 182, 168 BC (*ORF*[4] 12)] daughter, Scipio's [P. Cornelius Scipio Aemilianus Africanus minor, cos. 147, 134, censor 142 BC (*ORF*[4] 21)] sister, and he himself, being widowed, was intimate with a slave girl who secretly visited him. . . . [*Op. cet.* F 75] . . . [9] When Cato had got married [to his second wife], to him a son was born, who was given the name Salonius, after his mother [daughter of Salonius; T 79]. The elder son died when praetor [prob. praetor-elect (*MRR* 1:454), ca. 152 BC; cf. T 79; Cic. *Tusc.* 3.70], and Cato often speaks of him in his books as someone who had become an excellent man [cf. Cic. *Sen.* 84]. [10] And he [Cato] is said to have borne the loss calmly and philosophically and not to have become less vigorous in any way with regard to political activity because of it [cf. T 7c].

T 63 Plut. *Cat. Mai.* 25.1–4

συνετάττετο μὲν οὖν λόγους τε παντοδαποὺς καὶ ἱστορίας· γεωργίᾳ δὲ προσεῖχε νέος μὲν ὢν ἔτι καὶ διὰ τὴν χρείαν—φησὶ γὰρ δυσὶ κεχρῆσθαι μόνοις πορισμοῖς, γεωργίᾳ καὶ φειδοῖ—, τότε δὲ διαγωγὴν καὶ θεωρίαν αὐτῷ τὰ γινόμενα κατ' ἀγρὸν παρεῖχε· [2] *καὶ συντέτακταί γε βιβλίον γεωργικόν, ἐν ᾧ καὶ περὶ πλακούντων σκευασίας*[1] *καὶ τηρήσεως ὀπώρας γέγραφεν, ἐν παντὶ φιλοτιμούμενος περιττὸς εἶναι καὶ ἴδιος.* [3] *ἦν δὲ καὶ τὸ δεῖπνον ἐν ἀγρῷ δαψιλέστερον· ἐκάλει γὰρ ἑκάστοτε τῶν ἀγρογειτόνων καὶ περιχώρων τοὺς συνήθεις καὶ συνδιῆγεν ἱλαρῶς, οὐ τοῖς καθ' ἡλικίαν μόνον ἡδὺς ὢν συγγενέσθαι καὶ ποθεινός, ἀλλὰ καὶ τοῖς νέοις, ἅτε δὴ πολλῶν μὲν ἔμπειρος πραγμάτων γεγονώς, πολλοῖς δὲ γράμμασι*[2] *καὶ λόγοις ἀξίοις ἀκοῆς ἐντετυχηκώς.* [4] *τὴν δὲ τράπεζαν ἐν τοῖς μάλιστα φιλοποιὸν ἡγεῖτο, καὶ πολλὴ μὲν εὐφημία τῶν καλῶν καὶ ἀγαθῶν πολιτῶν ἐπεισήγετο, πολλὴ δ' ἦν ἀμνηστία τῶν ἀχρήστων καὶ πονηρῶν, μήτε ψόγῳ μήτ' ἐπαίνῳ πάροδον ὑπὲρ αὐτῶν τοῦ Κάτωνος εἰς τὸ συμπόσιον διδόντος.*

[1] *σκευασίας vel ἐργασίας codd.*
[2] *γράμμασι Sintenis: πράγμασι codd.*

T 64 Plut. *Cat. Mai.* 29 (= *Comp. Arist. et Cat. Mai.* 2).1–5

ἔτι δ' Ἀριστείδης μὲν ἐν Μαραθῶνι καὶ πάλιν ἐν Πλαταιαῖς δέκατος ἦν στρατηγός, Κάτων δὲ δεύτερος μὲν

T 63 Plutarch, *Life of Cato the Elder*

He [Cato], then, composed speeches of all kinds and histories; and as for farming, he followed it in earnest when he was still young and out of need—indeed, he says he had only two ways of making money, farming and frugality—; later, matters concerning the fields provided pastime and intellectual activity for him. [2] And he put together a book on farming, in which he has written down recipes for cakes and for preserving fruit, eager to be eccentric and peculiar in everything. [3] Also the dinners in the country were rather plentiful. For each time he would ask friends from among his neighbors and those living round about and would make merry with them, being agreeable, and desirable company not only to those of his own age, but also to the young, since he had experience in many matters and had come across many texts and stories well worth listening to. [4] He considered the table to be among the best promoters of friendship, and much praise of honorable and worthy citizens used to be introduced, but there was much passing over of the worthless and base since Cato allowed entry to the dinner to neither blame nor praise of those individuals.

T 64 Plutarch, *Life of Cato the Elder*

Further, at Marathon and again at Plataea Aristides [Athenian statesman, fl. ca. 500 BC] was one of ten generals, while Cato was elected one of two consuls out of many

ὕπατος ᾑρέθη πολλῶν ἀντιμετιόντων, δεύτερος δὲ τιμητής, ἑπτὰ[1] τοὺς ἐπιφανεστάτους καὶ πρώτους ἁμιλλωμένους ὑπερβαλόμενος. [2] . . . [3] Κάτων δ' οὐ μόνον αὐτὸς ὑπατεύων ἐπρώτευσε καὶ χειρὶ και γνώμῃ κατὰ τὸν Ἰβηρικὸν πόλεμον, ἀλλὰ καὶ χιλιαρχῶν περὶ Θερμοπύλας ὑπατεύοντος ἑτέρου τὴν δόξαν ἔσχε τῆς νίκης, μεγάλας ἐπ' Ἀντίοχον Ῥωμαίοις ἀναπετάσας κλισιάδας[2] καὶ πρόσω μόνον ὁρῶντι τῷ βασιλεῖ περιστήσας κατὰ νώτου τὸν πόλεμον. ἐκείνη γὰρ ἡ νίκη, περιφανῶς ἔργον οὖσα Κάτωνος, ἐξήλασε τῆς Ἑλλάδος τὴν Ἀσίαν, παρέσχε δ'[3] ἐπιβατὴν αὖθις Σκηπίωνι. [4] πολεμοῦντες μὲν οὖν ἀήττητοι γεγόνασιν ἀμφότεροι, τὰ δὲ περὶ[4] τὴν πολιτείαν Ἀριστείδης μὲν ἔπταισεν ἐξοστρακισθεὶς καὶ καταστασιασθεὶς ὑπὸ Θεμιστοκλέους, Κάτων δ', οἵπερ ἦσαν ἐν Ῥώμῃ δυνατώτατοι καὶ μέγιστοι, πᾶσιν ὡς ἔπος εἰπεῖν, ἀντιπάλοις χρώμενος, καὶ μέχρι γήρως ὥσπερ ἀθλητὴς ἀγωνιζόμενος, ἀπτῶτα διετήρησεν αὑτόν· [5] πλείστας δὲ καὶ φυγὼν δημοσίας δίκας καὶ διώξας, πολλὰς μὲν εἷλε, πάσας δ' ἀπέφυγε, πρόβλημα τοῦ βίου καὶ δραστήριον ὄργανον ἔχων τὸν λόγον, ᾧ δικαιότερον ἄν τις ἢ τύχῃ καὶ δαίμονι τοῦ ἀνδρὸς τὸ μηδὲν παθεῖν παρ' ἀξίαν ἀνατιθείη.

[1] ἑπτὰ *vel* ἔπειτα *codd.*
[2] κλισιάδας *vel* κλεισιάδας *codd.*
[3] παρέσχε δὲ *vel* καὶ παρέσχε *codd.*
[4] τὰ δὲ περὶ *vel* περὶ δὲ *codd.*

competitors [for 195 BC], and one of two censors [for 184 BC], surpassing seven most illustrious and foremost men, who stood for the office in competition with him. [2] . . . [3] Cato was not only chief in actions and plans in relation to the Iberian war, when he was consul himself; but also, as a military tribune at Thermopylae [in 191 BC], when another was consul [M'. Acilius Glabrio], he secured the glory of the victory, having opened up wide gates for the Romans toward Antiochus [Antiochus III the Great] and, while the king was watching only the front, having brought the war around to his back. For that victory, manifestly the work of Cato, drove Asia out of Greece and in turn laid it open for Scipio [L. Cornelius Scipio Asiaticus, cos. 190 BC]. [4] In battle, then, both [Aristides and Cato] were undefeated, but in politics Aristides fell, ostracized and overpowered by Themistocles. Cato, on the contrary, though he had almost all the greatest and most powerful men in Rome as opponents and wrestled with them like an athlete up to his old age, kept himself untoppled. [5] He was involved in countless public proceedings, as both plaintiff and defendant; as plaintiff, he won many, as defendant, he avoided defeat in all, as he had eloquence as a bulwark and efficacious instrument of his life: to this, more justly than to fortune and the guardian genius of the man, one may ascribe the fact that he suffered nothing in violation of his dignity.

T 65 Suet. *Gram. et rhet.* 15.2

ac tanto amore erga patroni memoriam extitit [Lenaeus, Cn. Pompei Magni libertus] ut Sallustium historicum, quod eum oris probi animo inverecundo scripsisset, acerbissima satura laceraverit, lastaurum et lurconem et nebulonem popinonemque appellans, et vita scriptisque monstrosum, praeterea priscorum Catonis verborum ineruditissimum furem.

T 66 Suet. *Aug.* 86.2–3

M. quidem Antonium ut insanum increpat, quasi ea scribentem quae mirentur potius homines quam intellegant, deinde ludens malum et inconstans in eligendo genere dicendi ingenium eius addit haec: [3] "tuque dubitas Cimberne Annius ac Veranius Flaccus imitandi sint tibi, ita ut verbis quae Crispus Sallustius excerpsit ex Originibus Catonis utaris, an potius Asiaticorum oratorum inanis[1] sententiis verborum volubilitas in nostrum sermonem transferenda?"

[1] inanis *Gronovius*: inanibus *vel* manibus *vel* immanibus *codd.*

T 65 Suetonius, *Lives of Illustrious Men. Grammarians and Rhetoricians*

And he [Lenaeus, a freedman of Cn. Pompeius Magnus] demonstrated such great love for the memory of his patron that, because Sallust [C. Sallustius Crispus (*ORF*[4] 152)], the historian, had written that he [Pompey] had an honest face and a shameless mind, he tore him [Sallust] to pieces in a most severe satire, calling him a catamite, a glutton, a rascal, and a customer in insalubrious restaurants, as well as monstrous in his life and writings, and, what is more, a completely uneducated thief of the old words of Cato [cf. T 49, 66, 71].[1]

[1] Scholz (1989) suggests that, for example, Cato's speech given in the trial on his consulship (*Orat.* F 21–55) inspired Sallust in the *Histories* with regard to the letter he has Pompey send to the Senate during the fight against Sertorius (Sall. *Hist.* 2.98 M. = 2.86 R.).

T 66 Suetonius, *Life of Augustus*

As for M. Antonius [M. Antonius triumvir (*ORF*[4] 159)], he [Augustus] berates him as a madman, on the grounds that he was writing what people would admire rather than understand; then, ridiculing his perverse and inconsistent judgment in choosing a style of speaking, he adds the following: [3] "And can you doubt whether you should imitate Annius Cimber [T. Annius Cimber, praet. prob. 43 BC] and Veranius Flaccus [identity uncertain], so that you use words that Sallustius Crispus [C. Sallustius Crispus (*ORF*[4] 152)] excerpted from Cato's *Origines* [cf. T 49, 65, 71], or rather whether you should introduce into our language the meaningless volubility of the Asiatic orators in discourse?"

T 67 Fronto, *Ad M. Caes.* 1.7.3–4 (p. 15.10–17 van den Hout)

[FRONTO:] quot litterae istic sunt, totidem consulatus mihi, totidem laureas, triumphos, togas pictas arbitror contigisse. [4] quid tale M. Porcio aut Quinto Ennio, C. Graccho aut Titio poetae, quid Scipioni aut Numidico, quid M. Tullio tale usuvenit? quorum libri pretiosiores habentur et summam gloriam retinent, si sunt Lampadionis aut Staberii, Plautii aut D. Aurelii, Autriconis aut Aelii manu scripta e<xem>pla aut a Tirone emendata aut a Domitio Balbo descripta aut ab Attico aut Nepote. mea oratio extabit M. Caesaris manu scripta.

T 68 Fronto, *Ad M. Caes.* 2.6.1 (p. 27.3–5 van den Hout)

[M. AURELIUS CAESAR:] sane si quid Graeci veteres tale scripserunt, viderint qui sciunt; ego, si fas est dicere, nec M. Porcium tam bene vituperantem quam tu laudasti usquam advorti.

T 67 Fronto, *Correspondence*

[FRONTO:] As many letters as there are here,[1] so many consulships, so many laurels, triumphs, ceremonial robes, I believe, have been granted to me. [4] What of this kind happened to M. Porcius [Cato] or Quintus Ennius, to C. Gracchus [C. Sempronius Gracchus (*ORF*^{4} 48)] or the poet Titius, what to Scipio [P. Cornelius Scipio Aemilianus Africanus minor (*ORF*^{4} 21)] or Numidicus [Q. Caecilius Metellus Numidicus (*ORF*^{4} 58)], what to M. Tullius [Cicero]? Their books are regarded as more precious and retain the greatest distinction if copies have been written by the hand of Lampadio or Staberius, Plautius or D. Aurelius, Autrico or Aelius or corrected by Tiro or transcribed by Domitius Balbus or by Atticus or Nepos [ancient editors]. My speech will be extant written by the hand of M. Caesar.

1 The letters (characters) are those in a copy of one of Fronto's speeches: Marcus Aurelius has written out the speech in his own hand and sent this copy to Fronto.

T 68 Fronto, *Correspondence*

[M. AURELIUS CAESAR:] Indeed, if the old Greeks have written anything like this, they who have knowledge should see to it; I, if it is permissible to say so, have not even noticed M. Porcius [Cato] criticizing anywhere so well as you have praised.

T 69 Fronto, *Ad M. Caes.* 2.17.1 (p. 34.18–22 van den Hout)

[M. Aurelius Caesar:] ego tibi de patrono meo M. Porcio gratias ago, quod eum crebro lectitas. tu mihi de C. Crispo timeo ut umquam gratias agere possis, nam uni M. Porcio me dedicavi atque despondi atque delegavi. hoc etiam ipsum "atque" unde putas? ex ipso furore.

T 70a Fronto, *Ad M. Caes.* 3.17.3 (p. 49.18–21 van den Hout)

[Fronto:] meministi autem tu[1] plurimas lectiones, quibus usque adhuc versatus es, comoedias, Atellan<a>s,[2] oratores veteres, quorum aut pauci aut praeter Catonem et Gracchum nemo tubam inflat; omnes autem mugiunt vel stridunt potius.

[1] tu *Mai*: te *cod.* [2] atellans *cod.*

T 70b Fronto, *Ad M. Antoninum de eloquentia* 4.4 (p. 148.10–12 van den Hout)

[Fronto:] Ennium deinde et Accium et Lucretium ampliore iam mugitu personantis tamen tolerant. at ubi Catonis et Sallustii et Tulli tuba exaudita est, trepidant et pavent et fugam frustra meditantur.

T 69 Fronto, *Correspondence*

[M. AURELIUS CAESAR:] I offer gratitude to you as regards my patron M. Porcius [Cato], since you read him frequently. I fear that you might never be able to offer gratitude to me as regards C. Crispus [C. Sallustius Crispus (*ORF*[4] 152)]; for I have dedicated, and devoted, and entrusted myself to M. Porcius alone. Where do you think this very "and" [*atque*] is coming from? From this very folly.[1]

[1] The comment alludes to Cato's preference for *atque* (over other conjunctions) to express "and" in the *Origines* and the speeches (see e.g., Till 1937, 82; Fraenkel 1968, 130; Sblendorio 1971, 8; Sblendorio Cugusi 1982, 39; Calboli 1996, 20; Courtney 1999, 75, 80; Schönberger 2000, 360; Cugusi and Sblendorio Cugusi 2001, 1:84; von Albrecht 2012, 32 [with further references and figures]).

T 70a Fronto, *Correspondence*

[FRONTO:] And you remember very many readings, with which you have been occupied up to now, comedies, Atellanae, old orators, of whom either few or nobody except Cato and Gracchus [C. Sempronius Gracchus (*ORF*[4] 48)] blows the tuba; but all rather bellow or hiss.

T 70b Fronto, *Correspondence*

[FRONTO:] Then they still accept that Ennius, and Accius, and Lucretius resound already with more bellowing. But as soon as the tuba of Cato, and Sallust [C. Sallustius Crispus (*ORF*[4] 152)], and Tullius [Cicero] has been heard, they tremble, and are frightened, and think in vain of flight.

T 71 Fronto, *Ad M. Caes.* 4.3.2 (pp. 56.18–57.1 van den Hout)

[FRONTO:] quamobrem rari admodum veterum scriptorum in eum laborem studiumque et periculum verba industriosius quaerendi sese commisere, oratorum post homines natos unus omnium M. Porcius eiusque frequens sectator C. Sallustius, poetarum maxime Plautus, multo maxime Q. Ennius eumque studiose aemulatus L. Coelius nec non Naevius, Lucretius, Accius etiam, Caecilius, Laberius quoque.

T 72 Fronto, *Ad M. Caes.* 4.6.1 (p. 62.10–12 van den Hout)

[M. AURELIUS CAESAR:] ergo ab undecima noctis in tertiam diei partim legi ex agri cultura Catonis, partim scripsi, minus misere, mercule, quam heri.

T 73 Fronto, *Ad M. Antoninum de eloquentia* 1.2 (p. 134.1–6 van den Hout)

[FRONTO:] historiam quoque scripsere Sallustius structe, Pictor incondite, Claudius lepide, Antias invenuste, Seisenna longinque,[1] verbis Cato multiiugis, Coelius singulis. contionatur autem Cato infeste, Gracchus turbulente, Tullius gloriose; iam in iudiciis saevit idem Cato, triumphat Cicero, tumultuatur Gracchus, Calvus rixatur.

[1] concinne *Cornelissen* *post* longinque *nomen auctoris, fort.* Rutilius, *intercidisse putat Klussmann*

T 71 Fronto, *Correspondence*

[Fronto:] For that reason only few of the old writers have committed themselves to that labor, effort, and risk of seeking words more diligently, of all the orators since the beginning of humankind M. Porcius [Cato] alone and his assiduous follower C. Sallustius [C. Sallustius Crispus (*ORF*[4] 152); cf. T 49, 65, 66], of the poets especially Plautus, more particularly Q. Ennius, and his eager emulator L. Coelius [L. Coelius Antipater (*FRHist* 15)], and also Naevius, Lucretius, Accius as well, Caecilius [Statius], also [Decimus] Laberius.

T 72 Fronto, *Correspondence*

[M. Aurelius Caesar:] Thus from the eleventh hour of the night until the third of the day I have spent some time reading from Cato's [work on] agriculture and some time writing, less miserably, by Hercules, than yesterday.

T 73 Fronto, *Correspondence*

[Fronto:] And history was written by Sallust [C. Sallustius Crispus (*ORF*[4] 152)] in an orderly way, by Pictor [Q. Fabius Pictor (*FRHist* 1)] clumsily, by Claudius [Q. Claudius Quadrigarius (*FRHist* 24)] charmingly, by Antias [Valerius Antias (*FRHist* 25)] inelegantly, by Sisenna [L. Cornelius Sisenna (*FRHist* 26)] in a longwinded way, by Cato with many and varied words, by Coelius [L. Coelius Antipater (*FRHist* 15)] with one word apiece. And to the People Cato speaks aggressively, Gracchus [C. Sempronius Gracchus (*ORF*[4] 48)] provocatively, Tullius [Cicero] magnificently; further, in the courts the same Cato rages, Cicero triumphs, Gracchus creates an uproar, Calvus [C. Licinius Macer Calvus (*ORF*[4] 165)] brawls.

T 74 Fronto, *Ad M. Antoninum de orationibus* 2 (p. 153.11–14 van den Hout)

[Fronto:] confusam eam[1] ego eloquentiam, cata‹c›hannae[2] ritu partim pineis nucibus Catonis, partim Senecae mollibus et febriculosis[3] prunuleis insitam, subvertendam censeo radicitus, immo vero Plautino ‹e›t rato[4] verbo "exradicitus."

[1] confusaneam *Haupt*: confusiciam *Studemund*: confusam (*vel* contusam) enim ego *Hauler* [2] catahannae *cod.; cf. marg.*: catachenae *Unger*: m^2 *in margine* catachanna [3] vermiculosis *Cornelissen* [4] Plautino ‹e›t rato *Baehrens*: plautinotrato *cod.*: Plautino irato *Mai*: Plautino facto *Allen*: Plautino utar *Jordan*: *alii alia*

T 75 Fronto, *Principia historiae* 4 (p. 204.3–4 van den Hout)

[Fronto:] * * * ‹eni›mvero fandi ‹agendique› laudibus longe praestantissimus omnium Cato Porcius Censorius . . .

T 76 Fronto, *Principia historiae* 4 (p. 204.14–16 van den Hout, m^2 *in margine*)

[Fronto:] . . . catus . . . Cato ‹Censorius a› p‹a›tria oppidatim statuis ornandus, qui prima sollertiarum et Latini nominis subolem et Italicarum origines ‹urbium et Ab›originum pueritias inlustravit

T 74 Fronto, *Correspondence*

[FRONTO:] This confused eloquence, in the manner of a tree on which several different fruits have been grafted, partly grafted with pine nuts of Cato, partly with Seneca's soft little plums giving rise to fever, I believe, must be destroyed by the roots, or rather, with a Plautine and approved word, "by the very roots" [Plaut. *Most.* 1112].

T 75 Fronto, *Correspondence*

[FRONTO:] . . . for, in relation to the praise received for speaking ‹and acting in court›, by far the most outstanding of all, Porcius Cato, the ex-censor . . .

T 76 Fronto, *Correspondence*

[FRONTO:] . . . clever . . . Cato, ‹the ex-censor›, to be honored ‹by› his fatherland with statues in every town, the man who cast light on the beginnings of resourcefulness, and the progeny of the Latin name, and the origins of the Italic ‹cities, and› the infancy of the indigenous peoples

T 77 Fronto, *Laudes fumi et pulveris* 1.5 (p. 216.24–25 van den Hout, m^2 *in margine*)

[Fronto:] modo dulce illud incorruptum sit et pudicum, Tusculanum et Ionicum, id est Catonis et Herodoti

T 78 Apul. *Apol.* 95.5–6

quamcumque ora<tio>nem struxerit Avitus, ita illa erit undique sui perfecte absoluta, ut in illa neque Cato gravitatem requirat neque Laelius lenitatem nec Gracchus impetum nec Caesar calorem nec <H>ortensius distributionem nec Calvus argutias nec parsimoniam Salustius nec opulentiam Cicero. [6] prorsus, inquam, ne omnis persequar, si Avitum audias, neque additum quicquam velis neque detractum neque autem aliquid commutatum.

T 79 Gell. *NA* 13.20.6–10

[Apollinaris:] non unus autem, sed conplures M. illius Catonis Censorii nepotes fuerunt, geniti non eodem patre; [7] duos enim M. ille Cato, qui et orator et censor fuit, filios habuit et matribus diversos et aetatibus longe dispares. [8] nam iam adulescente altero matre eius amissa ipse quoque iam multum senex Saloni clientis sui filiam virginem duxit in matrimonium, ex qua natus est ei M. Cato Salonianus; hoc enim illi cognomentum fuit a

T 77 Fronto, *Correspondence*

[FRONTO:] only be that sweetness uncorrupted and pure, in the Tusculan and the Ionic manner, that is [in the manner] of Cato and Herodotus

T 78 Apuleius, *Apologia*

Any speech that Avitus [L. Hedius Rufus Lollianus Avitus, cos. 144 AD] has composed will be so perfectly finished in all respects that Cato could not miss solemnity in it, nor Laelius [C. Laelius Sapiens (*ORF*[4] 20)] smoothness, nor Gracchus [C. Sempronius Gracchus (*ORF*[4] 48)] force, nor Caesar [C. Iulius Caesar (*ORF*[4] 121)] ardor, nor Hortensius [Q. Hortensius Hortalus (*ORF*[4] 92)] structure, nor Calvus [C. Licinius Macer Calvus (*ORF*[4] 165)] animation, nor Sallust [C. Sallustius Crispus (*ORF*[4] 152)] economy, nor Cicero richness. [6] In sum, I say, so as not to run through them all, if you were to hear Avitus, you would not want anything added, nor removed, nor indeed anything altered.

T 79 Gellius, *Attic Nights*

[APOLLINARIS:] For there was not just one, but there were several grandsons of the famous M. Cato, the ex-censor, though not sprung from the same father. [7] For that M. Cato, who was both an orator and a censor, had two sons, having different mothers and very far apart in terms of their ages. [8] For, when one of them was already a young man and his mother had passed away, he [Cato], himself too already well advanced in age, married the maiden daughter of his client Salonius, and from her was born to him M. Cato Salonianus; for this additional name was

Salonio, patre matris, datum. [9] ex maiore autem Catonis filio, qui praetor designatus patre vivo mortuus est et egregios de iuris disciplina libros reliquit, nascitur hic de quo quaeritur M. Cato M. filius M. nepos. [10] is satis vehemens orator fuit multasque orationes ad exemplum avi scriptas reliquit et consul cum Q. Marcio Rege fuit, inque eo consulatu in Africam profectus in ea provincia mortem obit.

T 80 Fest., p. 216.20–23 L.

Originum libros quod inscripsit Cato, non satis plenum titulum propositi sui[1] videtur amplexus, quando praegravant ea, quae sunt rerum gestarum populi Romani.

[1] propositi sui *ed. princ.*: propositis ut *codd.*

T 81 Ampel. *Lib. mem.* 19.8

Cato Censorius qui totiens accusatus {est}[1] quoad vixit nocentis accusare non destitit. hic est omnium rerum peritissimus et, ut Sallustio Crispo videtur, Romani generis disertissimus {Cato}.[2]

[1] est *del. Assmann*: est <et> *Woelfflin* [2] *del. Halm*

T 82 [Aurel. Vict.] *Vir. ill.* 47.1–9

Marcus Porcius Cato, genere Tusculanus, a Valerio Flacco Romam sollicitatus, tribunus militum in Sicilia, quaestor

given to him from Salonius, his mother's father [*Op. cet.* F 75]. [9] But to Cato's elder son, who died when praetor-elect, while his father was still alive [cf. T 7c, 62], and left admirable books on the science of law [T 97], there was born the man about whom we are inquiring, M. Cato, Marcus' son, Marcus' grandson [cos. 118 BC]. [10] That man was an orator of some power and left many speeches written up, according to the model of his grandfather; and he was consul with Q. Marcius Rex [cos. 118 BC], and during that consulship he went to Africa and died in that province.

T 80 Festus

As for the books of *Origines*, as Cato entitled them, he does not seem to have adopted a sufficiently comprehensive title for his endeavor, since the parts that are dedicated to the deeds of the Roman People outweigh [the description of the origins].

T 81 Ampelius

Cato, the ex-censor, who, having been so frequently prosecuted {is}, did not stop prosecuting the guilty as long as he was alive. He is the most knowledgeable in all matters and, as it seems to Sallustius Crispus [C. Sallustius Crispus (*ORF*^{4} 152)], the most eloquent of the Roman nation {Cato} [cf. T 85].

T 82 [Aurelius Victor], *On Famous Men*

Marcus Porcius Cato, a Tusculan by birth, having been encouraged [to move] to Rome by Valerius Flaccus [L. Valerius Flaccus, cos. 195 BC], was a military tribune in

sub Scipione fortissimus, praetor iustissimus fuit: in praetura Sardiniam subegit, ubi ab Ennio Graecis litteris institutus. [2] consul Celtiberos domuit et, ne rebellare possent, litteras ad singulas civitates misit, ut muros diruerent. [3] cum unaquaeque sibi soli imperari putaret, fecerunt. Syriaco bello tribunus militum sub M'.[1] Acilio Glabrione occupatis Thermopylarum iugis praesidium hostium depulit. [4] censor L. Flaminium[2] consularem senatu movit, quod ille in Gallia ad cuiusdam scorti spectaculum eiectum quondam e carcere in convivio iugulari iussisset. [5] basilicam suo nomine primus fecit. [6] matronis ornamenta erepta Oppia lege repetentibus restitit. [7] accusator assiduus malorum Galbam octogenarius accusavit, ipse quadragies quater accusatus gloriose absolutus. [8] Carthaginem delendam censuit. [9] post octoginta annos filium genuit. imago huius funeris gratia produci solet.

[1] M'. *Schott*
[2] Flamininum *vulgo*

Sicily [214 BC], a very valiant quaestor [204 BC] under Scipio [P. Cornelius Scipio Africanus maior, cos. 205, 194, censor 199 BC (*ORF*[4] 4)], and a very just praetor [198 BC]: during his praetorship he subdued Sardinia, where he was instructed in Greek literature by Ennius [cf. T 26]. [2] As consul [195 BC], he subdued the Celtiberians [peoples in the Iberian peninsula], and, so that they could not rebel, he sent letters to each individual community asking them to demolish their walls. [3] Since each of them believed that the order was addressed to it alone, they did so [cf. Frontin. *Str.* 1.1.1; App. *Hisp.* 41.167–70; Zonar. 9.17]. In the Syrian war, as a military tribune [191 BC] under M'. Acilius Glabrio [cos. 191 BC], having occupied the ridge of Thermopylae, he routed the garrison of the enemy. [4] As censor [184 BC], he removed L. Flaminius, an ex-consul [L. Quinctius Flamininus, cos. 192 BC], from the Senate, since, while in Gaul, for the entertainment of some prostitute, he had ordered that someone previously taken out of the prison be strangled during a banquet [*Orat.* F 69–71; *Op. cet.* F 70]. [5] He [Cato] was the first to erect a basilica bearing his name [T 33; *Orat.* F 87]. [6] He opposed the married women who were claiming the return of their adornments that had been taken away by *Lex Oppia* [*Orat.* F 17A]. [7] As an eager prosecutor of evil individuals, as an octogenarian [*Orat.* F 196–99A], he prosecuted Galba [Ser. Sulpicius Galba (*ORF*[4] 19)]; he himself was prosecuted and, to his glory, was acquitted forty-four times [cf. T 42, 60]. [8] He was of the opinion that Carthage should be destroyed [*Op. cet.* F 76]. [9] Beyond the age of eighty he fathered a son [cf. T 41]. His image is generally carried in procession on the occasion of a funeral.

T 83 Solin. 2.2

sed Italia tanta cura ab omnibus dicta, praecipue M. Catone, ut iam inveniri non sit quod non veterum auctorum praesumpserit diligentia, largiter in laudem excellentis terrae materia suppetente, dum scriptores praestantissimi reputant locorum salubritatem, caeli temperiem, ubertatem soli, aprica collium, opaca nemorum, innoxios saltus, vitium olearumque proventus, nobilia pecuaria, tot amnes, lacus tantos, bifera violaria: . . .

T 84 Diom., *GL* I, p. 472.2–4

si paenultimus fuerit tribrachys vel pyrrichius et paeones successerint primus et novissimus, erit antiqua structura, quae dicitur confragosa; qua usus est Cato.

T 85 Fab. Laur. Vict. *In Rhet. Cic.* 1.20, *RLM*, p. 203.24–28

namque historia et brevis esse debet in expositione et aperta et probabilis, ut Sallustius sibi omnia in Catilina tribuit: "quam verissime potero, paucis absolvam," cum aliis historiographis singula tradidisset in libro primo His-

T 83 Solinus

But Italy has been described with so much attention by all, especially by M. Cato, that nothing can be found any longer that the diligence of the old authorities has not anticipated, with material abundantly available for the praise of the excellent country, while the most outstanding writers reflect upon the healthiness of places, the temperateness of the climate, the fertility of the soil, the sunny places on the hills, the shady places in the groves, the pastures free from poison, the yields of vines and olive trees, excellent herds of cattle, so many rivers, such great lakes, twice-flowering flower beds: . . .

T 84 Diomedes

If the penultimate [foot in rhythmical prose] is a tribrach [⏑⏑⏑] or pyrrhic [⏑⏑] and the first [–⏑⏑⏑] and the last paeon [⏑⏑⏑–] follow, this will be an ancient structure, which is called "rough," and which Cato has used.[1]

[1] On the types and frequency of clausulae in Cato's oratory (including examples of ⏑⏑⏑–), see Habinek 1985, 190.

T 85 Fabius Laurentius Victorinus

For history should be concise in the presentation, and clear, and plausible, as Sallust [C. Sallustius Crispus (*ORF*[4] 152)] ascribes all these qualities to himself in *Catilina* [Sall. *Cat.* 4.3]: "as truthfully as I will be able to, I will describe briefly," when he had assigned them individually to other historiographers in the first book of the *Histories* [Sall. *Hist.* F 1.4 M. = 1.3 R.]: he attributes brevity to Cato,

toriarum: dat Catoni brevitatem "Romani generis disertissimus paucis absolvit," Fannio vero veritatem.

T 86 Sulp. Vict., *Inst. or.* 21, *RLM*, pp. 323.34–24.2

partitio est, qua causam dividimus in partes: hoc in controversiis non fere fit,[1] sed in causis veris, etsi non semper, at[2] tamen saepe. apud Catonem assidua partitio est, apud M. Tullium rarior.

[1] fit *Halm*: sit *vulg.* [2] at *vel* ut *edd. vet.*

T 87 Iul. Vict., *Ars* 4.4, *RLM*, p. 389.19–21 (= p. 24.24–26 Giomini / Celentano)

dividuntur negotiales, quae in legum et rogationum lationibus reperiuntur, primo quidem ab obscuritate, si nobis materia largitur, ut Marcus Tullius de lege agraria facit, et Cato saepe et saepissime Gracchus.

T 88 SHA (Ael. Spart.), 1 *Hadr.* 16.6

Ciceroni Catonem, Vergilio En‹n›ium, Salustio Coelium praetulit . . .

T 89a Hieron. *Ep.* 52.3.6

nec mirum, cum etiam Cato, Romani generis disertissimus, censorius iam et senex, Graecas litteras nec erubuerit nec desperaverit discere.

"the most eloquent of the Roman nation has described briefly," and truthfulness to Fannius [C. Fannius (*FRHist* 12 T 6)].

T 86 Sulpicius Victor

partitio ["division"] is where we divide the case into parts: this does not usually occur in forensic exercises, but in real cases, even though not always, but still frequently. In Cato *partitio* is constantly present, in M. Tullius [Cicero] more rarely.

T 87 Iulius Victor

Legal issues, which are found in relation to proposals of laws and decrees, can be subdivided: firstly, on the basis of obscurity, if the material permits that to us, as Marcus Tullius does [in the speech] on the agrarian law [Cic. *Leg. Agr.*], and Cato often, and Gracchus [C. Sempronius Gracchus (*ORF*^{4} 48)] most frequently.

T 88 *Historia Augusta* (Aelius Spartianus), *Life of Hadrian*

He [the emperor Hadrian] preferred Cato to Cicero, Ennius to Vergil, Coelius [L. Coelius Antipater (*FRHist* 15)] to Sallust [C. Sallustius Crispus (*ORF*^{4} 152)] . . .

T 89a Jerome, *Letters*

And it [display of intellectual accomplishments in old age] is not surprising, when even Cato, the most eloquent of the Roman nation, already an ex-censor and of advanced age, felt no shame or despair in studying Greek literature.

T 89b Hieron. *Ep.* 61.3.3

solus es Cato, Romani generis disertissimus, qui testimonio tuo et prudentiae velis credi.

T 90 Serv. ad Verg. *Aen.* 6.841

"magne Cato": Censorium dicit, qui scripsit historias, multa etiam bella confecit: nam Uticensem praesente Augusto, contra quem pater eius Caesar et dimicavit et Anticatones scripsit, laudare non poterat.

T 91a Serv. ad Verg. *Aen.* 7.259

"di nostra incepta secundent": antiquo more locuturus de publicis rebus, id est de pace et nuptiis filiae, facit ante deorum commemorationem, sicut etiam in omnibus Catonis orationibus legimus. hinc est in divinatione Ciceronis: "si quid ex aliqua vetere oratione 'Iovem ego optimum maximum.'" ipse etiam Vergilius: "praefatus divos solio rex infit ab alto."

T 91b Serv. ad Verg. *Aen.* 11.301

"praefatus divos" more antiquo: nam maiores nullam orationem nisi invocatis numinibus inchoabant, sicut sunt

T 89b Jerome, *Letters*

You alone are Cato, the most eloquent of the Roman nation, you who wish to trust your own evidence and sagacity [i.e., said ironically to the addressee].

T 90 Servius, *Commentary on Virgil*

"great Cato": He [Virgil] means the ex-censor, who wrote histories and also completed many wars. For in the presence of Augustus he could not praise the one of Utica [M. Porcius Cato Uticensis / Cato the Younger, 95–46 BC], against whom his [Augustus' adoptive] father Caesar [C. Iulius Caesar (*ORF*^{4} 121)] both fought and wrote *Anticatones*.

T 91a Servius, *Commentary on Virgil*

"may the gods favor our activities": In old-fashioned manner, about to speak on political matters, i.e., on peace and the marriage of his daughter [Lavinia], he [Latinus] first makes a reference to the gods, as we also read in all speeches of Cato. Hence there is in a pre-trial speech by Cicero [Cic. *Div. Caec.* 43]: "if something from some old speech [like] 'I [call on] Iuppiter Optimus Maximus.'" Virgil himself also [says] [Verg. *Aen.* 11.301]: "after having first addressed the gods, the king begins to speak from his elevated seat."

T 91b Servius, *Commentary on Virgil*

"after having first addressed the gods," in old-fashioned manner: for the ancients did not begin any speech without having invoked the gods; such are all the orations of Cato

omnes orationes Catonis et Gracchi; nam generale caput in omnibus legimus.

T 91c Symm. *Ep.* 3.44.2

an si nobis scribenda sit forensis oratio, Iovem deosque ceteros Catonis lege praefabimur, ne nobis vitio detur vel negligentia antiquitatis vel inscitia? atqui praestat Tullium sequi, qui ignorata maioribus usurpat exordia.

T 92 Serv. ad Verg. *Aen.* 7.678

"nec Praenestinae fundator defuit urbis": de civitatibus totius orbis multi quidem ex parte scripserunt, ad plenum tamen Ptolomaeus Graece, Latine Plinius. de Italicis etiam urbibus Hyginus plenissime scripsit, et Cato in Originibus. apud omnes tamen si diligenter advertas, de auctoribus conditarum urbium dissensio invenitur, adeo ut ne urbis quidem Romae origo possit diligenter agnosci.

T 93 Serv. ad Verg. *Aen.* 9.600

"durum a stirpe genus": Italiae disciplina et vita laudatur: quam et Cato in Originibus et Varro in gente populi Romani commemorat.

and of Gracchus [C. Sempronius Gracchus (*ORF*[4] 48)]; for we read a generic opening in all of them.

T 91c Symmachus, *Letters*

Won't we, if we should have to write a forensic speech, first mention Jupiter and other gods by way of preface according to a law of Cato, so that neither neglect nor ignorance of antiquity could be reckoned as a fault on our part? And yet it is better to follow Tullius [Cicero], who frequently employs openings unknown to predecessors.

T 92 Servius, *Commentary on Virgil*

"and the founder of the city of Praeneste [Caeculus] was not missing": On the communities of the entire world many have written a partial account, but only Ptolemy in Greek and Pliny in Latin have done so comprehensively. On the Italic towns Hyginus [C. Iulius Hyginus (*FRHist* 63 T 4)] has also written very comprehensively, and Cato in the *Origines*. Still, among all of them, if you carefully pay attention, disagreement is found as to the individuals responsible for establishing cities, to the extent that not even the origin of the city of Rome can be known accurately.

T 93 Servius, *Commentary on Virgil*

"an austere nation from the root": Italy's discipline and way of life are praised: which both Cato in the *Origines* and Varro in *On the descent of the Roman People* [M. Terentius Varro (F 20 *HRR*)] recall.

T 94 Grillius, ad Cic. *Inv. rhet.* 1.4 (p. 30.11–17 Jakobi)

in politia sua dicit Tullius rectorem rei publicae summum virum et doctissimum esse debere ita, ut sapiens sit et iustus et temperans et eloquens, ut possit facile currente oratione animi secreta ad regendam plebem exprimere. scire etiam debet ius, Graecas nosse litteras, quod Catonis facto probatur, qui in summa senectute Graecis litteris operam dans indicavit, quantum utilitatis haberent.

T 95 Cassiod. *Orat.*, p. 467 Mommsen / Traube (*MGH, AA* XII)

quid Catonem repetam disciplinarum libros moribus transeuntem?

T 96 *Excerpta rhetorica e codice Parisino 7530 edita* (*RLM*, pp. 588.31–89.2)

principiorum ad historiam pertinentium species sunt tres: de historia, de persona, de materia. aut enim historiam bonum generaliter commendamus, ut Cato, aut pro persona scribentis rationem eius quod hoc officium adsumpserit reddimus, ut Sallustius eo loco, ubi dicit [Sall. *Cat.* 3.3]: . . . , aut eam rem, quam relaturi sumus, dignam quae et scribatur et legatur ostendimus, ut Livius ab urbe condita.

T 94 Grillius, *Commentary on Cicero*

In his *State* Tullius [Cicero] says [cf. Cic. *Rep.* 5.2 Ziegler; ad 5.4 Powell] that the leader of a state should be the best and most learned man, so that he is wise, and just, and moderate, and eloquent, so that he can easily express in fluent speech the secrets of his mind for the purpose of ruling the People. He should also know the law and have become familiar with Greek literature: this is demonstrated by what Cato did, when he, devoting his efforts to Greek literature, at a very advanced age, showed how great its utility was.

T 95 Cassiodorus, *Speeches*

Why shall I call to mind Cato, who surpasses the books of instruction by his morals?

T 96 Rhetorical excerpts

There are three types of beginnings pertaining to history: concerning history, concerning the person [of the author], concerning the subject matter. For we can praise history as a good in general, like Cato, or we can provide an account on behalf of the person of the writer of why they have taken on that task, as Sallust [C. Sallustius Crispus (*ORF*^{4} 152)] does in that passage where he says [Sall. *Cat.* 3.3]: . . . , or we can show that the matter that we are about to tell is worthy both to be written of and to be read, as Livy does in *From the Foundation of the City* [Liv. 1, *praef.*].[1]

[1] Some editors assign this passage as a fragment to Cato's *Origines* (e.g., *Orig.* F 3 Peter); others reject this attribution since the reference to Cato is regarded as too vague (e.g., Chassignet 1986, xxxvii–xxxviii).

T 97 *Dig.* 1.2.2.38

hos sectatus ad aliquid est Cato. deinde Marcus Cato princeps Porciae familiae, cuius et libri extant, sed plurimi filii eius, ex quibus ceteri oriuntur.

T 98 Isid. *Orig.* 17.1.1

apud Romanos autem de agricultura primus Cato instituit; quam deinde Marcus Terentius expolivit; mox Vergilius laude carminum extulit. nec minorem studium habuerunt postmodum Cornelius Celsus et Iulius Atticus, Aemilianus, sive Columella insignis orator, qui totum corpus disciplinae eiusdem conplexus est.

T 99 *CLE* 1251

D. M. M. Romani Iovini rhetoris eloquii Latini (M. Iunius Severus et Romania Marcia heredes bene merenti fecerunt): conditus hac Romanius est tellure Iovinus / docta loqui doctus quique loqui docuit. / manibus infernis si vita est gloria vitae, / vivit et hic nobis ut Cato vel Cicero.

T 97 *Digest*

Those [the Aelii and their legal writings] were followed to some extent by Cato. Then Marcus Cato, the foremost member of the Porcian family, by whom books are also extant, but most numerous are those by his son [T 79], from which others have originated.

T 98 Isidore, *Origins*

Among the Romans, however, Cato was the first to instruct about agriculture; then Marcus Terentius [Varro] elaborated on it; soon Vergil exalted it by the praise of his poems. No less effort was displayed a little later by Cornelius Celsus [A. Cornelius Celsus] and Iulius Atticus [author of monograph on viticulture], Aemilianus [Palladius Rutilius Taurus Aemilianus], or Columella, an outstanding orator, who embraced the whole body of this same discipline.

T 99 Inscription from Rome

To the spirits of M. Romanius Iovinus, a rhetor of Latin eloquence (M. Iunius Severus and Romania Marcia, the heirs, have erected this for him who deserved it): Romanius Iovinus is buried in this soil, taught to speak about learned matters and who taught speaking. If for the shades of the dead in the underworld glory acquired in life is life, this man too is alive for us like Cato or Cicero.

ORIGINES (F 1–156)

While Cato was not the first historiographer in Rome, the Origines *("*Origins*") is the first attested historical work in Latin, since other early Roman historians wrote in Greek. By using the Latin language and adopting a more comprehensive approach, Cato sets himself apart from his predecessors in historiography and creates a "Roman" historical perspective within the contemporary political and intellectual context. (On Cato's role in the development of Roman historiography, see, e.g., Timpe 1970–1971; Kierdorf 1980; Mehl 2011, esp. 49–55.)*

Although the Origines *may have been composed over a longer period, Cato is said to have been working on the piece mainly in his old age and until close to his death (T 22, 26;* Orat. *F 198). A reference to the war against Perseus (171–168 BC) implies that the section including this comment (F 55) must have been written after the time of that war (if the notice is correctly assigned to the* Origines*). Testimonia that might seem to present the* Origines *as an early work are not regarded as clear evidence to the contrary (T 31: reference probably anachronistic;* Inc. *F 12: history written in large characters for the education of the son seen as a different work, an early version, or a construction of later tradition).*

ORIGINES (F 1–156)

In its final form the Origines *consisted of seven books (cf. T 26; introductions to each book): Book 1 deals with the early history of Rome, Books 2 and 3 with the early history of other places in Italy, and Books 4 to 7 with the historical period from the First Punic War (264–241 BC) to Cato's death (149 BC), as the final book includes a speech Cato gave in the last year of his life. Thus, as already noted in antiquity, the work's established title is fully appropriate only for the first three books (T 26, 80). This title* Origines *is first attested in Cicero (T 13, 15, 22; cf. T 10) and Cornelius Nepos (T 26); occasionally, the terms* Annales *(T 34, 43),* Origo generis Romani *(*Orig. *F 10),* ktiseis *("foundation stories of cities") (*Orig. *F 75), and* Peri Romaikes archaiotetos *("On Roman ancient history") (*Orig. *F 3) are found with reference to Cato's work (cf. also T 29:* genealogiai, *"pedigrees"). In those contexts* Annales *is probably used as a generic designation of a historical work (as* historia(e) *appears as a category for Cato's work: e.g., T 20b, 26, 63, 73, 85, 90, 96) and does not literally indicate a strict annalistic structure; the other terms refer in different ways to the outline of the origins of Rome and other places: so, these words do not seem to function as alternative titles and are rather used descriptively.*

The Origines *is not limited to Rome; instead, it includes the early history of other towns and nations in Italy (T 26, 29, 76, 83, 92, 93), though these two elements may have been less distinct than it appears if Rome was regarded as part of Italy and if Italy was presented as a unity, at least geographically. Thus, the work illustrates the history of the Roman People in the context of the history of other peoples they encountered. Latin seems to have been understood and used sufficiently widely across Italy by the time the* Origines *was completed so that this first historiographical work in Latin would have been accessible to non-Roman readers in Italy too. Cato's account of peoples and places, partly probably based on personal observation, is fairly comprehensive. It goes beyond the presentation of foundation legends and also covers physical geography (e.g.,* Orig. *F 62, 99, 111, 150); weather phenomena (e.g.,* Orig. *F 116, 141); flora and fauna (e.g.,* Orig. *F 31, 47, 75, 121, 122 142); agricultural practices and natural produce (e.g.,* Orig. *F 38, 40, 46, 48, 100, 116); customs, national characteristics and ways of life (e.g.,* Orig. *F 30, 33, 84, 109, 128); political, military, religious, and legal rules and conventions (e.g.,* Orig. *F 35, 85, 112); as well as amazing natural phenomena (e.g.,* Orig. *F 47, 75, 116). Such details display a certain level of interest (on the part of the author and perhaps also on that of the intended primary audience) in the nature and history of each region. Providing such information contributes to illustrating the traditions and key features of the peoples in Italy, which might be useful for assessing the military and economic position of the territory (see also Thuc. 1.2) in relation to the creation of a Roman empire. (On the information about Italy compiled by Cato, his potential sources, and his aims in presenting the material in this way, see, e.g., Dench 1995,*

17–19; Hantos 1998; Williams 2001, esp. 35–99; Jefferson 2012; on aspects of date, title, and structure, see also Sbardella 2001a; 2003).

The overall content points to a unifying concept consisting of the sequential outline of the history of Rome and Italy as well as the presentation of a broad range of factual information. According to Cornelius Nepos' overview (T 26), the material was given "in summary fashion" or "according to the main points" (depending on the translation and the interpretation of the key term in Cornelius Nepos' text; see, e.g., Astin 1978, 218): this method probably means that not all details of all events are included and instead an overview of important developments is presented. This procedure does not exclude emphasizing certain items and describing key events in a more specific and extensive manner. Such a method of writing suggests that the Origines *did not just list major incidents per year in serial fashion and instead provided more than records of basic facts, thus being distinguished from pontifical chronicles, against which Cato sets off his own writing in a fragment (*Orig. *F 80). Cornelius Nepos' wording and the identifiable historical incidents across the various books may indicate that this format is particularly prominent in the first five books, while the last two are more expansive and detailed, covering a shorter period of time. The extant records of dates (*Orig. *F 13, 52, 55, 77a) show that Cato employed a relative system of dating, placing events in relation to each other. Overall, there seems to be an emphasis on foundation stories and then on contemporary history and Cato's own deeds.*

Moreover, there was presumably also a certain didactic aim on Cato's part, so as to highlight core Roman morals and acquaint his fellow citizens with details of Roman his-

tory, as history is said to have been described as a good at the beginning (T 96). Such an intention might mirror the focus of other known works, like the writings for Cato's son (cf. Inc. *F 12).*

While there is broad agreement on the general shape of the Origines *by now, the work's specific nature and structure mean that there are still open questions, on which scholars have put forward different theories. For instance, it has been suggested that the* Origines *might have originally consisted of five books, three on origins and two on the more recent history up to 167 BC, and that the final two books were added later, presenting contemporary history in more discursive (and perhaps unfinished) form, or that the work consists of two essentially different parts and perhaps even originally separate pieces. Others assume a more developed overall plan for a single piece from the start.*

In antiquity Cato was regarded as one of the early writers in Rome, particularly because of his historiography; and his writing style in the Origines *(and other writings) was assessed accordingly. While some readers in Cicero's time found it simple and ancient (T 6, 11, 13, 15), Cicero defended it as clear, pleasingly straightforward, and displaying all the ornaments available at the time (T 13). It was favored by Sallust (T 49, 65, 66, 71, 81, 85) and the archaists of the second century AD (e.g., T 69, 75, 77).*

A remarkable feature of Cato's narrative style in the Origines *is that he is said to have identified individual commanders not by name, but by their functions (T 26, 43); that this was at least a general principle is confirmed by fragments referring to "the military tribune" or "the dictator of the Carthaginians" (e.g.,* Orig. *F 76, 78). This*

*way of presentation reduces the glory of individuals and rather highlights that they serve the community and thus that the achievements are those of the Roman People. As a result, Cato's historiographical work is a description of the deeds of the Roman People (*populi Romani gesta*) rather than those of individuals (*Orig. *F 1b). Still, scholars regard it as unlikely that Cato never used any names (or failed to identify himself), as such a method would make the narrative difficult to follow. He may have given the names of individuals involved as factual information at the start of the description of a sequence of events and left them out in the narrative. At any rate, this principle seems to apply mainly to the more "historical" later books (4–7); the review of facts in the early books (1–3) includes names of individuals (e.g., *Orig. *F 5, 6, 7, 8, 9, 10, 11, 15, 16, 25, 36, 50, 51, 61, 65, 67, 69, 70, 74) as well as place-names (e.g., *Orig. *F 4, 16, 23, 36, 45, 46, 47, 50, 61, 62, 65, 68, 69, 70, 71, 73).*

*Another unusual characteristic is that Cato included copies of some of his speeches in the *Origines* (T 34; *Orig. *F 104, 106c, 107a, 107b; *Orat. *F 163, 171). While the precise extent to which any written version of a Roman orator's speech matches the delivered version must remain uncertain, these speeches may be assigned a higher level of authenticity than can generally be attributed to speeches appearing in historiographical works when those have been composed by historians and put into the mouth of other historical individuals. Since the transfer into the *Origines* is explicitly attested for two of Cato's orations, only these are marked as part of the *Origines*; further items, such as orations delivered by Cato to soldiers, may also have been included.*

The effect for the entire work is that, although it is rightly classified as historiography, it also displays elements associated with other literary genres, such as oratory, ethnography, autobiography, or political memoir; thus, the resulting text may be seen as the expression of an individual writer's personality and the product of a period when boundaries were still fluid (see Chassignet 2005; Cornell 2009).

Cato's sources for the Origines *will have been earlier prose works by Greek and Roman writers, and perhaps early Latin historical epics, as well as local and oral traditions, town chronicles, pontifical acts, inscriptions, and also Cato's own experiences and inquiries.*

For convenience, in this edition the fragments of the Origines *are presented in the order of* FRHist: *i.e., the sequence starts with fragments assigned to a particular*

BOOK 1 (F 1–26)

The first book of the Origines *starts with a proem (F 1–2; cf. T 96; on the potential content and structure of the proem as well as its influence see Cugusi 1994) and then covers the early history of Rome from its legendary origins. It describes Aeneas' coming to Italy with his father, Anchises, his founding of a city, on land received from Latinus, the fighting against Turnus and Mezentius, Aeneas' son Ascanius' accession to power, the story of Romulus, the war with Alba Longa (near mod. Castel Gandolfo), and the regal period (not only this last item, as T 26 says). The version of Rome's early history Cato promotes, as far as it can be reconstructed, provides glimpses into Cato's*

book in the order of the books; then there are the fragments transmitted for the Origines, *but not attributed to a particular book, followed by fragments that might belong to the work, but are not attested for it (see General Introduction: Organization of This Edition). The testimonia in* FRHist *have been inserted into the Testimonia section with a different numbering (see Concordances).* FRHist *also provides extensive bibliographical references on the work as a whole and on the problems associated with individual fragments. (On the origin and nature of the* Origines, *the style, structure, and role in Roman society and Latin literature, see, e.g., Bömer 1953; Leeman 1963, 68–72; Meister 1964; Timpe 1970–1971; Astin 1978, 211–39; Letta 1984; Chassignet 1987; Flach 1998, 68–74; Gotter 2003; 2009; Sciarrino 2004; Jefferson 2012; Elliott 2020.)*

BOOK 1 (F 1–26)

views on Rome's development (and thus potentially into those of his contemporaries).

For commentary on fragments from this book and discussion of the versions of early Roman history followed by Cato, in addition to FRHist, *see Schröder 1971; Scholz 1978; Richard 1983a; Sbardella 2002. A number of the stories Cato reports are also attested in further places without reference to Cato, and there are alternative versions transmitted elsewhere. To keep this edition manageable, it does not give a full record of those passages as parallels or for comparison and only mentions what is relevant for defining Cato's version.*

F 1a [Sergius], *Expl. in art. Don.* 1, *GL* IV, p. 502.12–17

et nominativus tamen pluralis, qui apud veteres geminus fuit, hodie ab usu recessit: dicebant enim veteres qui et ques. . . . et necesse erat ita dicere, ques. nam ablativus singularis i littera terminatus nominativum pluralem in es mittit. Cato quoque Origines sic inchoat, "si ques sunt homines."[1]

[1] homines *del. Cardinali*

F 1b Pomp., *Comm. art. Don.*, *GL* V, p. 208.25–32

sed huius declinationis nominativus erit ques: huius declinationis, id est quando dicis dativo et ablativo plurali a quibus. siqui tibi dicat, fac inde nominativum pluralem, necesse habes facere hi ques: "si ques[1] homines sunt,[2] quos delectat populi Romani gesta[3] discribere," si ques homines pro eo quod est si qui. et iuste secundum regulam: ablativus enim i terminatus nominativum pluralem semper in es mittit, puppi puppes, agili agiles, docili do-

[1] queis *Jordan*

[2] homines *del. Cardinali*: sunt homines *Churchill, Scholz (cf. F 1a)*

[3] populi R. gesta(s) *vel* populi respondit gesta *vel* populi res gestas *codd.*: populi Romani res gestas *Jordan*

F 1a [Sergius]

And yet the nominative plural, which was twofold among the ancients, has today receded from use: for the ancients used to say *qui* and *ques* ["any"]. . . . And it was necessary to say so, *ques*. For an ablative singular ending in the letter *-i* creates a nominative plural ending in *-es* [cf. F 32, 123]. Cato too begins the *Origines* thus: "if there are any [*ques*] individuals."

F 1b Pompeius

But the nominative of this declension will be *ques* ["any"]: of this declension, that is when you say in the dative and ablative plural *a quibus*. If anyone should say to you, create the nominative plural from there, you will have to create necessarily *hi ques* [cf. F 32, 123]: "if there are any individuals whom it pleases to portray the deeds of the Roman People,"[1] "if any individuals" [*si ques homines*] for what is "if any" [*si qui*]. And rightly according to the rule: for an ablative ending in *-i* always creates a nominative plural ending in *-es*: *puppi*, *puppes* ["stern, boat"; abl. sg.,

1 Cardinali (1988) interprets *homines* ("individuals") as a gloss that should be deleted and analyzes the remaining sequence of the first few words as a hexametric structure with a preponderance of spondees (see also Churchill 1995, 100–101). Thereby, he argues, Cato highlights the work's connection with historical epic and provides a precedent for later Roman historians (see also Sbardella 2001b). On the reading and meaning of the fragment, see Scholz 1979, 243–44; on the structure of the passage, the potential connotations of the chosen wording, and the implications of such a statement, see Sciarrino 2004, 334–40.

ciles. sic si dixeris a qui, hi ques erit nominativo plurali, nec potest aliter.

F 2a Cic. *Planc.* 66

ecquid[1] ego dicam de occupatis meis temporibus, cui fuerit ne otium quidem umquam otiosum? nam quas tu commemoras, Cassi, legere te solere orationes, cum otiosus sis, has ego scripsi ludis et feriis, ne omnino umquam essem otiosus. etenim M. Catonis illud quod in principio scripsit Originum suarum semper magnificum et praeclarum putavi, clarorum virorum[2] atque magnorum non minus oti quam negoti rationem exstare oportere.

[1] ecquid *ed. Gryph.*: et quid *codd.*: sed quid *Lambinus*
[2] virorum *vel* hominum *codd.*

F 2b Iust. *Epit.*, *praef.* 5

quod ad te non tam cognoscendi magis quam emendandi causa transmisi, simul ut et otii mei, cuius et Cato reddendam operam putat, apud te ratio constaret.

Cf. Xen. *Symp.* 1.1: *ἀλλ' ἐμοὶ δοκεῖ τῶν καλῶν κἀγαθῶν ἀνδρῶν ἔργα οὐ μόνον τὰ μετὰ σπουδῆς πραττόμενα ἀξιομνημόνευτα εἶναι ἀλλὰ καὶ τὰ ἐν ταῖς παιδιαῖς;* Cic. *Att.* 5.20.9; Columella, *Rust.* 2.21.1; Suet. *Galb.* 9.1; Symm. *Ep.* 1.1.2; Ennod. *Carm.* 1.9, *praef.* 3; Ambros. *Off. ministr.* 1.3.9.

nom. pl.]; *agili*, *agiles* ["nimble, agile"; abl. sg., nom. pl.]; *docili*, *dociles* ["teachable, skillful"; abl. sg., nom. pl.]. Thus, if you should say *a qui*, it will be *hi ques* in the nominative plural, and it cannot be otherwise.

F 2a Cicero, *Pro Plancio*

What shall I say about my busy periods of time, I for whom not even leisure was ever leisurely? For those speeches, Cassius [L. Cassius Longinus (*ORF*[4] 168), one of the prosecutors], which you say it is your custom to read when you are at leisure, I have written during festivals and holidays, so that I was never completely at leisure. And indeed, I have always regarded that [phrase] of M. Cato that he wrote in the opening section of his *Origines* as magnificent and splendid: that, as regards famous and great men, there should be available an account no less of their leisure than of their activity.

F 2b Justin, *Epitome*

This [work] I have passed on to you not so much for the sake of studying rather than emending, at the same time so that there exists with you an account also of my leisure, to which Cato too believes that attention should be paid.

Cf. Xenophon, *Symposium*: "But it seems to me that, as regards the deeds of good and great men, not only what was achieved with earnest zeal is worth mentioning, but also what was done in pastime"; the thought recurs in later writers (see list of examples quoted opposite).

F 3 Lydus, *Mag.* 1.5

ὥστε τύραννος ἦν ὁ Ῥωμύλος, πρῶτον μὲν τὸν ἀδελφὸν ἀνελὼν καὶ τὸν μείζονα, καὶ πράττων ἀλόγως τὰ προσπίπτοντα· ταύτῃ καὶ Κυρῖνος προσηγορεύθη, οἷον εἰ κύριος, κἂν εἰ Διογενιανῷ τῷ λεξογράφῳ ἄλλως δοκεῖ. οὐδὲ γὰρ ἀγνοήσας ὁ Ῥωμύλος, ἢ οἱ κατ' αὐτόν, δείκνυται κατ' ἐκεῖνο καιροῦ τὴν Ἑλλάδα φωνήν, τὴν Αἰολίδα λέγω, ὥς φασιν ὅ τε Κάτων ἐν τῷ περὶ Ῥωμαικῆς ἀρχαιότητος Βάρρων τε ὁ πολυμαθέστατος ἐν προοιμίοις τῶν πρὸς Πομπήιον αὐτῷ γεγραμμένων, Εὐάνδρου καὶ τῶν ἄλλων Ἀρκάδων εἰς Ἰταλίαν ἐλθόντων ποτὲ καὶ τὴν Αἰολίδα τοῖς βαρβάροις ἐνσπειράντων φωνήν.

F 4a Serv. ad Verg. *Aen.* 1.5

"dum conderet urbem": tres hic sunt significationes. aut enim Troiam dicit, quam ut primum in Italiam venit, fecit Aeneas, de qua ait . . .—Troiam autem dici quam primum fecit Aeneas, et Livius in primo et Cato in Originibus[1] testantur—. . .

[1] *post* originibus *tres vel quattuor litterae erasae sunt in cod.* hoc *fuisse Bergkius coniecit. sed* tes *vel* tres *litterae a correctore deletae sunt.*

F 4b Serv. ad Verg. *Aen.* 7.158–59

"primasque in litore sedes": ideo "primas" quia imperium Lavinium translaturus est. et sciendum civitatem, quam primo fecit Aeneas, Troiam dictam secundum Catonem et Livium: quod et ipse dicit "nec te Troia capit."

F 3 Lydus, *On the Magistracies of the Roman Republic*

Thus Romulus was a tyrant, in particular because he removed his brother, the older one, and also because he dealt with events in an unreasonable way. For that reason he was also called Quirinus, as if he were a "master" [Gk. *kyrios*], even if it seems differently to Diogenianos the lexicographer. For Romulus, or those around him, cannot be shown to have been ignorant of the Greek language at that time, I mean the Aeolian, as Cato says in the work on Roman ancient history and the very learned Varro in the introductions to the writings he dedicated to Pompeius [M. Terentius Varro (F 295 *GRF*)], since Evander and the other Arcadians had come to Italy at some point and spread the Aeolian [language] among the "barbarians."

F 4a Servius, *Commentary on Virgil*

"until he [Aeneas] founded the city": Here are three meanings. For either he [Virgil] means Troy, which Aeneas established, when he had first come to Italy, about which he says . . .—and that [the city] that Aeneas first established is called Troy is attested by both Livy in the first [book] [Liv. 1.1.4–5] and Cato in the *Origines*—. . .

F 4b Servius, *Commentary on Virgil*

"and the first settlements on the shore": For that reason "first" because he [Aeneas] was to transfer the realm to Lavinium. And one should know that the settlement that Aeneas first established was called Troy according to Cato and Livy [Liv. 1.1.4–5], which he [Virgil] also says himself: "and Troy cannot contain you [Ascanius]" [Verg. *Aen.* 9.644].

F 5 Serv. ad Verg. *Aen.* 11.316

"est antiquus ager Tusco mihi proximus amni": . . . unde sequenda est potius Livii, Sisennae et Catonis auctoritas: nam paene omnes antiquae historiae scriptores in hoc consentiunt. Cato enim in Originibus dicit Troianos a Latino accepisse agrum, qui est inter Laurentum et castra Troiana. hic etiam modum agri commemorat et dicit eum habuisse iugera $\overline{\text{II}}$DCC.

F 6a Serv. et Serv. auct. ad Verg. *Aen.* 1.267

"cui nunc cognomen Iulo / additur": secundum Catonem historiae hoc habet fides: Aeneam cum patre ad Italiam venisse et propter invasos agros contra Latinum Turnumque pugnasse, in quo proelio periit Latinus. Turnum postea ad Mezentium confugisse eiusque fretum auxilio bella renovasse, quibus Aeneas Turnusque pariter rapti sunt. migrasse postea in Ascanium et Mezentium bella, sed eos singulari certamine dimicasse. et occiso Mezentio Ascanium sicut I. Caesar scribit Iulum coeptum vocari, vel quasi *ἰόβολον*, id est sagittandi peritum, vel a prima barbae lanugine quam *ἴουλον* Graeci dicunt, quae ei tempore victoriae nascebatur.

F 5 Servius, *Commentary on Virgil*

"there is an ancient district of mine [of Latinus] very close to the Etruscan river [i.e., Tiber]": . . . For that reason the authority of Livy [Liv. 1.1], Sisenna [L. Cornelius Sisenna (*FRHist* 26 F 2)], and Cato should rather be followed: for almost all writers of ancient history agree on this. For Cato says in the *Origines* that the Trojans received from Latinus the territory that lies between Laurentum and the Trojan camp. He also mentions the size of the territory and says that it comprised 2,700 *iugera* [ca. 1,800 acres or 680 hectares].

F 6a Servius and Servius Danielis, *Commentary on Virgil*

"[Ascanius] to whom now the name Iulus is added": According to Cato, credence applies to this element of the story: that Aeneas had come to Italy with his father [Anchises] and, because of the invasion of the territories, had fought against Latinus and Turnus; that Latinus died in that battle. That Turnus had later fled to Mezentius and, trusting in his help, had renewed the wars, in which Aeneas and Turnus had both been carried off. That the wars had later transferred to Ascanius and Mezentius, but they had fought in single combat. And that, after Mezentius had been killed, Ascanius, as I. Caesar writes [C. Iulius Caesar (F susp. et spur. 6 Klotz)], had begun to be called Iulus, either as if *iobolos*, that is skilled in archery, or from the first down of the beard, which the Greeks call *ioulos*, which in his case was beginning to grow at the time of the victory.

F 6b Hyg. *Fab.* 260

Eryx Veneris et Butae filius fuit, qui occisus ab Hercule est. monti ex sepultura sua nomen imposuit, in quo Aeneas Veneris templum constituit. in hoc autem monte dicitur etiam Anchises sepultus, licet secundum Catonem ad Italiam venerit.

F 6c Serv. ad Verg. *Aen.* 1.570

"sive Erycis fines": . . . in quo matris fecerat templum, quod Aeneae adscribit poeta dicens "tum vicina astris Erycino in vertice sedes / fundatur Veneri Idaliae." in hoc autem monte dicitur etiam Anchises sepultus, licet secundum Catonem ad Italiam venerit.

F 6d Serv. ad Verg. *Aen.* 3.711

"fessum / deseris": ut supra diximus, secundum Vergilium: nam Cato eum in Originibus ad Italiam venisse docet; unde etiam in sexto illud amphibolon est "quo magis Italia mecum laetere reperta."

F 6e Serv. ad Verg. *Aen.* 4.427

"Anchisae cineres manesve revelli": . . . sciendum sane Varronem dicere, Diomedem eruta Anchisae ossa filio reddidisse, Catonem autem adfirmare, quod Anchises ad

F 6b Hyginus

Eryx was a son of Venus and Butes, and he was killed by Hercules. From his burial he conferred his name to the mountain [Mount Eryx, mod. Monte Erice, on Sicily], on which Aeneas set up a temple for Venus. And on this mountain Anchises is also said to have been buried [cf. Verg. *Aen.* 3.707–11, 5.23–34], even though, according to Cato, he came to Italy.

F 6c Servius, *Commentary on Virgil*

"or the region of Eryx": . . . There he had set up a temple for his mother, which the poet ascribes to Aeneas, saying "then, close to the stars, on the summit of Eryx, a dwelling for Idalian Venus is founded" [Verg. *Aen.* 5.759–60]. And on this mountain Anchises is also said to have been buried, even though, according to Cato, he came to Italy.

F 6d Servius, *Commentary on Virgil*

"you [Anchises] leave me, exhausted": As we have said above [on Verg. *Aen.* 1.267: F 6a], according to Virgil: for Cato in the *Origines* reports that he [Anchises] came to Italy; hence also in the sixth [book] there is that ambiguous statement [Verg. *Aen.* 6.718]: "so that you may rejoice with me all the more on the discovery of Italy."

F 6e Servius, *Commentary on Virgil*

"I have disturbed the ashes and remains of Anchises": . . . One must certainly know that Varro [M. Terentius Varro] says that Diomedes, after having dug up Anchises' bones, returned them to his son, but that Cato affirms that An-

Italiam venit. tanta est inter ipsos varietas et historiarium confusio.

F 7a Serv. et Serv. auct. ad Verg. *Aen.* 4.620

"sed cadat ante diem": Cato dicit iuxta Laurolavinium cum Aeneae socii praedas agerent, proelium commissum, in quo Latinus occisus est, fugit Turnus: et Mezentii auxilio conparato renovavit proelium, quo victus quidem est ab Aenea; qui tamen {Aeneas}[1] in ipso proelio non conparuit. Ascanius vero postea Mezentium interemit. alii dicunt . . .

[1] qui tamen Aeneas *vel* aeneas autem *vel* Aeneas *om. codd.*

F 7b Serv. et Serv. auct. ad Verg. *Aen.* 9.742

"vulnus Saturnia Iuno / detorsit veniens": . . . plerique, sed non idonei commentatores dicunt, hoc loco occisum Turnum, sed causa oeconomiae gloriam a poeta Aeneae esse servatam: quod falsum est. nam si veritatem historiae requiras, primo proelio interemptus Latinus est in arce:[1] inde ubi Turnus Aenean vidit superiorem, Mezentii imploravit auxilium: secundo proelio Turnus occisus est, et nihilo minus Aeneas postea non conparuit: tertio proelio Mezentium occidit Ascanius. hoc Livius dicit et Cato in Originibus.

[1] acie *Roth*

F 8a Serv. ad Verg. *Aen.* 6.760

"ille vides pura iuvenis qui nititur hasta": Aeneas, ut Cato dicit, simul ac venit ad Italiam, Laviniam accepit uxorem. propter quod Turnus iratus, tam in Latinum, quam in

chises came to Italy. So great is the variety and confusion of the accounts among [the writers] themselves.

F 7a Servius and Servius Danielis, *Commentary on Virgil*

"but let him [Aeneas] die before his day": Cato says that near Laurolavinium, when Aeneas' companions were driving off booty, a battle was joined, in which Latinus was killed and Turnus fled. And, having acquired Mezentius' help, he [Turnus] renewed the fight, in which he was certainly defeated by Aeneas; yet he {Aeneas} disappeared in the battle itself. But Ascanius later killed Mezentius. Others say . . .

F 7b Servius and Servius Danielis, *Commentary on Virgil*

"Saturnian Juno deflected the coming wound": . . . Many, but unqualified commentators say that Turnus was killed at this point, but for reasons of economy the glory was reserved by the poet for Aeneas: this is false. For if you ask about the truth of the story, Latinus was killed in the first fight on the citadel; when Turnus saw from this that Aeneas was superior, he called on Mezentius for help; in the second fight Turnus was killed, and nonetheless Aeneas disappeared afterward; in the third fight Ascanius killed Mezentius. This is what Livy says [Liv. 1.2] and Cato in the *Origines*.

F 8a Servius, *Commentary on Virgil*

"that young man [Silvius], you see, who is leaning on a spear without an iron point": Aeneas, as Cato says, as soon as he had come to Italy, took Lavinia as his wife. Angered because of this, Turnus started wars against Latinus as well

Aenean bella suscepit a Mezentio impetratis auxiliis: quod et ipse ostendit dicens "se satis ambobus Teucrisque venire Latinisque." sed, ut supra diximus, primo bello periit Latinus, secundo pariter Turnus et Aeneas, postea Mezentium interemit Ascanius et Laurolavinium tenuit. cuius Lavinia timens insidias, gravida confugit ad silvas et latuit in casa pastoris Tyrrhi: ad quod adludens ait "Tyrrhusque pater, cui regia parent / armenta": et illic enixa est Silvium. sed cum Ascanius flagraret invidia, evocavit novercam et ei concessit Laurolavinium, sibi vero Albam constituit. qui quoniam sine liberis periit, Silvio, qui et ipse Ascanius dictus est, suum reliquit imperium; unde apud Livium est error, qui Ascanius Albam condiderit. postea Albani omnes reges Silvii dicti sunt ab huius nomine, sicut hodieque Romani imperatores Augusti vocantur, . . .

F 8b Myth. Vat. Prim. 2.100.11–15

idem Aeneas, ut Cato dicit, postquam Laviniam, Latini regis filiam, accepit uxorem vivente marito Turno, idem Turnus iratus tam in Latinum quam in Aeneam bella suscepit, a Mezentio impetratis auxiliis; in quorum primo bello periit Latinus, in secundo pariter ‹Turnus›[1] et Aeneas. [12] postea Mezentium interemit Ascanius et Laurolavinium tenuit. [13] cuius Lavinia timens insidias, gravida confugit in silvas et latuit in casa pastoris Tyri—ad

[1] *add Serv.*

as against Aeneas, having obtained additional forces from Mezentius: he [Virgil] himself even shows this, saying "that he [Turnus] was going against the Teucrians and the Latins, a match for both" [Verg. *Aen.* 7.470]. But, as we have said above [on Verg. *Aen.* 1.267: F 6a; 4.620: F 7a], in the first war Latinus died, in the second both Turnus and Aeneas, later Ascanius killed Mezentius and took hold of Laurolavinium. Fearing his snares, Lavinia, pregnant, fled into the woods and hid in the hut of the shepherd Tyrrhus; alluding to this, he [Virgil] says "and father Tyrrhus, whom the royal herds obey" [Verg. *Aen.* 7.485–86]. And there she gave birth to Silvius. But although Ascanius was burning with envy, he summoned his stepmother and conceded Laurolavinium to her, but for himself he founded Alba. Since he died without children, he left his realm to Silvius, who himself was also called Ascanius; hence there is uncertainty in Livy [Liv. 1.3.1–4] as to which Ascanius founded Alba. Later all the Alban kings were called Silvii from his name, just as today too the Roman emperors are called Augusti, . . .

F 8b Mythographus Vaticanus Primus

After the same Aeneas, as Cato says, had taken Lavinia, king Latinus' daughter, as his wife while her husband Turnus was still alive, this very Turnus, in anger, started a war against Latinus as well as against Aeneas, having obtained additional forces from Mezentius; in their first war Latinus died, in the second both ‹Turnus› and Aeneas. [12] Later Ascanius killed Mezentius and took hold of Laurolavinium. [13] Fearing his snares, Lavinia, pregnant, fled into the woods and hid in the hut of the shepherd Tyrus—al-

quam[2] alludens "Tyrus pater": recepit eam et fovit—; et illic enixa est Silvium. [14] sed cum Ascanius flagraret invidia, evocavit novercam et ei concessit Laurolavinium; sibi vero Albam constituit. [15] qui quoniam sine liberis periit, Silvi<i>o,[3] qui et ipse Ascanius dictus est, suum reliquit imperium.

[2] quam *cod.*: quod *Serv.* [3] Silvio *Serv.*

F 9 Macrob. *Sat.* 3.5.10

sed veram huius contumacissimi nominis causam in primo libro Originum Catonis diligens lector inveniet: ait enim Mezentium Rutulis imperasse ut sibi offerrent quas dis primitias offerebant, et Latinos omnes similis imperii metu ita vovisse: "Iuppiter, si tibi magis cordi est nos ea tibi dare potius quam Mezentio, uti nos victores facias."

F 10 *Orig. gent. Rom.* 12.5–13.8

at Cato in Origine generis Romani ita docet: suem triginta porculos peperisse in eo loco, ubi nunc est Lavinium, cumque Aeneas ibi urbem condere constituisset propterque agri sterilitatem maereret,[1] per quietem ei visa deorum penatum simulacra adhortantium, ut perseveraret in condenda urbe, quam coeperat; nam post annos totidem, quot foetus illius suis essent, Troianos in loca fertilia atque uberiorem agrum transmigraturos et urbem

[1] maereret *Jordan*: mereret *codd.*: metueret *Schott*: haereret *Damsté*

luding to her [him?] "father Tyrus" [Verg. *Aen.* 7.485]: he took her in and attended to her needs—; and there she gave birth to Silvius. [14] But although Ascanius was burning with envy, he summoned his stepmother and conceded Laurolavinium to her, but for himself founded Alba. [15] Since he died without children, he left his empire to Silvius, who himself was also called Ascanius.

F 9 Macrobius, *Saturnalia*

But an attentive reader will find the true origin of this description [of Mezentius] as most contumacious [*contemptor divum*: Verg. *Aen.* 7.648] in the first book of Cato's *Origines*: for he [Cato] says that Mezentius ordered the Rutulians to offer to him the first fruits that they usually offered to the gods, and that all the people of Latium, in fear of a similar command, made the following vow: "Jupiter, if it is more pleasing to you that we offer these things to you rather than to Mezentius, [we pray] that you make us victorious."

F 10 *Origin of the Roman People*

But Cato in the *Origin of the Roman People* outlines as follows: that a sow had given birth to thirty piglets in that place where Lavinium now is and that, when Aeneas had decided to found a city there and was in despair because of the infertility of the land, in his sleep the images of the Penate gods had appeared to him, encouraging him to persevere in founding the city that he had begun; for after as many years as the litter of that sow were, the Trojans would migrate to fertile places and a richer territory and

clarissimi nominis in Italia condituros. [13.1] igitur Latinum Aboriginum regem, cum ei nuntiatum esset multitudinem advenarum classe advectam occupavisse agrum Laurentem, adversum subitos inopinatosque hostes incunctanter suas copias eduxisse ac priusquam signum dimicandi daret, animadvertisse Troianos militariter instructos, cum sui lapidibus ac sudibus armati, tum etiam veste aut pellibus, quae eis integumento erant, sinistris manibus involutis processissent. [2] itaque suspenso certamine per colloquium inquisito, qui essent quidve peterent, utpote qui in hoc consilium auctoritate numinum cogebatur (namque extis ac somniis saepe admonitus erat tutiorem se adversum hostes fore, si copias suas cum advenis coniunxisset) [3] cumque cognovisset Aeneam et Anchisen bello patria[2] pulsos cum simulacris deorum errantes sedem quaerere, amicitiam foedere inisse dato invicem iureiurando, ut communes quosque hostes amicosve haberent. [4] itaque coeptum a Troianis muniri locum, quem Aeneas ex nomine uxoris suae, Latini regis filiae, quae iam ante desponsata Turno Herdonio fuerat, Lavinium cognominavit. [5] at vero Amatam, Latini regis uxorem, cum indigne ferret Laviniam repudiato Turno, consobrino suo, Troiano advenae collocatam, Turnum ad arma concitavisse; eumque mox coacto Rutulorum exer-

[2] patria *Schott*: patrio *codd.*

found a city of the most illustrious repute in Italy. [13.1] Therefore Latinus, the king of the original settlers [*Aborigines*], when it had been reported to him that a large number of newcomers had arrived with a fleet and occupied the Laurentian territory, had, without hesitation, led out his troops against the sudden and unexpected enemy and, before he had given the sign to fight, had noticed that the Trojans had been drawn up in military fashion while his men had proceeded, equipped with stones and sticks, and also with clothing and hides, which they had as cover, wrapped around their left hands. [2] And so, after the contest had been suspended, after in a meeting the question had been put who they were and what they wanted, since he was forced to this course of action by the authority of the divine (for he had often been admonished by entrails and dreams that he would be safer against enemies if he had joined his troops with newcomers), [3] and when he had learned that Aeneas and Anchises had been driven from their fatherland by war and, wandering around with the images of gods, were looking for a place to settle, he had entered friendship by treaty, with each swearing an oath to the other that they would have a common view on others as enemies or friends. [4] And thus a start had been made by the Trojans to fortify the place that Aeneas named Lavinium from the name of his wife, king Latinus' daughter, who had earlier already been promised in marriage to Turnus Herdonius. [5] But Amata, king Latinus' wife, since she took it amiss that Turnus, her cousin [son of maternal aunt], was rejected and Lavinia was given in marriage to a Trojan newcomer, had urged Turnus to arms; and soon afterward he, after having brought together an army of the Rutuli, had directed his

citu tetendisse in agrum Laurentem et adversus eum Latinum pariter cum Aenea progressum inter proeliantes circumventum occisumque. [6] nec tamen amisso socero Aeneas Rutulis obsistere desiit, namque et Turnum interemit. [7] hostibus[3] fusis fugatisque victor Lavinium se cum suis recepit consensuque omnium Latinorum rex declaratus est, ut scribit Lutatius libro tertio. [8] Piso quidem Turnum matruelem Amatae fuisse tradit interfectoque Latino mortem ipsam sibimet conscivisse.

[3] interemit <et> hostibus *Damsté*

F 11 *Orig. gent. Rom.* 15.5

igitur Latini Ascanium ob insignem virtutem non solum Iove ortum crediderunt, sed etiam per diminutionem declinato paululum nomine primo Iolum, dein postea Iulum appellarunt; a quo Iulia familia manavit, ut scribunt Caesar libro secundo et Cato in Originibus.

F 12 Serv. auct. ad Verg. *Aen.* 1.269–70

"triginta": vel quod XXX. tantum annos regnavit, vel quod Cato ait XXX. annis expletis eum Albam condidisse.

course toward the Laurentian district, and Latinus, having advanced against him along with Aeneas, had been surrounded among the fighters and killed. [6] Still, not even after losing his father-in-law did Aeneas stop opposing the Rutuli; for he killed Turnus as well. [7] When the enemy had been routed and put to flight, he withdrew as victor to Lavinium with his men and, with the agreement of all, was declared king of the Latins, as Lutatius writes in the third book [Lutatius (*FRHist* 32 F 4)]. [8] Yet Piso [L. Calpurnius Piso Frugi (*FRHist* 9 F 4)] reports that Turnus was Amata's cousin [son of maternal uncle] and that, after Latinus had been killed, she brought death upon herself.

F 11 *Origin of the Roman People*

Thus the Latins not only believed Ascanius, because of his outstanding virtue, to be descended from Jupiter, but, by modifying the name a little, also called him, by a diminutive, first Iolus, then later Iulus.[1] From him the Julian family descended, as Caesar writes in the second book [C. Iulius Caesar (F susp. et spur. 5 Klotz)] and Cato in the *Origines* [cf. Liv. 1.3.2; Ov. *Fast.* 4.39–40].

[1] On the etymologies of the name Iulus and their possible sources, see Richard 1983b.

F 12 Servius Danielis, *Commentary on Virgil*

"thirty": either because he [Iulus / Ascanius] reigned for thirty years only or because Cato says that, after thirty years had been completed, he founded Alba.

F 13a Dion. Hal. *Ant. Rom.* 1.74.1–2

τὸν δὲ τελευταῖον γενόμενον τῆς Ῥώμης οἰκισμὸν ἢ κτίσιν ἢ ὅτι δήποτε χρὴ καλεῖν Τίμαιος μὲν ὁ Σικελιώτης οὐκ οἶδ' ὅτῳ κανόνι χρησάμενος ἅμα Καρχηδόνι κτιζομένῃ γενέσθαι φησὶν ὀγδόῳ καὶ τριακοστῷ πρότερον ἔτει τῆς πρώτης ὀλυμπιάδος. Λεύκιος δὲ Κίγκιος ἀνὴρ τῶν ἐκ τοῦ βουλευτικοῦ συνεδρίου περὶ τὸ τέταρτον ἔτος τῆς δωδεκάτης ὀλυμπιάδος. Κόϊντος δὲ Φάβιος κατὰ τὸ πρῶτον ἔτος τῆς ὀγδόης ὀλυμπιάδος. [2] Κάτων δὲ Πόρκιος Ἑλληνικὸν μὲν οὐχ ὁρίζει χρόνον, ἐπιμελὴς δὲ γενόμενος, εἰ καί τις ἄλλος, περὶ τὴν συναγωγὴν τῆς ἀρχαιολογουμένης ἱστορίας ἔτεσιν ἀποφαίνει δυσὶ καὶ τριάκοντα καὶ τετρακοσίοις ὑστεροῦσαν τῶν Ἰλιακῶν. ὁ δὲ χρόνος οὗτος ἀναμετρηθεὶς ταῖς Ἐρατοσθένους χρονογραφίαις κατὰ τὸ πρῶτον ἔτος πίπτει τῆς ἑβδόμης ὀλυμπιάδος.

Cf. Syncell. 364–65 (p. 228.21–28 Mosshammer); Euseb. *Chron.*, p. 135 Karst (Arm.).

F 13b Lydus, *Mag.* 1.2

ἀνύονται τοιγαροῦν ἐκ τῆς Αἰνείου ἐπὶ τὴν Ἰταλίαν παρόδου ἕως τοῦ πολισμοῦ τῆς Ῥώμης ἐνιαυτοὶ ἐννέα καὶ τριάκοντα καὶ τετρακόσιοι κατὰ Κάτωνα τὸν πρῶτον καὶ Βάρρωνα, τοὺς Ῥωμαίους· . . .

F 14 Dion. Hal. *Ant. Rom.* 1.75.4–84.8

τὰ μὲν δὴ περὶ τοῦ χρόνου καθ' ὃν ἡ νῦν δυναστεύουσα πόλις ᾠκίσθη τοῖς τε πρὸ ἐμοῦ γενομένοις εἰρη-

F 13a Dionysius of Halicarnassus, *Roman Antiquities*

As for the final founding or settling of Rome, or whatever it ought to be called, Timaeus the Sicilian [Greek historian, fl. ca. 300 BC (*FGrHist / BNJ* 566 F 60)], following what principle I do not know, says that it happened at the same time as the founding of Carthage, in the thirty-eighth year before the first Olympiad [814/13 BC]. Lucius Cincius [L. Cincius Alimentus (*FRHist* 2 F 2)], a member of the senate, [places it] about the fourth year of the twelfth Olympiad [729/28 BC], and Quintus Fabius [Q. Fabius Pictor (*FRHist* 1 F 5a)] in the first year of the eighth Olympiad [748/47 BC]. [2] Porcius Cato does not define the time in Greek style, but being as careful as any writer in gathering the facts of ancient history [*FRHist* 5 T 14b], he declares it to be four hundred and thirty-two years after the Trojan War. And that time, measured according to the *Chronicles* of Eratosthenes, falls into the first year of the seventh Olympiad [752/51 BC].

F 13b Lydus, *On the Magistracies of the Roman Republic*

Thus, there were accomplished from Aeneas' journey to Italy until the building of Rome four hundred and thirty-nine years according to Cato the Elder and Varro [M. Terentius Varro], the Romans; . . .

F 14 Dionysius of Halicarnassus, *Roman Antiquities*

This, then, is what is said by those who lived before me and seems good to me concerning the time at which the

μένα κἀμοὶ δοκοῦντα τοιάδ᾽ ἐστίν. οἰκισταὶ δ᾽ αὐτῆς οἵτινες ἦσαν καὶ τίσι τύχαις χρησάμενοι τὴν ἀποικίαν ἔστειλαν ὅσα τε ἄλλα περὶ τὴν κτίσιν ταύτην ἱστόρηται πολλοῖς μὲν εἴρηται καὶ διαφόρως τὰ πλεῖστα ἐνίοις, λεχθήσεται δὲ κἀμοὶ τὰ πιθανώτατα τῶν μνημονευομένων. ἔχει δὲ ὧδε· [1.76.1] . . . [1.79.4] *περὶ δὲ τῶν ἐκ τῆς Ἰλίας γενομένων Κόιντος μὲν Φάβιος ὁ Πίκτωρ λεγόμενος, ᾧ Λεύκιός τε Κίγκιος καὶ Κάτων Πόρκιος καὶ Πείσων Καλπούρνιος καὶ τῶν ἄλλων συγγραφέων οἱ πλείους ἠκολούθησαν, γέγραφε·* . . . [1.84.8] . . . *περὶ μὲν οὖν γενέσεως καὶ τροφῆς τῶν οἰκιστῶν τῆς Ῥώμης ταῦτα λέγεται.*

F 15 Fest., p. 196.9–21 L.

‹ORATORES› ex Graeco quod est *ἀρητῆρ›ες* dictos existimant . . . gentes qui missi[1] . . . ‹m›agistratus populo Romano . . . ‹solerent›[2] *ἀρᾶσθαι*, ‹id est testari›[3] . . . est ab aequitate; eos nostri alii[4] pro legatis appellant, ut Cato . . . . [*Orat.* F 130]. et in Originum lib. I: "propter id bellum coepit. Cloelius praetor[5] Albanus oratores misit Romam cum . . ."

1 *fort.* gentesque missi *Lindsay in app.*
2 *suppl. Epit.*
3 *suppl. Epit.*
4 antiqui *Mueller*
5 coelius PR *cod.*

Cf. Paul. *Fest.*, p. 197.1–3 L.

city [i.e., Rome], now powerful, was settled. Who its founders were and induced by what turns of fortune they led out the colony, and whatever else is told concerning this settlement, this has been related by many, and the greatest part of it in a variety of ways by some; and I, too, shall relate the most probable of what has been recorded. It is as follows: [1.76.1] . . . [1.79.4] Concerning the offspring born of Ilia [i.e., Romulus and Remus], Quintus Fabius, called Pictor [*FRHist* 1 F 4a], whom Lucius Cincius [L. Cincius Alimentus (*FRHist* 2 F 1)], Porcius Cato, Calpurnius Piso [L. Calpurnius Piso Frugi (*FRHist* 9 F 5)], and most of the other historians have followed, writes: . . . [1.84.8] . . . This, then, is told about the birth and rearing of the founders of Rome [*after a long summary of the well-known stories on the origin of Rome*].

F 15 Festus

They believe that ‹*oratores*› ["speakers / envoys"] are called thus on the basis of the Greek term that is *arētēr›es* ["people who pray"] . . . nations, those who have been sent . . . ‹m›agistrates to the Roman People . . . ‹were accustomed› to pray [*arasthai*], ‹that is to invoke› . . . is from equity; others of our people call them thus instead of "envoys" [*legati*], as Cato . . . [*Orat*. F 130]. And in Book 1 of the *Origines*: "For that reason war began. Cloelius [C. Cluilius], the Alban praetor, sent speakers / envoys to Rome when / with . . ."[1]

1 On this conflict between Alba Longa and Rome in the time of king Tullus Hostilius see, e.g., Liv. 1.22.3–23.4; Dion. Hal. *Ant. Rom.* 3.2.1–5.3; Diod. Sic. 8.25.1–4 (for an analysis of the sources see Mensching 1966). For the fragment, different interpretations have been suggested, depending on the respective views of its structure and thus the appropriate punctuation.

F 16 Macrob. *Sat.* 1.10.11–16

decimo Kalendas feriae sunt Iovis quae appellantur Larentinalia, de quibus—quia fabulari libet—hae fere opiniones sunt. [12] . . . [16] Cato ait Larentiam meretricio quaestu locupletatam post excessum suum populo Romano agros Turacem, Semurium, Lintirium et Solonium reliquisse et ideo sepulcri magnificentia et annuae parentationis honore dignatam.

F 17 Dion. Hal. *Ant. Rom.* 4.15.1

διεῖλε δὲ καὶ τὴν χώραν ἅπασαν, ὡς μὲν Φάβιός φησιν, εἰς μοίρας ἕξ τε καὶ εἴκοσιν, ἃς καὶ αὐτὰς καλεῖ φυλὰς καὶ τὰς ἀστικὰς προστιθεὶς αὐταῖς τέτταρας·[1] ὡς δὲ Οὐεννώνιος ἱστόρηκεν, εἰς μίαν τε καὶ τριάκοντα, ὥστε σὺν ταῖς κατὰ πόλιν οὔσαις ἐκπεπληρῶσθαι τὰς ἔτι καὶ εἰς ἡμᾶς ὑπαρχούσας τριάκοντα καὶ πέντε φυλάς· Κάτων μέντοι τούτων ἀμφοτέρων ἀξιοπιστότερος ὢν τριάκοντα φυλὰς ἐπὶ

[1] *post* τέτταρας *sequuntur in codd. haec verba*: τριάκοντα φυλὰς ἀμφοτέρων Κάτων μέντοι τούτων ἐπὶ Τυλλίου τὰς πάσας γενέσθαι λέγει, *in codd. quibusdam ante* τριάκοντα *legitur* καί. *verba* Κάτων μέντοι τούτων ἀμφοτέρων *Sigonio auctore Niebuhrius post* φυλὰς *transposuit, quem secutus est Kiesslingius. Jacoby verba hoc modo collocanda esse censuit.*

F 16 Macrobius, *Saturnalia*

On the tenth day before the Kalends [i.e., Dec. 23] there is the festival of Jupiter that is called Larentinalia, about which—since it is a pleasure to talk—there are roughly the following views. [12] . . . [16] Cato says that Larentia, made wealthy by her prostitution business, after her death left to the Roman People the *ager Turax*, the *ager Semurius*, the *ager Lintirius*, and the *ager Solonius*, and was for that reason deemed worthy of a splendid tomb and the honor of annual obsequies as for a family member.[1]

[1] On the different traditions about Larentia, see, e.g., Gell. *NA* 7.7.5–8; Plut. *Rom.* 4–5; *Mor.* 272F–73B (*Quaest. Rom.* 35); Dion. Hal. *Ant. Rom.* 1.84.4. *ager Turax* and *ager Lintirius* are not mentioned elsewhere. *ager Turax* might be an area by the Campus Martius (*LTUR Sub.* V 210, s.v. *Turax ager*); *ager Semurius* is once referred to elsewhere, by Cicero (Cic. *Phil.* 6.14), and is probably an area close to Rome; and *ager Solonius* is a region in Latium.

F 17 Dionysius of Halicarnassus, *Roman Antiquities*

He [Servius Tullius, Roman king] also divided the entire country, as Fabius [Q. Fabius Pictor (*FRHist* 1 F 9)] says, into twenty-six parts, which he also calls tribes, and having added the four city tribes to them. But as Vennonius [*FRHist* 13 F 2] reports, [he divided the country] into thirty-one parts, so that with those in the city there were made up the thirty-five tribes that exist down to our day. Cato, however, who is more trustworthy than both of those

Τυλλίου τὰς πάσας γενέσθαι λέγει καὶ οὐ χωρίζει τῶν μοιρῶν τὸν ἀριθμόν.

F 18a Fest., p. 160.6–12 L.

NEQUITUM et NEQUITUR pro non posse dicebant, ut . . . ; et Cato Originum lib. I: "fana in eo loco conpluria fuere: ea exauguravit, prae<ter>quam[1] quod Termino fanum fuit; id nequitum exaugurari."

[1] prae<ter>quam *Augustinus*: praequam *cod.*

F 18b Donat. ad Ter. *Phorm.* 611 (2)

<compluria>[1] sic veteres, quod nostri dempta syllaba complura dicunt. sic et Cato Originum V: "fana in eo loco compluria" et . . .

[1] *add. Stephanus*

[*FRHist* 5 T 15], says that, under Tullius, thirty tribes made up the full number, and he does not divide up the number of the parts.[1]

[1] The general sense of the passage is clear (on the number of "tribes" [*tribus*] in the city and in total, see also Dion. Hal. *Ant. Rom.* 4.14.1; Liv. 1.43.12–13; Plin. *HN* 18.13; Paul. *Fest.*, p. 506.5–7 L.), but details of the constitution of the text are uncertain. Thus, establishing its precise meaning is difficult and controversial; on the context and the readings proposed, see, e.g., Gabba 1961, 103–7.

F 18a Festus

They used to say *nequitum* and *nequitur* [forms of *nequeo*, "I am unable, I cannot"] for "not to be able to," as . . . ; and Cato in Book 1 of the *Origines*: "There were a number of shrines in that place: he deconsecrated those, except for what was the shrine for Terminus [god of boundary markers]; that could not be deconsecrated."

F 18b Donatus, *Commentary on Terence*

<*compluria*> ["many"], thus the ancients, for which people of our time use *complura*, with a syllable taken away. Thus also Cato in [Book] 5[1] of the *Origines*: "many shrines in that place" and . . .

[1] The reference to Book 1 given by Festus (F 18a) is generally preferred because of the assumed context: the preparation of the Capitol on the part of the Tarquinian kings for the construction of the Temple of Iuppiter Optimus Maximus by the removal of existing shrines (cf. Liv. 1.55.1–4, 5.54.7; Dion. Hal. *Ant. Rom.* 3.69.5–6; Ov. *Fast.* 2.667–70; Serv. ad Verg. *Aen.* 9.446; Flor. 1.7.8–9).

F 18c Gell. *NA* 5.21.6

ibi ille amicus ridens: "amabo te," inquit, "vir bone, quia nunc mihi a magis[1] seriis rebus otium est, velim doceas nos cur 'pluria' sive 'compluria'—nihil enim differt—non Latine sed barbare dixerint M. Cato, Q. Claudius, Valerius Antias, L. Aelius,[2] P. Nigidius, M. Varro, quos subscriptores approbatoresque huius verbi habemus praeter poetarum oratorumque veterum multam copiam."

[1] magis *codd. rec.*: magnis *codd.*
[2] Aelius *Carrio*: lelius *codd.*

F 19 Gell. *NA* 1.16.4

M. Cato in primo Originum: "inde est ferme mille passum."

F 20 Non., p. 64.18–21 M. = 89 L.

Cf. *Orat.* F 57.

F 18c Gellius, *Attic Nights*

Thereupon that friend said with a smile: "My good sir, please, since I now have leisure from more serious affairs, I wish you would explain to us why *pluria* or *compluria*—for there is no difference—are used not in a correct Latin way, but 'barbarously' [as the interlocutor had claimed], by M. Cato, Q. Claudius [Q. Claudius Quadrigarius (*FRHist* 24 F 92)], Valerius Antias [*FRHist* 25 F 68], L. Aelius [L. Aelius Stilo (F 48 *GRF*)], P. Nigidius [P. Nigidius Figulus, late Republican scholar (F 41 *GRF* = LXVIIII Swoboda)], and M. Varro [M. Terentius Varro], whom we have as endorsers and approvers of this word, besides a great number of the early poets and orators."[1]

[1] The speaker goes on to justify the use of *pluria* and *compluria* (and the related adverb *compluriens*; cf. F 81; *Orat*. F 251). Examples are only given for the compound forms (see Lebek 1971).

F 19 Gellius, *Attic Nights*

M. Cato in the first [book] of the *Origines*: "from there it is nearly a thousand steps" [example of *mille*, "a thousand," used with a singular verb].

F 20 Nonius Marcellus

Cf. *Orat*. F 57.

F 21 Non., p. 67.25–27 M. = 94 L.

PROSAPIA est[1] generis longitudo: dicta a prosupando aut proserendo. Cato Originum I: "veteres prosapia."

[1] prosapia est *Onions*: prosapie (*pro* -a ê, *i.e.* -a est) *vel* prosapies *codd.*

F 22 Charis., *GL* I, p. 72.6–7 = p. 91.7–8 B.

lignum singulariter dici semper debet in multitudine. Cato Originum I: "vehes" ait "ligni" . . .

F 23 Prisc., *GL* II, p. 129.7–15

et testis eius Caper, qui diversorum de huiscemodi nominibus ponit usus auctorum, confirmans tam in is quam in as huiuscemodi nomina solere proferri. Cato Censorius in I Originum: "sed lucus Capenatis." in II: "si quis mortuus est Arpinatis, eius heredem sacra non secuntur." ibidem:

F 21 Nonius Marcellus

prosapia ["lineage"] is the extent [into the past] of the family: it is derived from spreading or generating offspring. Cato [says] in [Book] 1 of the *Origines*: "ancient [pl.] by lineage."[1]

[1] Such an expression perhaps inspired the phrase *hominem veteris prosapiae* ("a person of old lineage") in Sallust (Sall. *Iug.* 85.10), who is said to have borrowed from Cato (T 49, 65, 66, 71). *prosapia* is defined as an old-fashioned word by Cicero (Cic. *Tim.* 39) and Quintilian (Quint. *Inst.* 1.6.40, 8.3.26).

F 22 Charisius

lignum ["wood"] ought always to be used in the singular with reference to a large number. Cato says in [Book] 1 of the *Origines*: "wagonloads of wood" . . .

F 23 Priscian

And a witness for this is Caper [Flavius Caper, 2nd cent. AD], who puts down the usage of diverse writers concerning nouns of this kind, confirming that it was customary to use nouns of this kind ending in both *-is* and in *-as* [cf. *Orat.* F 230]. Cato the ex-censor [says] in [Book] 1 of the *Origines*: "but the grove of Capena [*Capenatis*; Capena: town in Latium, just north of Rome; cf. F 69]." In [Book] 2 [F 35]:[1] "if anyone from Arpinum [*Arpinatis*; Arpinum: mod. Arpino] has died, the responsibility for family rites

[1] The attribution of F 35 and F 36 to Book 2 as suggested in this passage is usually regarded as more probable than their attribution to Book 1, as in Priscian's second quotation of the three pieces, where the third one appears in shortened form.

"lucum Dianium in nemore Aricino Egerius B<a>ebius[1] Tusculanus dedicavit dictator[2] Latinus. hi populi communiter: Tusculanus, Aricinus, Lanuvinus, Laurens, Coranus, Tiburtis, Pometinus, Ardeatis, Rutulus," "Ardeatis" dixit pro eo, quod nunc dicimus "Ardeas."

1 B<a>ebius *Wagner*: bebius *vel* brevius *vel* laebius *vel* lebius *codd.*: Laebius *def. Grotefend*: Laevius *Keil cunctanter in app.*

2 dictator *codd. rel.*: dicator *unus cod.*

Cf. Prisc., *GL* II, p. 337.19–23: Cato in I Originum: "sed lucus Capenatis." idem in eodem: "si quis mortuus est Arpinatis, eius heredem sacra non secuntur." idem in eodem: "populus communiter Tusculanus, Aricinus, Lanuvinus, Laurens, Coranus, Tiburtis, Pometinus, Ardeatis."

F 24a Prisc., *GL* II, p. 182.1–8

vetustissimi tamen et "altera utra" et "alterum utrum" et "alterius utrius" solebant proferre et "plerus plera plerum" absque "que" additione. . . . Cato de ambitu: . . . . idem in I Originum: "agrum quem Volsci habuerunt campestris plerus[1] Aboriginum fuit."

1 plerus *vel* plenus *codd.*

Cf. Prisc., *GL* II, p. 230.20–24.

does not get passed on to their heir." In the same place [F 36]: "Egerius Baebius of Tusculum, the Latin dictator, consecrated the grove of Diana in the wood at Aricia [mod. Ariccia, just outside Rome in Latium]. These peoples jointly: the Tusculan, Aricinian, Lanuvinian, Laurentian, Coranan, Tiburtine, Pometinian, Ardeatic [*Ardeatis*], Rutulan [nation]."[2] He used *Ardeatis* in place of where we now use *Ardeas* ["Ardeatic," of Ardea, town in Latium, just south of Rome].

[2] The name of the founder is given as Manius Egerius elsewhere (Fest., p. 128.15–18 L.). The list of groups forming the Latin league (all based in central Italy) is not complete (cf. Liv. 2.18.3; Dion. Hal. *Ant. Rom.* 5.61.3).

F 24a Priscian

Yet the earliest writers were accustomed to use *altera utra* and *alterum utrum* and *alterius utrius* ["either of two"; nom. sg. fem., nom. sg. neut., gen. sg.], and *plerus*, *plera*, *plerum*, and without the addition of *-que* [instead of *plerusque*, "the greater part, most of"; nom. sg. masc., fem., neut.]. . . . Cato [says in the speech] on electioneering: . . . [*Orat.* F 136]. The same [Cato] [says] in [Book] 1 of the *Origines*: "the land that the Volsci [Italic people] had, situated on a plain, for the most part [*plerus*], was that of the original settlers [of Latium, *Aborigines*]."[1]

[1] The subject of the sentence (*ager*) is not in the nominative and rather attracted into the case of the relative (*agrum quem*), which emphasizes the word (on this construction see Briscoe 2010, 155–56).

F 24b Osbern, *Derivationes* O 4.13 (p. 466 Bertini)

et componitur pluraliter[1] aborigines num .i. superflue quedam frutices que non naturaliter sed vitiose in arboribus vel etiam in campis oriuntur, unde Cato "ager," inquit, "quem Volci habuerunt plenus aboriginum fuit"; et dicuntur aborigines quasi seorsum ab origine.

[1] pluralis *Mai*

Cf. Osbern, *Derivationes* A 471 (p. 65 Bertini): aborigines, arbutus non plantata sed sponte crescens. Cato "ager quem Volsci habuerunt, aboriginum plenus fuit."

F 25 Prisc., *GL* II, p. 227.11–12

"soli" pro "solius" Cato in I Originum: "nam de omni Tusculana civitate soli Lucii Mamilii beneficium gratum fuit."

Cf. Prisc., *GL* II, p. 266.10–11.

F 24b Osbern

And in the plural the form is *aborigines*, *-num* ["bushes growing wildly"; nom., gen. pl.]; certain surplus shrubs that do not originate naturally but parasitically on trees or even in fields, whence Cato says: "the land that the Volsci [Italic people] had was full of bushes growing wildly [*aborigines*]"; and they are called *aborigines* as if separately from the [natural] origin [*ab origine*].[1]

[1] The Benedictine monk Osbern of Gloucester (12th cent.) seems to have misunderstood the passage from Cato and thus explains the meaning of the term *Aborigines* differently. Since Priscian was one of his sources, the example might have been taken from Priscian's discussion (F 24a).

Cf. Osbern: *aborigines* ["bushes growing wildly"], a shrub not planted, but growing of its own accord. Cato: "the land that the Volsci had was full of bushes growing wildly [*aborigines*]."

F 25 Priscian

soli ["of someone alone"; less common form of gen. sg.] instead of *solius* [standard form] [is used by] Cato in [Book] 1 of the *Origines*: "for concerning the entire citizenry of Tusculum the service of Lucius Mamilius alone was welcome"[1] [cf. F 153].

[1] According to Roman tradition, in 460 BC Lucius Mamilius of Tusculum provided military assistance to the Romans in confronting an uprising of the Sabine Appius Herdonius, who had seized the Capitol (Liv. 3.18; Dion. Hal. *Ant. Rom.* 10.14–16); Lucius Mamilius was rewarded with Roman citizenship two years later (Liv. 3.29.6).

F 26 Prisc., *GL* II, p. 264.7–18

nam "vetus veteris" commune est trium generum . . . quamvis "veter" etiam analogia exigit, ut bene sit dictum. . . . pro "vetus." quod Capro quoque prudentissime videtur, cum comparativus "veterior" et superlativus "veterrimus" "veter" desiderent positivum. Cato in I Originibus: "Antemna[1] veterior est quam Roma."

[1] antemna *vel* Antempna *vel* Antemnantia *codd.*: Antemnatium *Roth*: Antemna etiam *Bormann*

BOOK 2 (F 27–40)

The second and third books cover cities and peoples of Italy (T 26, 29, 76, 83, 92, 93), providing foundation stories, but also items of geography, ethnography, culture and

F 27 Gell. *NA* 17.13.1–4

"quin" particula, quam grammatici coniunctionem appellant, variis modis sententiisque conectere orationem videtur. [2] . . . aliter autem cum sic componimus, quod quasi priori videtur contrarium: "non idcirco causas Isocrates non defendit, quin id utile esse et honestum existumarit"; [3] a quo illa significatio non abhorret, quae est in tertia Origine M. Catonis: "haut eos" inquit "eo postremum scribo quin populi et boni et strenui sient."[1] [4] in secunda quoque Origine M. Cato non longe secus hac particula

[1] sient *vel* sint *vel* fient *codd.*

F 26 Priscian

For *vetus, veteris* ["old"; nom., gen.] is the same for the three genders . . . Though analogy also demands *veter* ["old"], so that it is said well. . . . , instead of *vetus* [standard form]. That seemed very prudent also to Caper [Flavius Caper, 2nd cent. AD], since the comparative *veterior* and the superlative *veterrimus* require the positive *veter*. Cato in [Book] 1 of the *Origines*: "Antemna [town in Latium, just north of Rome, at the confluence of Anio and Tiber] is older [*veterior*] than Rome."

BOOK 2 (F 27–40)

customs, etymology, law, and agriculture. The precise coverage of each of these books and their exact internal organization are unclear.

F 27 Gellius, *Attic Nights*

The particle *quin*, which the grammarians call a conjunction, seems to function as a connecting link of discourses in various ways and meanings. [2] . . . and in yet another way, when we thus put together what seems almost contradictory to a former [statement]: "it was not for that reason that Isocrates refrained from pleading cases, that he did not believe that to be useful and honorable." [3] Not very different from this is that meaning that is found in the third book of M. Cato's *Origines* [F 41]: "It is not for that reason," he says, "that I describe those last that they are not good and valiant peoples." [4] Also in the second book of the *Origines* M. Cato has used this particle in a not far different manner: "He did not consider it suf-

usus est: "neque satis" inquit "habuit quod eam[2] in occulto vitiaverat, quin eius famam prostitueret."

[2] eam *unus cod.*[2]: eum *codd. rel.*

F 28 Fest., p. 400.22–27 L.

SUBLIMAVIT dixit <Cato>,[1] id est in altum extulit, Originum lib. II: "in maximum decus atque in excelsissimam claritudinem sublimavit." id autem dicitur a limine superiore, quia supra nos est.

[1] *add. Augustinus*

F 29 Non., p. 152.18–21 M. = 223 L.

PUTIDUM, putre. . . . Cato Originum lib. II:[1] "si inde in{de} {ig}navis[2] putidas atque sentinosas commeatum oner<ar>e[3] volebant."

[1] V *Mueller*
[2] in{de} {ig}navis *Roth*: inde ignavis *codd.*: indu n. *Scaliger*
[3] oner<ar>e *Scaliger*: onere *codd.*: ponere *Lipsius*

F 30 Non., pp. 207.32–8.6 M. = 306 L.

GELU neutri generis. . . . masculini. . . . Cato Originum lib. II: "{Libii}[1] qui aquatum ut[2] lignatum videntur[3] ire; secu-

[1] Libii *vel* libri *vel om. codd.* (*pro* lib. II): Libui *Roth*: Ligui *Gerlach*
[2] ut *Lipsius*: et *codd.*
[3] iubentur *Lipsius*

ficient," he says, "that he had violated her[1] in secret, unless he openly defamed her reputation."

[1] Editors of Cato usually adopt the correction *eam* ("her") for *eum* ("him") in one manuscript and refer the remark to Lucumo, who seduced the wife of his guardian Arruns of Clusium (Liv. 5.33.2–4; Dion. Hal. *Ant. Rom.* 13.10; Plut. *Cam.* 15.3–4).

F 28 Festus

<Cato> said *sublimavit* ["he raised up"], that is "he lifted up to the sky," in Book 2 of the *Origines*: "he raised up to greatest honor and to outstanding fame." And that is said derived from lintel [*limen*] since it is above us.

F 29 Nonius Marcellus

putidum ["rotting"], rotten. . . . Cato in Book 2 of the *Origines*: "if they were willing to load provisions from there onto ships rotten and full of bilge water."

F 30 Nonius Marcellus

gelu ["frost, cold, ice"], of neuter gender. . . . Of masculine [gender]. . . . Cato in Book 2 of the *Origines*: ". . . [?],[1] who are seen to go to fetch water in the same way as to fetch

[1] If the (omitted / deleted) word at the start of the quotation is not an erroneous repetition of the indication of the book and rather the subject of the sentence, it could be interpreted as *Libui*, referring to the Libui (Liv. 5.35.2, 21.38.7, 33.37.6), a people in northern Italy and probably the same as the Libicii based around Vercellae (mod. Vercelli) (cf. F 57); or, if read as *Ligui*, the word could be interpreted as an alternative version of the name for the Ligurians, a people in northwestern Italy.

rim atque lorum[4] ferunt, gelum crassum excidunt, eum loro conligatum auferunt."

[4] lorum *Lipsius*: solum folum *vel* solum *codd.*

F 31 Charis., *GL* I, p. 83.26–28 = p. 105.15–19 B.

papaver neutri generis est; sed masculino genere Plautus dixit . . . et Cato Originum secundo: "papaver Gallicanus," et . . .

F 32 Charis., *GL* I, p. 91.16–18 = p. 115.27–29 B.

ques autem dixisse veteres testimonio est Cato, qui ait Originum II: "quescumque Romae regnavissent," et . . .

Cf. Prisc., *GL* III, p. 9.13–17.

F 33 Charis., *GL* I, p. 202.20–22 = p. 263.2–4 B.

industriosissime M. Cato Originum II: "pleraque Gallia duas res industriosissime persequitur, rem militarem et argute loqui."

F 34a Serv. ad Verg. *Aen.* 11.700

"Appenninicolae bellator filius Auni": . . . Ligures autem omnes fallaces sunt, sicut ait Cato in secundo Originum libro.

wood; they carry an ax and a leather strap, they cut out [a piece of] thick ice, they carry it away, tied up with a leather strap."

F 31 Charisius

papaver ["poppy"] is of neuter gender, but Plautus used it in the masculine gender [Plaut. *Trin.* 410] . . . and Cato in the second [book] of the *Origines*: "Gallican poppy," and . . .

F 32 Charisius

And that the ancients used *ques* ["who / any"; nom. pl. instead of *qui*], for that Cato bears testimony [cf. F 1, 123], as he says in [Book] 2 of the *Origines*: "whoever had reigned at Rome," and . . .

F 33 Charisius

industriosissime ["most assiduously"; rare and archaic form of superlative], M. Cato [uses it in Book] 2 of the *Origines*: "most of Gaul pursues two things most assiduously, military affairs and to speak shrewdly."[1]

[1] For a discussion of the meaning and context of this fragment and a defense of the transmitted text, see Fo 1979.

F 34a Servius, *Commentary on Virgil*

"the warlike son of Aunus, a dweller in the Apennines": . . . And the Ligurians [people in northwestern Italy][1] are all deceitful, as Cato says in the second book of the *Origines*.

[1] On the views on and the presentation of the Ligurians both here and in F 34b, see Dubuisson 1990.

F 34b Serv. auct. ad Verg. *Aen.* 11.715

"vane Ligus": . . . Nigidius[1] de terris "nam et Ligures, qui Appenninum tenuerunt, latrones, insidiosi, fallaces, mendaces," Cato Originum cum de Liguribus loqueretur "sed ipsi, unde oriundi sunt, exacta memoria inliterati mendacesque sunt et vera minus meminere."

[1] Nigidius *Daniel*: nigius *unus cod.*

F 35 Prisc., *GL* II, p. 129.7–15

Cf. F 23.

F 36a Prisc., *GL* II, p. 129.7–15

Cf. F 23.

F 36b Prisc., *GL* II, p. 337.19–23

Cf. F 23 n.

F 37 Prisc., *GL* II, pp. 151.14–52.17

alia vero omnia masculina sunt, ut . . . , exceptis duobus, quae ipsa natura defendit femineo generi, "mater" et "mulier" (. . .) et adiectivis, quae si non in "is" facient feminina, necessario communia sunt (ut "celer" masculinum

F 34b Servius Danielis, *Commentary on Virgil*

"you vain Ligurian": . . . Nigidius [says in the work] on lands [P. Nigidius Figulus, late Republican scholar (F CI Swoboda)]: "for the Ligurians too, who were in control of the Apennine mountains, bandits, treacherous, deceitful, liars," Cato in the *Origines*, when he spoke about the Ligurians [people in northwestern Italy], [said]: "but they themselves, having lost the memory of where they originate from, are uneducated and liars, and remember the truth less."

F 35 Priscian

Cf. F 23.[1]

[1] A comment on inheritance law at Arpinum as it differed from conventions at Rome.

F 36a Priscian

Cf. F 23.

F 36b Priscian

Cf. F 23 n. 1.

F 37 Priscian

But all others [nouns ending in *-er*] are masculine, like . . . , with the exception of two, with regard to which nature itself acts in defense of the feminine gender, *mater* ["mother"] and *mulier* ["wife"] (. . .), and of adjectives, which, if they do not form feminine versions ending in *-is*, are necessarily common (as masculine *celer* ["fast"] forms

"celeris" facit femininum, cuius neutrum in e invenitur . . .) . . . "uber" . . . Cato in II Originum: "itaque res uber fuit, antequam legiones . . ."[1]

[1] s. accederent *gloss. cod. unius*: vastassent regiones *edd. ante ed. Aldinam Venetam a. 1527*: vastassent legiones *edd. inde ab ed. Aldina Veneta a. 1527 usque at Putschianam*

F 38 Prisc., *GL* II, p. 171.6–9

. . . "hic" et "haec retis" et "hoc rete," "hic" et "hoc sexus," "hic" et "haec" et "hoc specus," "hic" et "hoc sal." Cato in II:[1] "ex sale, qui apud Carthaginienses fit."

[1] II *vel* secundo *vel* III *codd.*

Cf. Alcuinus, *Grammatica* (*PL* 101, p. 862B): hic et hoc sal. Cato: "ex sale, qui apud Carthaginienses fit."

F 39 Prisc., *GL* II, p. 487.8–11

"torsi" quoque et "tortum" et "torsum" facit, itaque "tortores" et "torsores" dicuntur. Cato in II Originum:[1] "Marsus hostem occidit prius quam Paelignus, propterea Marrucini vocantur, de Marso detorsum nomen."

[1] in IIII originum *om. unus cod.* IIII *vel* secundo *codd. rel.*

feminine *celeris*, whose neuter is found ending in *-e* . . .) . . . *uber* ["abundant, rich"] . . . Cato in [Book] 2 of the *Origines*: "and thus the matter was prosperous [*uber*: nom. fem. sg.], before the legions . . ."

F 38 Priscian

. . . masculine, feminine and neuter *retis / rete* ["net"], masculine and neuter *sexus* ["gender"], masculine, feminine and neuter *specus* ["cave"], masculine and neuter *sal* ["salt"]. Cato in [Book] 2:[1] "from salt [masc.] that is produced among the Carthaginians."

[1] The work by Cato from which the quotation comes is not identified; but since a book number is given, it must be the *Origines*.

F 39 Priscian

torsi ["I have twisted"] too forms both *tortum* and *torsum* [different forms of past participle]; accordingly, *tortores* and *torsores* ["torturers"] are in use. Cato in [Book] 2[1] of the *Origines*: "The Marsian killed the enemy before the Paelignian [could]; therefore, they are called Marrucini [various Italic peoples], a name derived with distortion [*detorsum*] from Marsian."

[1] Most editors of Cato assign this fragment to Book 2, although the editor of Priscian follows the majority of the manuscripts and opts for Book 4.

F 40 Prisc., *GL* II, p. 537.6–10

e brevi antecedente in "to" desinentia duo inveni: "peto petivi" et "meto messui." Cato in II Originum: "in campo Tiburti ubi hordeum demessuit, idem in montibus serit, ubi hordeum idem iterum metit." Cassius Emina in III annalium: "in campo Tiburte ubi hordeum demessuerunt."

Cf. Prisc., *GL* III, pp. 489.37–90.3.

BOOK 3 (F 41–45)

The third book continues the description of Italy (T 26; see Book 2), most clearly shown by F 45, on southern Italy. As for Book 2, the coverage is difficult to determine precisely.

F 41 Gell. *NA* 17.13.2–4

Cf. F 27.

F 42 Fest., pp. 196.36–98.5 L.

OREAE, freni quod ori inseruntur. . . . Cato Originum lib. III: "equos respondit: oreas mihi inde, tibi cape flagellum."

F 40 Priscian

I have found two [words] ending in *-to* with a short preceding *e*: *peto*, *petivi* ["I seek," "I sought"] and *meto*, *messui* ["I harvest," "I harvested"]. Cato in [Book] 2 of the *Origines*: "when someone has harvested barley in the Tiburtine plain, they then sow it in the mountains, where they harvest an equivalent [crop of] barley a second time." Cassius Hemina [L. Cassius Hemina (*FRHist* 6 F 30)] in [Book] 3 of the *Annals*: "in the Tiburtine plain, where they have harvested barley."

BOOK 3 (F 41–45)

Only a small number of fragments are clearly attested for this book.

F 41 Gellius, *Attic Nights*

Cf. F 27.

F 42 Festus

oreae ["mouthpiece of a bridle, bit"], since bridles are inserted into the mouth [*os*, *oris*]. . . . Cato in Book 3 of the *Origines*: "The horse replied: 'Insert the bit for me; take the whip for yourself.'"[1]

[1] The fragment might be connected with a version of a fable attributed to Stesichorus: a horse is aiming for a pact with a man and then brought under the man's control (Arist. *Rh.* 2.20, 1393b).

F 43–44 Charis., *GL* I, p. 73.7–8 = p. 92.16–18 B.

pulmentum et pulmentarium dicitur. nam Cato Originum III "laserpitium pro pulmenta|rio <suo>[1] habet," idem[2] "multo pulmento usi."

[1] *add. Putschen ex deperdito cod.*: *om. Beda*

[2] idem *Beda*: in eodem *cod. descr.* (*"quod minus spatio lacunae convenit" Barwick*)

Cf. Beda, *Orth.*, *GL* VII, p. 285.13–14.

F 45 Probus, ad Verg. *Ecl.*, *praef.* (p. 326.2–17 Hagen)

huius autem fluminis, apud quod purgatus est Orestes, Varro meminit humanarum XI[1] sic: "iuxta Rhegium fluvii sunt continui septem: Latapadon, Micodes, Eugiton, Stracteos, Polie, Molee, Argeades. in his matris nece purgatus dicitur Orestes ibique ahenum eius diu fuisse ensem et ab eo aedificatum Apollinis templum, e cuius luco Rheginos, cum Delphos proficiscerentur, re divina facta lauream decerpere solitos, quam ferrent secum." item Cato Originum III: "Thesunti Tauriani[2] vocantur de fluvio, qui propter fluit, id oppidum Aurunci primo possiderunt, inde Achaei Troia domum redeuntes. in eorum agro fluvii sunt sex; septimus finem Rheginum atque Taurinum dispescit:

[1] X *ed. Bipontina*

[2] Thesunti *vel* Theseunti *vel* Rhegini *codd.*: Thesunti *Duebner* Tauriani *vel* thauriani *vel* Taurocini *codd.*

F 43–44 Charisius

pulmentum ["small savory dish"] et *pulmentarium* ["anything used to flavor *pulmentum*"] are in use. For Cato [says in Book] 3 of the *Origines*: "he/she has asafoetida [produce of the *silphium* plant; a spice used for savory dishes] for ‹his/her› *pulmentarium*;" the same[1] [Cato]: "having used much *pulmentum*."

[1] If *idem* is read rather than *in eodem* ("in the same"; see textual note), the attribution of the second fragment to Book 3 is uncertain. In either case, the piece is identified as a fragment of Cato's.

F 45 Probus, *Commentary on Virgil*

But of this river, at which Orestes was cleansed, Varro makes mention in [Book] 11 of *Human* [*Matters*] as follows [M. Terentius Varro (*Ant. rer. hum.*, F X.XI Mirsch)]: "Next to Rhegium [mod. Reggio Calabria] there is a series of seven rivers: Latapadon, Micodes, Eugiton, Stracteos, Polie, Molee, and Argeades. In these Orestes is said to have been cleansed from the killing of his mother, and that his bronze sword was there for a long time, and that there was built by him a temple of Apollo, from whose grove the inhabitants of Rhegium, when they set off for Delphi, were accustomed, after having completed divine rites, to pluck a laurel branch, which they took with them." Likewise Cato in [Book] 3 of the *Origines*: "The Thesunti are called Tauriani from the river that flows nearby [probably Metaurus]; Aurunci [Italic people in southern Italy] first had that town in their control, then Achaeans, returning home from Troy. In their territory there are six rivers; a seventh separates the area of Rhegium and that of Tauri-

fluvii nomen est Pecoli. eo[3] Orestem cum Iphigenia atque Pylade dicunt maternam necem expiatum venisse et non longinqua memoria est, cum in arbore ensem viderint, quem Orestes abiens reliquisse dicitur."

3 Pecoli. eo *Duebner*: Pecolieo *vel* Paccolico *codd.*: Phacelini *Hermann*: Phacelino *Bergk*: *an* Polie *(cf. Varro)*? *Hagen*

FROM BOOKS 1–3 (F 46–75)

The fragments in this section are not assigned to a specific book of the Origines *in the transmission (some not even to the* Origines, *though all are attributed to Cato; see also* Incertorum operum reliquiae*). Since they describe details concerning the political and settlement history of Italy, its*

F 46a Varro, *Rust.* 1.2.7

an non M. Cato scribit in libro Originum sic: "ager Gallicus Romanus vocatur, qui viritim c{e}<i>s Ar{e}<i>minu{n}<m> datus[1] est ultra agrum Picentium.[2] in eo agro aliquotfariam[3] in singula iugera dena cullea vini fiunt"?

1 c{e}<i>s Ar{e}<i>minu{n}<m> datus *Vettori (1541)*: cis Aremin. datus *Poliziano*: Caesarem inundatus *vel* Cesarem inundatus *vel* Cesarem mundatus *codd.* 2 Picentinum *Leo*: Pincentium *vel* Picenum *codd.* 3 aliquotfariam *Merula*: aliquod fariam *vel* aliquod far ita *codd.*

---

1 A section of *ager Gallicus* that had remained *ager publicus* was handed out in individual allotments as a result of *Lex Flaminia de agro (Piceno et) Gallico viritim dividendo* (*LPPR*, pp. 247–48; Elster 2003, 171–75) in 232/28 BC (Pol. 2.21.7–8;

num: the name of the river is Pecoli.[1] There, they say, Orestes came with Iphigenia and Pylades to expiate the killing of his mother, and it is not a distant memory when people saw in a tree the sword that Orestes is said to have left when going away."

[1] The precise geographical identification of the places and rivers mentioned is difficult and controversial (for discussion, see the commentary on F 45 in *FRHist*).

FROM BOOKS 1–3 (F 46–75)

geography, and its natural produce, they are likely to come from the early books of the Origines, *most probably from Books 2 or 3. (On Cato's comments on Gallia cisalpina and their background, see Heurgon 1974.)*

F 46a Varro, *On Agriculture*

Or does not M. Cato write in a book of the *Origines* as follows: "*ager Gallicus Romanus* is the name [for the area] that has been given out to men in individual lots on this side of Ariminum [mod. Rimini] beyond the district of Picenum [in northeastern central Italy between the Apennines and the Adriatic Sea]. In that area in several places ten *cullea* [liquid measure, here used as neuter; one *culleus* = 20 amphorae] of wine are produced for each *iugerum* [land measure, ca. two-thirds of an acre]"?[1]

Cic. *Sen.* 11; *Acad. Pr.* 13; *Brut.* 57). The yield should be seen in relation to what Columella (*Rust.* 3.3.10) seems to regard as standard, that even the worst vineyards, if properly taken care of, will yield one *culleus* of wine per *iugerum* (for considerations on the yields of ancient vineyards, see Günther 1996).

F 46b Plin. *HN* 14.52

ac ne quis victam in hoc antiquitatem arbitretur, idem Cato denos culleos redire ex iugeribus scripsit, efficacibus exemplis non maria plus temerata conferre mercatori, non in Rubrum litus Indicumve merces petitas quam sedulum ruris larem.

Cf. Columella, *Rust.* 3.3.2–3, 3.9.2–3; Non., p. 197.22–23 M. = 290 L.; *De dubiis nominibus*, *GL* V, p. 576.19–20.

F 47 Varro, *Rust.* 2.3.3

de quarum velocitate in Originum libro Cato scribit haec: "in Sauracti ‹et›[1] Fiscello caprae ferae sunt, quae saliunt e saxo pedes plus sexagenos." oves enim quas pascimus ortae sunt ob ovibus feris; sic caprae quas alimus a capris feris ortae, . . .

[1] *add. Clüver*

F 48 Varro, *Rust.* 2.4.11

de magnitudine Gallicarum succidiarum Cato scribit his verbis: "in Italia Ins{cro}‹u›b‹r›es[1] terna atque quaterna milia auli‹coct›a‹rum› succidia‹rum salli›vere.[2] sus usque adeo pinguitudine crescere solet, ut se ipsa stans sustinere non possit neque progredi usquam; itaque eas siquis quo traicere vol{e}t,[3] in plaustrum inponit."

[1] Ins{cro}‹u›b‹r›es *Turnebus*: in scrobes *codd.*

[2] auli‹coct›a‹rum› succidia‹rum salli›vere *Flach*: aulia succidia vere *codd.*: succidiarum vendere *Brakman*

[3] vol{e}t *Jordan*: volet *vel* nolet *codd.*

F 46b Pliny the Elder, *Natural History*

And so that nobody believes that antiquity was beaten in this respect, Cato also wrote that there were returns of ten *cullei* [liquid measure; one *culleus* = 20 amphorae] from each *iugerum* [land measure, ca. two-thirds of an acre], with impressive examples [to show] that the seas violated do not bring more profit to the merchant, nor merchandise sought out as far as the coast of the Red Sea or of the Indian Ocean, than does a diligently cultivated rural homestead.

F 47 Varro, *On Agriculture*

About their [the goats'] swiftness Cato writes this in a book of the *Origines*: "on Soracte ‹and› Fiscellus [mountains in central Italy] there are wild goats [cf. Varro, *Rust.* 2.1.5], which jump from a rock more than sixty feet." For the sheep that we pasture has originated from wild sheep; likewise, the goats that we raise have originated from wild goats, . . .

F 48 Varro, *On Agriculture*

On the volume / size of Gallic joints of pork Cato writes in the following words: "In Italy the Insubres[1] [people in the area of mod. Lombardy] have salted three or four thousand boiled joints of pork. A sow usually grows so much in fatness that she cannot support herself standing nor move anywhere; therefore, if anyone wishes to transport them anywhere, they put them onto a cart."

[1] The text at the beginning of the fragment and thus the attribution of these customs to the Insubres are based on a conjectural restoration of the transmission.

F 49a Dion. Hal. *Ant. Rom.* 1.11.1

οἱ δὲ λογιώτατοι τῶν Ῥωμαϊκῶν συγγραφέων, ἐν οἷς ἐστι Πόρκιός τε Κάτων ὁ τὰς γενεαλογίας τῶν ἐν Ἰταλίᾳ πόλεων ἐπιμελέστατα συναγαγὼν καὶ Γάϊος Σεμπρώνιος καὶ ἄλλοι συχνοί, Ἕλληνας αὐτοὺς εἶναι λέγουσι τῶν ἐν Ἀχαΐᾳ ποτὲ οἰκησάντων, πολλαῖς γενεαῖς πρότερον τοῦ πολέμου τοῦ Τρωικοῦ μεταναστάντας. οὐκέτι μέντοι διορίζουσιν οὔτε φῦλον Ἑλληνικὸν οὗ μετεῖχον, οὔτε πόλιν ἐξ ἧς ἀπανέστησαν, οὔτε χρόνον οὔθ᾽ ἡγεμόνα τῆς ἀποικίας, οὔθ᾽ ὁποίαις τύχαις χρησάμενοι τὴν μητρόπολιν ἀπέλιπον· Ἑλληνικῷ τε μύθῳ χρησάμενοι οὐδένα τῶν τὰ Ἑλληνικὰ γραψάντων βεβαιωτὴν παρέσχοντο. τὸ μὲν οὖν ἀληθὲς ὅπως ποτ᾽ ἔχει, ἄδηλον· . . .

F 49b Dion. Hal. *Ant. Rom.* 1.13.2

τὰ μὲν οὖν ὑπὸ τῶν παλαιῶν εἰρημένα ποιητῶν τε καὶ μυθογράφων περί τε οἰκήσεως καὶ γένους τῶν Οἰνώτρων τοιαῦτά ἐστιν· οἷς ἐγὼ πειθόμενος, εἰ τῷ ὄντι Ἑλληνικὸν φῦλον ἦν τὸ τῶν Ἀβοριγίνων, ὡς Κάτωνι καὶ Σεμπρωνίῳ καὶ πολλοῖς ἄλλοις εἴρηται, τούτων ἔγγονον αὐτῶν τῶν Οἰνώτρων ὑποτίθεμαι. τὸ γὰρ δὴ Πελασγικὸν καὶ τὸ Κρητικὸν καὶ ὅσα ἄλλα ἐν Ἰταλίᾳ ᾤκησεν, ὑστέροις εὑρίσκω χρόνοις ἀφικόμενα. παλαιότερον δὲ τούτου στόλον ἀπαναστάντα τῆς Ἑλλάδος εἰς τὰ προσεσπέρια τῆς Εὐρώπης οὐδένα δύναμαι καταμαθεῖν.

F 49a Dionysius of Halicarnassus, *Roman Antiquities*

But the most learned of the Roman historians, among whom is Porcius Cato, who compiled the pedigrees of the cities in Italy with the greatest care, Gaius Sempronius [C. Sempronius Tuditanus (*FRHist* 10 F 4)], and a great many others, say that they [i.e., the people from whom the Romans originally descended] were Greeks, of those who had once dwelt in Achaea, and migrated many generations before the Trojan War. But they do not also define the Greek subgroup to which they belonged, or the city from which they set off, or the date, or the leader of the migration, or what kinds of misfortune they had suffered before they left their mother city. And, though following a Greek story, they have cited no one of those writing Greek history as their authority. Thus, what the truth is remains unclear; . . .

F 49b Dionysius of Halicarnassus, *Roman Antiquities*

Such, then, are the accounts by the ancient poets and writers of legends concerning the abode and ancestry of the Oenotrians [people of Greek origin, settling in southern Italy]; trusting them, I suggest that, if that of the original settlers [*Aborigines*] was indeed a Greek group, as is stated by Cato, Sempronius [C. Sempronius Tuditanus (*FRHist* 10 F 4)], and many others, it was a descendant of these very Oenotrians. For I find that the Pelasgian, and the Cretan, and any other [nations] that lived in Italy arrived in later times, nor can I discover any other expedition more ancient than this that came from Greece to the western parts of Europe.

F 50 Dion. Hal. *Ant. Rom.* 2.49.1–5

Ζηνόδοτος δ' ὁ[1] Τροιζήνιος, συγγραφεὺς * * *[2] Ὀμβρικοὺς ἔθνος αὐθιγενὲς[3] ἱστορεῖ τὸ μὲν πρῶτον οἰκῆσαι περὶ τὴν καλουμένην Ῥεατίνην· ἐκεῖθεν δὲ ὑπὸ Πελασγῶν ἐξελασθέντας[4] εἰς ταύτην ἀφικέσθαι τὴν γῆν ἔνθα νῦν οἰκοῦσι καὶ μεταβαλόντας[5] ἅμα τῷ τόπῳ τοὔνομα Σαβίνους ἐξ Ὀμβρικῶν προσαγορευθῆναι. [2] Κάτων δὲ Πόρκιος τὸ μὲν ὄνομα τῷ Σαβίνων ἔθνει τεθῆναί φησιν ἐπὶ Σάβου τοῦ Σάγκου[6] δαίμονος ἐπιχωρίου, τοῦτον δὲ τὸν Σάγκον ὑπό τινων πίστιον καλεῖσθαι Δία. πρώτην δ' αὐτῶν οἴκησιν ἀποφαίνει γενέσθαι κώμην τινὰ καλουμένην Τεστροῦναν ἀγχοῦ πόλεως Ἀμιτέρνης κειμένην, ἐξ ἧς ὁρμηθέντας τότε Σαβίνους εἰς τὴν Ῥεατίνην ἐμβαλεῖν Ἀβοριγίνων ἅμα <Πελασγοῖς>[7] κατοικούντων καὶ πόλιν αὐτῶν τὴν ἐπιφανεστάτην Κοτυλίας[8] πολέμῳ χειρωσαμένους κατασχεῖν. [3] ἐκ δὲ τῆς Ῥεατίνης ἀποικίας ἀποστείλαντας ἄλλας τε πόλεις κτίσαι πολλάς, ἐν αἷς οἰκεῖν ἀτειχίστοις, καὶ δὴ καὶ τὰς προσαγορευομένας

[1] δ' ὁ *Kiessling*: δὲ *codd.* [2] *post* συγγραφεὺς *excidisse* οὐδενὸς δεύτερος, Σαβίνους μοῖραν εἶναι ἀποφαίνων τοῦ *Ambrosch*, παλαιὸς *vel* λόγου ἄξιος *Kiessling* [3] Ὀμβρικοὺς ἔθνος αὐθιγενὲς *Reiske* ὀμβρικοῦ ἔθνους αὐθιγενεὶς *codd.* [4] ἐξελασθέντας *vel* ἐξελα<θ>έντας *vel* ἐξελαθέντας *codd.* [5] μεταβαλόντας *vel* <μετα>βαλόντας *vel* καταβάντας *codd.* [6] Σάβου τοῦ Σάγκου *Sylburg*: σαβίνου τοῦ σάγκου *codd.* [7] *add. Reiske* [8] Κοτυλίας *Gelenius*: κοτύνας *codd.*

F 50 Dionysius of Halicarnassus, *Roman Antiquities*

But Zenodotus of Troezen, a historiographer [Greek historian of Hellenistic period (*FGrHist / BNJ* 821 F 3)], . . . reports that the Umbrians, a native people, first dwelt in the Reatine territory [around mod. Rieti], as it is called, and that, being driven from there by the Pelasgians, they came to the land where they now live and, changing their name with their place of habitation, from Umbrians were called Sabines. [2] But Porcius Cato says that the name was given to the Sabine nation from Sabus, the son of Sancus, an indigenous divinity, and that this Sancus is by some called Dius Fidius. He points out that their first place of abode was a certain village called Testruna [also: Testrina], situated near the city of Amiternum; that, setting out from there, the Sabines then made an incursion into the Reatine territory, when the original settlers [*Aborigines*] lived there together with ‹the Pelasgians›, and took hold of their most famous city, Cutiliae, overpowering them in battle; [3] that, sending out colonies from the Reatine territory, they founded many other cities, in which they lived without city walls, among others the so-called

Κύρεις· χώραν δὲ κατασχεῖν τῆς μὲν Ἀδριανῆς θαλάττης ἀπέχουσαν ἀμφὶ τοὺς ὀγδοήκοντα καὶ διακοσίους σταδίους, τῆς δὲ Τυρρηνικῆς τετταράκοντα πρὸς διακοσίοις· μῆκος δὲ αὐτῆς εἶναί φησιν ὀλίγῳ μεῖον σταδίων χιλίων. [4] ἔστι δέ τις καὶ ἄλλος ὑπὲρ τῶν Σαβίνων ἐν ἱστορίαις ἐπιχωρίοις λεγόμενος λόγος, ὡς Λακεδαιμονίων ἐποικησάντων αὐτοῖς καθ' ὃν χρόνον ἐπιτροπεύων Εὔνομον τὸν ἀδελφιδοῦν Λυκοῦργος ἔθετο τῇ Σπάρτῃ τοὺς νόμους. ἀχθομένους γάρ τινας τῇ σκληρότητι τῆς νομοθεσίας καὶ διαστάντας ἀπὸ τῶν ἑτέρων οἴχεσθαι τὸ παράπαν ἐκ τῆς πόλεως· ἔπειτα διὰ πελάγους πολλοῦ φερομένους εὔξασθαι τοῖς θεοῖς (πόθον γάρ τινα ὑπελθεῖν αὐτοὺς ὁποιασδήποτε γῆς) εἰς ἣν ἂν ἔλθωσι πρώτην, ἐν ταύτῃ[9] κατοικήσειν. [5] καταχθέντας δὲ τῆς Ἰταλίας περὶ τὰ καλούμενα Πωμεντῖνα πεδία τό τε χωρίον, ἐν ᾧ πρῶτον ὡρμίσαντο, Φορωνίαν[10] ἀπὸ τῆς πελαγίου φορήσεως ὀνομάσαι καὶ θεᾶς ἱερὸν ἱδρύσασθαι Φορωνίας, ᾗ τὰς εὐχὰς ἔθεντο· ἣν νῦν ἑνὸς ἀλλαγῇ γράμματος Φερωνίαν καλοῦσιν. ἐκεῖθεν δ' ὁρμηθέντας αὐτῶν τινας συνοίκους τοῖς Σαβίνοις γενέσθαι· καὶ διὰ τοῦτο πολλὰ τῶν νομίμων εἶναι Σαβίνων[11] Λακωνικά, μάλιστα δὲ τὸ φιλοπόλεμόν τε καὶ τὸ λιτοδίαιτον καὶ παρὰ πάντα τὰ ἔργα τοῦ βίου σκληρόν. ὑπὲρ μὲν δὴ τοῦ Σαβίνων γένους ταῦθ' ἱκανά.

[9] *ταύτῃ Reiske*: *ἐν αὐτῇ codd.*

[10] *Φορωνίαν Ambrosch*: *φερωνείαν vel φερωνίαν codd. praeter unum*: *Σαβίνοις Bücheler*

[11] *σαβίνων om. codd.*

Cures [ancient Sabine town, just north of Rome]. He further says that they occupied a country distant from the Adriatic Sea about two hundred and eighty stadia [280 x ca. 180 m = ca. 50 km] and from the Tyrrhenian two hundred and forty [240 x ca. 180 m = ca. 43 km], and that its length was a little less than a thousand stadia [1,000 x ca. 180 m = ca. 180 km]. [4] There is also another account given of the Sabines in the local histories, that Lacedaemonians settled among them at the time when Lycurgus, being guardian to his nephew Eunomus, gave laws to Sparta [Sparta's legendary lawgiver]. For the story goes that some, unhappy with the harshness of the law code and separating from the others, left the city entirely; then, being borne across a vast stretch of sea, they made a vow to the gods to settle in the land whichever they should reach first (for a longing came upon them for any land whatsoever). [5] That at last they gained possession of the area of Italy around the so-called Pomentine plains, and they called the place where they first landed Foronia, from their being borne [*phoresis*] across the sea, and built a temple to the goddess Foronia, to whom they had addressed their vows; this goddess, by the alteration of one letter, they now call Feronia [goddess of fertility]. And that some of them, setting out from there, became fellow settlers with the Sabines. And that for this reason many of the customs of the Sabines are Lacedaemonian, particularly the fondness for war, the frugality, and the austerity in all the actions of their lives. This then is enough about the Sabine nation.[1]

[1] On Cato's views on the origin of the Sabines and their context, see Letta 1985.

F 51 Serv. auct. ad Verg. *Aen.* 8.638

"Curibusque severis": . . . aut "severis" disciplina: aut rem hoc verbo reconditam dixit, quia Sabini a Lacedaemoniis originem ducunt, ut Hyginus ait de origine urbium Italicarum, . . . Cato autem et Gellius a Sabo[1] Lacedaemonio trahere eos originem referunt. porro Lacedaemonios durissimos fuisse omnis lectio docet. Sabinorum etiam m{ai}ores[2] populum Romanum secutum idem Cato dicit: merito ergo "severis," qui et a duris parentibus orti sunt, et quorum disciplinam victores Romani in multis secuti sunt.

[1] a Sabo *Daniel*: asco *cod.* [2] m{ai}ores *Daniel*: maiores *cod.*

F 52 Vell. Pat. 1.7.2–4

dum in externis moror, incidi in rem domesticam maximique[1] erroris et multum discrepantem auctorum opinionibus; nam quidam huius temporis tractu aiunt a Tuscis Capuam Nolamque conditam ante annos fere DCCCXXX. [3] quibus equidem adsenserim; sed M. Cato quantum differt! qui dicat Capuam ab eisdem Tuscis conditam ac subinde Nolam; stetisse autem Capuam, antequam a Romanis caperetur, annis circiter CCLX. [4] quod si ita est, cum sint a Capua capta anni CCXL, ut condita est, anni

[1] maximique *Rhenanus*: maximeque *cod. deperditus*

---

[1] Velleius Paterculus' calculation is based on the capture of Capua in the Second Punic War in 211 BC. Cato could have referred to 338 BC, when Capua became a *civitas sine suffragio* in relation to Rome (a community with Roman citizenship, albeit without voting rights).

F 51 Servius Danielis, *Commentary on Virgil*

"and for the austere men of Cures [ancient Sabine town, just north of Rome]": . . . either "austere" with respect to training, or he [Virgil] mentioned a recondite matter with this word since the Sabines trace their origin from the Lacedaemonians, as Hyginus says [in the work] on the origin of the Italic cities [C. Iulius Hyginus (*FRHist* 63 F 9)], . . . But Cato and Gellius [Cn. Gellius (*FRHist* 14 F 20)] report that they trace their origin from Sabus, a Lacedaemonian. Further, all reading demonstrates that the Lacedaemonians were extremely hardy. The same Cato says that the Roman People even followed the customs of the Sabines: deservedly therefore "austere," those who were born from hardy parents and whose practice the victorious Romans followed in many respects.

F 52 Velleius Paterculus, *Compendium of Roman History*

While I was dwelling on foreign affairs, I came upon a domestic matter, characterized by great error and by much discrepancy in the views of the authorities. For some say that in the course of this period [i.e., time of Hesiod] Capua and Nola [towns in Campania] were founded by the Etruscans, about 830 years ago. [3] With these I myself am inclined to agree; but how much does M. Cato's view differ! He says that Capua was founded by the same Etruscans and shortly afterward Nola, but that Capua had been in existence for about 260 years before it was captured by the Romans. [4] If this is so, as it is 240 years since Capua was captured,[1] it is about 500 years

sunt fere D. ego, pace diligentiae Catonis dixerim, vix crediderim tam mature tantam urbem crevisse floruisse concidisse resurrexisse.

F 53 Plin. *HN* 3.51

intus coloniae Falisca Argis orta, ut auctor est Cato, quae cognominatur Etruscorum, Lucus Feroniae,[1] Rusellana, Seniensis, Sutrina.[2]

[1] feroniae *Gelenius*: foro- *vel* colo- *codd.* [2] sutrina *vel* uricina *vel* tricina *vel* tritina *codd.*: cirtona *edd. vet.*

F 54 Plin. *HN* 3.98

praeterea interisse Thebas Lucanas Cato auctor est, et . . .

F 55 Plin. *HN* 3.114

Ameriam supra scriptam Cato ante Persei bellum conditam annis DCCCCLXIII[1] prodit.[2]

[1] DCCCCLXIII *vel* DCCCCLXIIII *codd.* [2] prodit *vel* prodidit *codd.*

F 56 Plin. *HN* 3.116

in hoc tractu interierunt Boi quorum tribus CXII fuisse auctor est Cato, item Senones qui ceperunt[1] Romam.

[1] ceperunt *vel* ceperant *vel* coeperant *codd.*

since it was founded. For my own part, if I may say this with due regard for Cato's diligence [*FRHist* 5 T 14c], I could scarcely believe that in such a short space of time such a great city could have grown, flourished, fallen, and risen again.

F 53 Pliny the Elder, *Natural History*

Inland are the colonies of Falisca [Falerii, mod. Cività Castellana, originally town of the Falisci], taking its origin from the Argives, as Cato testifies, which was given the additional name "of the Etruscans," Lucus Feroniae, Rusellae, Siena, and Sutrium [places in Etruria].

F 54 Pliny the Elder, *Natural History*

In addition, Cato testifies that Thebes in Lucania [area in southern Italy] has disappeared, and . . .

F 55 Pliny the Elder, *Natural History*

Cato records that Ameria [town in Umbria, mod. Amelia], mentioned above [Plin. *HN* 2.148], was founded 963 years before the war with Perseus [king of Macedonia; 171–168 BC].

F 56 Pliny the Elder, *Natural History*

In this region [region 8, Cisalpine Gaul] the Boii [defeated by the Romans in 193 BC and deprived of some of their territory] have died out; according to Cato they had 112 units; likewise the Senones, who captured Rome [in 390 BC; defeated in 283 BC and their territory appropriated by the Romans], [have died out].

F 57 Plin. *HN* 3.123–25

Transpadana appellatur ab eo regio undecima, tota in mediterraneo, cui mari<n>a[1] cuncta fructuoso alveo inportat. oppida Vibi Forum, Segusio, coloniae ab Alpium radicibus Augusta Taurinorum—inde navigabili Pado—antiqua Ligurum stirpe, dein Salassorum Augusta Praetoria iuxta geminas Alpium fores,[2] Graias atque Poeninas—his Poenos, Grais Herculem transisse memorant—, oppidum Eporedia Sibyllinis a populo Romano conditum iussis. eporedias Galli bonos equorum domitores vocant. Vercellae Libiciorum ex Salluis ortae, [124] Novaria ex Vertamacoris, Vocontiorum hodieque pago, non, ut Cato existimat, Ligurum, ex quibus Laevi et Marici condidere Ticinum non procul a Pado, sicut Boi Transalpibus profecti Laudem Pompeiam, Insubres Mediolanum. Oromobiorum[3] stirpis esse Comum atque Bergomum et Licini Forum aliquotque circa populos auctor est Cato, sed originem gentis ignorare se fatetur, quam docet Cornelius Alexander ortam a Graecia interpretatione etiam nominis

[1] mari<n>a *Mayhoff*: maria *codd.*

[2] fores *vel* foras *codd.*

[3] oromobiorum *vel* -oviorum *vel* orumbiviorum *vel* orumbovi- *vel* orbovi- *codd.*: orobi- *edd. vet.*

F 57 Pliny the Elder, *Natural History*

The eleventh region is called Transpadana from that [river: Padus, mod. Po], situated entirely inland, whereto it [the river] carries all maritime products in its bounteous channel. Its towns are Forum Vibi [near mod. Saluzzo], Segusio [mod. Susa], and colonies at the foot of the Alps, Augusta Taurinorum [mod. Turin]—with the Padus navigable from there—, from ancient Ligurian stock, then Augusta Praetoria of the Salassi [mod. Aosta], near the twin passes of the Alps, the Graian and the Pennine—they say that the Carthaginians crossed the latter [cf. F 150] and Hercules the Graian [pass]—, and the town of Eporedia [mod. Ivrea], founded by the Roman People by order of the Sibylline [Books]. *eporediae* is what the Gauls call men good at taming horses. Vercellae of the Libicii [mod. Vercelli], taking the origin from the Salluii [also Salluvii or Salyes, people in Gaul], [124] Novaria [mod. Novara, in Piedmont region], from the Vertamacori, and today in the district of the Vocontii [Gallic people], not, as Cato thinks, of the Ligurians; from them [i.e., the Vocontii] the Laevi and Marici founded Ticinum [mod. Pavia] not far from the Padus, just as the Boii, setting out from beyond the Alps, founded Laus Pompeia [mod. Lodi Vecchio] and the Insubres Mediolanum [mod. Milan]. According to Cato, Comum [mod. Como], Bergamum [mod. Bergamo], Forum Licini [near mod. Incino], and some surrounding peoples are of Oromobian stock, but he confesses that he does not know the origin of the nation, which Cornelius Alexander [L. Cornelius Alexander Polyhistor / Alexandros Polyhistor (*FGrHist / BNJ* 273 F 104)] proclaims originated from Greece, with the interpretation also of the

vitam in montibus degentium. [125] in hoc situ interiit oppidum Oromobiorum[4] Parra, unde Bergomates Cato dixit ortos, etiamnum prodente se altius quam fortunatius situm. interiere et Caturiges,[5] Insubrum exsules, et Spina supra dicta, item Melpum opulentia praecipuum, quod ab Insubribus et Bois et Senonibus deletum eo die, quo Camillus Veios ceperit, Nepos Cornelius tradidit.

[4] oromobiorum *Mayhoff*: orub- *vel* oroboviorum *vel* orumb- *vel* bovi- *codd.*: orobi- *edd. vet.* [5] caturiges *Hermolaus Barbarus*: caturigens *vel* careges *vel* eaturi gens *codd.*

F 58 Plin. *HN* 3.130

Venetos Troiana stirpe ortos auctor est Cato, Cenomanos iuxta Massiliam habitasse in Volcis.

F 59 Plin. *HN* 3.133

verso[1] deinde ‹in›[2] Italiam pectore Alpium Latini iuris[3] Euganeae[4] gentes, quarum oppida XXXIIII enumerat Cato.

[1] verso *vel* versus *codd.* [2] *add. edd.* [3] iuris *vel* turis *codd.* [4] euganeae *edd.*: euganea *vel* eucaneae *vel* eucanaeae *vel* eucanee *codd.*

name as those who pass their lives in mountains [Gk. *oros*, "mountain" + *bios*, "life"]. [125] On this site a town of the Oromobii called Parra [mod. Parre, near Bergamo], whence Cato says the Bergomates originated, has perished, which even now reveals that it was located with greater height than good fortune. There have also perished the Caturiges [Ligurian people], exiles from the Insubres, and Spina [place in Umbria], mentioned above [Plin. *HN* 3.120], also Melpum [Etruscan town, near mod. Milan], conspicuous by its wealth, which is stated by Cornelius Nepos [*FRHist* 45 F 10] to have been destroyed by the Insubres, the Boii, and the Senones on that day on which Camillus captured Veii [town in Etruria, in 396 BC].

F 58 Pliny the Elder, *Natural History*

Cato testifies that the Veneti [people in northeastern Italy, mod. Veneto] are descended from Trojan stock and that the Cenomani [Celtic people] lived near Massilia [mod. Marseilles] in the territory of the Volcae [Gallic people].

F 59 Pliny the Elder, *Natural History*

Then, on the side of the Alps turned <toward> Italy, there are the Euganean peoples [ancient peoples dwelling just south of the Alps], with Latin right [a particular type of legal status in relation to Rome], of whom Cato enumerates thirty-four towns.

F 60 Plin. *HN* 3.134

Lepontios et Salassos Tauriscae[1] gentis idem Cato arbitratur; ceteri fere Lepontios relictos ex comitatu Herculis interpretatione Graeci nominis credunt, praeustis in transitu Alpium nive membris.

[1] tauriscae *vel* teutrisque *codd.*

F 61 Solin. 2.5–8

nam quis ignorat vel dicta vel condita . . . [7] . . . Tibur, sicut Cato facit testimonium, a Catillo Arcade praefecto classis Euandri; sicut Sextius, ab Argiva iuventute. [8] Catillus enim Amphiarai filius, post prodigialem patris apud Thebas interitum, Oeclei avi iussu cum omni fetu ver sacrum missus tres liberos in Italia procreavit, Tiburtum Coram Catillum, qui depulsis ex oppido Siciliae veteribus Sicanis a nomine Tiburti fratris natu maximi urbem vocaverunt.

F 62 Serv. ad Verg. *G.* 2.159

"te Lari maxime": Larius lacus est vicinus Alpibus, qui, iuxta Catonem in Originibus, per LX[1] tenditur milia.

[1] LX *vel* quadraginta *codd.*

---

[1] Nowadays, Lake Como is measured at ca. 46 km, since in antiquity Lake Como included Lago di Mezzola in the north; the latter is now a separate lake due to deposit of alluvium forming the Pian di Spagna between the two lakes.

F 60 Pliny the Elder, *Natural History*

Cato also considers the Lepontii and the Salassi [Celtic or Ligurian peoples in the Alps and northern Italy] to be of Tauriscan stock; other authors generally believe, through an interpretation of the name as Greek, that the Lepontii have been left behind from the companions of Hercules [Gk. *leipo*, "I leave"] because their limbs had been frostbitten by the snow in the crossing of the Alps.

F 61 Solinus

For who does not know that they have been named or founded . . . [7] . . . Tibur [mod. Tivoli], as Cato provides testimony, by Catillus, the Arcadian, the prefect of Evander's fleet; as Sextius [otherwise unknown] [says], by the Argive youth. [8] For Catillus, Amphiaraus' son, after his father's unnatural death at Thebes, had been sent on the order of his grandfather Oecleus with all progeny as a *ver sacrum* ["sacred spring"][1] and begat three children in Italy, Tiburtus, Coras, and Catillus, who, after expelling the ancient Sicanians from the town of Sicilia, called the city after the name of Tiburtus, the oldest brother.

[1] An Italic custom of sacrificing to a god all new life born in the spring, humans being allowed to grow to maturity and then getting banished.

F 62 Servius, *Commentary on Virgil*

"you, greatest Larius": Larius is a lake near the Alps [Lake Como]; according to Cato in the *Origines*, it extends for sixty miles [ca. 90 km; cf. Cassiod. *Var.* 11.14.2].[1]

F 63 Serv. ad Verg. *Aen.* 1.6

"genus unde Latinum": . . . tamen Cato in Originibus hoc dicit, cuius auctoritatem Sallustius sequitur in bello Catilinae, primo Italiam tenuisse quosdam qui appellabantur Aborigines. hos postea adventu Aeneae Phrygibus iunctos Latinos uno nomine nuncupatos. ergo descendunt Latini non tantum a Troianis, sed etiam ab Aboriginibus.

F 64 Serv. et Serv. auct. ad Verg. *Aen.* 3.402

"subnixa Petilia muro": . . . multi ita intellegunt, non "Philoctetae Petilia," sed "Philoctetae muro"; nam ait Cato, a Philocteta, condita iam pridem civitate, murum tantum factum.

F 65 Serv. ad Verg. *Aen.* 5.564

"Polite / progenies": illum dicit quem supra a Pyrrho introduxit occisum; de quo Cato in Originibus dicit, quod ad Italiam venerit et segregatus ab Aenea condiderit oppidum Politorium a suo nomine.

F 63 Servius, *Commentary on Virgil*

"whence the Latin nation": . . . Still Cato in the *Origines* says this, whose authority Sallust [C. Sallustius Crispus (*ORF*^{4} 152)] follows in *The War with Catiline* [Sall. *Cat.* 6.1–2], that certain people who were called *Aborigines* ["original settlers"] were the first to inhabit Italy. That afterward, after Aeneas' arrival, these [people] were joined with the Phrygians [i.e., Trojans] and were called Latins by a single name. Thus, the Latins are descended not only from the Trojans, but also from the *Aborigines*.

F 64 Servius and Servius Danielis, *Commentary on Virgil*

"Petelia [place in southern Italy], defended by a wall": . . . Many understand it thus, not "Philoctetes' Petelia," but "by Philoctetes' wall";[1] for Cato says that the settlement had been founded a long time ago and only the wall was built by Philoctetes.

[1] The question is whether in Virgil's line *parva Philoctetae subnixa Petelia muro* (Verg. *Aen.* 3.402) *Philoctetae* ("Philoctetes'") defines *Petelia* ("Petelia" [more common spelling]) or *muro* ("by a wall").

F 65 Servius, *Commentary on Virgil*

"Polites, your offspring": He [Virgil] means him [Polites, son of Priam] whom he introduced earlier [Verg. *Aen.* 2.526–32] as having been killed by Pyrrhus [Neoptolemus]; about him Cato says in the *Origines* that he came to Italy and, having been separated from Aeneas, founded the town Politorium [in Latium] after his own name [cf. Serv. auct. ad Verg. *Aen.* 1.2].

F 66a Serv. ad Verg. *Aen.* 5.755

"urbem designat aratro": quem Cato in Originibus dicit morem fuisse. conditores enim civitatis taurum in dexteram, vaccam intrinsecus iungebant, et incincti ritu Gabino,[1] id est togae parte caput velati, parte succincti, tenebant stivam incurvam, ut glebae omnes intrinsecus caderent, et ita sulco ducto loca murorum designabant, aratrum suspendentes circa loca portarum.

1 ritugabino *vel* ritu sauino *vel* ritu sabino *vel* libus auino *codd.*

F 66b Isid. *Orig.* 15.2.3

urbs vocata ab orbe, quod antiquae civitates in orbe fiebant; vel ab urbo[1] parte aratri, quo muri designabantur; unde est illud: "optavitque locum regno et concludere sulco." locus enim futurae civitatis sulco designabatur, id est aratro. Cato: "qui urbem," inquit, "novam condit,[2] tauro et vacca arat;[3] ubi araverit, murum facit;[4] ubi portam vult esse, aratrum substollit[5] et portat,[6] et portam vocat."

1 *i.e.* urvo: orvo *corr.* urve *vel* urbe *codd.*

2 condit *vel* condet *vel* condidit *codd.*

3 arat *vel* arit *vel* aret *codd.*

4 facit *vel* faciet *vel* faciat *codd.*

5 sustollit *vel* sustullit *vel* substollat *vel* sustollat *vel* subtollat *codd.*

6 portat *vel* portam *vel* portet *codd.*

F 66a Servius, *Commentary on Virgil*

"he marks out the city with a plow": Cato says in the *Origines* that this was a custom. For the founders of a settlement yoked a bull on the right side and a cow on the inner side, and, girded in the Gabian ritual style, that is, veiled at the head with a part of the toga, another part gathered up by a belt, they held the shaft of the plow handle in a curved way, so that all clods fell to the inside, and thus, with a furrow drawn, they designated the locations of the walls, lifting up the plow around the locations of the gates.[1]

[1] The veiled head is a characteristic of Roman religious ceremonies, in contrast to Greek ones. Mentions of *cinctus Gabinus* (rather than *ritus Gabinus*), referring to the girding of the toga, are more frequent (cf., e.g., Serv. ad Verg. *Aen.* 7.612). The divided transmission leaves it open whether *ritu Sabino* ("in the Sabine ritual style") should be read (see Schönberger 2000, 515). The custom of marking out the boundaries of a new settlement with a plow is widely attested in ancient writers.

F 66b Isidore, *Origins*

"City" [*urbs*] [has] been named from "circle" [*orbis*] since ancient settlements were constructed in a circle, or from the plow beam [*urvum* or *urbum*], a part of the plow, whereby the walls were designated; whence is that [Verg. *Aen.* 3.109, 1.425]: "and he selected a place for the realm, and they enclose it with a furrow." For the place of a future settlement was designated by a furrow, that is by a plow. Cato says: "who founds a new city, plows with a bull and a cow; where they have plowed, they erect a wall; where they want a gate to be, they lift the plow and carry it [*portat*], and they call it gate [*porta*]."

F 67 Schol. Veron. ad Verg. *Aen.* 7.681

<"Caeculus": Ca>to in Originibus ait Caeculum virgines aquam petentes in foco invenisse ideoque Vulcani <filium eum ex>istimasse et, quod oculos exiguos haberet, Caeculum appellatum. hic collecticiis pastoribus <urbem Praene>ste fundavit.

F 68 Serv. auct. ad Verg. *Aen.* 7.682

"altum Praeneste": Cato dicit quia is locus montibus praestet, Praeneste oppido nomen dedit. ergo "altum," quia in montibus locatum.

Cf. Paul. *Fest.*, p. 250.22–23 L.

F 69 Serv. et Serv. auct. ad Verg. *Aen.* 7.697

"lucosque Capenos": hos dicit Cato Veientum <iuvenes>[1] condidisse auxilio regis Propertii, qui eos Capenam cum adolevissent, miserat.

[1] *add. Wagner*

F 67 Scholia Veronensia to Virgil, *Aeneid*

<"Caeculus": Ca>to says in the *Origines* that maidens, fetching water, found Caeculus on a hearth and therefore belie<ved him> to be Vulcan's <son> [cf. Verg. *Aen.* 10.543] and that, because he had small / weak eyes, he was called Caeculus [from *caecus*, "blind"]. With shepherds haphazardly collected he founded <the city of Praene>ste [mod. Palestrina].[1]

[1] On the sources and traditions (e.g., Verg. *Aen.* 7.678–81; Serv. ad Verg. *Aen.* 7.678) concerning Caeculus and Praeneste, see Bremmer and Horsfall 1987.

F 68 Servius, *Commentary on Virgil*

"lofty Praeneste": Cato says: because this place stands out [*praestet*] in the mountains, it gave the name Praeneste [mod. Palestrina] to the town. Hence "lofty," because it is located in the mountains.

F 69 Servius and Servius Danielis, *Commentary on Virgil*

"and the groves of Capena": Cato says that <young men> of Veii [town in Etruria] established these [cf. F 23], with the aid of king Propertius, who had sent them to Capena [town in Latium, just north of Rome] after they had grown up.

F 70 Serv. auct. ad Verg. *Aen.* 10.179

"Alpheae ab origine Pisae": . . . Cato Originum[1] qui Pisas tenuerint ante adventum Etruscorum, negat sibi conpertum; sed inveniri[2] Tarchonem, Tyrrheno oriundum, postquam eorundem sermonem[3] ceperit, Pisas condidisse, cum ante regionem eandem Teutanes[4] quidam, Graece loquentes, possederint. alii . . .

[1] originum *vel* in originibus *codd.*: originum I *Commelinus*
[2] inveniri *vel* invenerit *codd.*: invenitur *Jordan*
[3] eorundem sermonem *vel* eurundem sermonum *codd.*: postquam eorum locorum dominium ceperit *Salmasius*: postquam eorundem regionem occupaverit *Cluverius*: *fort.* postquam locum desertum manu ceperit *Thilo*: † eurundem sermonem ceperit † *FRHist* [4] Teutanes *Salmasius (coll. Plin. HN 3.50: a Teutanis, Graeca gente)*: teutones *codd.*

F 71 Serv. ad Verg. *Aen.* 10.184

"intempestaeque Graviscae": Graviscanum oppidum alii intempestum dicunt ventis et tempestatibus carens: quod nulla potest ratione contingere. intempestas ergo Graviscas accipimus pestilentes secundum Plinium in naturali historia et Catonem in Originibus, ut intempestas intellegas sine temperie, id est tranquillitate: nam ut ait Cato, ideo Graviscae dictae sunt, quod gravem aerem sustinent.

F 70 Servius Danielis, *Commentary on Virgil*

"Pisa, Alphean in origin [from the river Alpheus]": . . . Cato, in the *Origines*, says that he had not ascertained who inhabited Pisa [town in Etruria] before the arrival of the Etruscans; but that it is found that Tarchon, descended from Tyrrhenus [figures in Etruscan foundation legends], after he had taken on the language of these same people, established Pisa, while previously certain Teutanes, Greek speakers, had possession of the same area. Others . . .

F 71 Servius, *Commentary on Virgil*

"and intemperate Graviscae": Some call the Graviscan town [port of the Etruscan city of Tarquinii; Roman colony established there in 181 BC] un-stormy [*intempestus*] as it lacks winds and tempests [*tempestates*]: this can happen in no way. Thus, we take in-temperate [*intempestus*] Graviscae as insalubrious according to Pliny in the *Natural History*[1] and Cato in the *Origines*, so that you understand "in-temperate" as without temperateness of climate [*temperies*], that is calm weather: for, as Cato says, it is for that reason that Graviscae is so named because it endures heavy [*gravis*] air.

[1] There are no extant references in Pliny's *Natural History*. An allusion to the climate in Graviscae is found in Rutilius Namatianus (*De reditu suo* 1.281–82).

F 72 Serv. ad Verg. *Aen.* 11.567

"non illum tectis ullae non moenibus urbes / accepere": non mirum a nulla hunc civitate susceptum: nam licet Privernas esset, tamen quia in Tuscorum iure paene omnis Italia fuerat, generaliter in Metabum omnium odia ferebantur. nam pulsus fuerat a gente Volscorum, quae etiam ipsa Etruscorum potestate regebatur: quod Cato plenissime exsecutus est.

F 73 Serv. ad Verg. *Aen.* 12.134

"nunc Albanus habetur": Catonem sequitur, qui Albanum montem ab Alba longa putat dictum.

F 74 Schol. ad Isid. *Orig.* 14.4.18 (p. 228 Lindsay)

Italia ob vini copiam Oenotria appellata est. Italiam Cato appellatam ait ab Italo rege, Timaeus, quod in ea boum quondam fuerit multitudo, Graecos autem antiquos solitos esse vocare tauros *ἰταλούς*; a quibus videntur dicti vituli.

Cf. Paul. *Fest.*, p. 94.9–10 L.: Italia dicta, quod magnos italos, hoc est boves, habeat. vituli enim ab Italis ‹itali›[1] sunt dicti. Italia ab Italo rege.

[1] *add. Mueller*

F 72 Servius, *Commentary on Virgil*

"no cities accepted that man [Metabus] in their buildings or their walls": Not surprising that this man was not received by any community: for, although he was a man from Privernum [mod. Priverno, in Latium, Volscian town], still, because almost the whole of Italy had been under the jurisdiction of the Etruscans, generally the hatred of all was directed against Metabus [king of the Volsci]. For he had been expelled from the nation of the Volsci, which itself was also ruled by the power of the Etruscans: Cato has detailed that very fully.

F 73 Servius, *Commentary on Virgil*

"now it [the hill] is called Alban": He [Virgil] follows Cato, who believes that the Alban Hill [near Rome] was named after Alba Longa [town in the Alban Hills near Rome].

F 74 Scholia to Isidore, *Origins*

Italy was called Oenotria because of its abundance of wine [Gk. *oinos*]. Cato says that Italy was named after king Italus, Timaeus [Timaeus the Sicilian, Greek historian, fl. ca. 300 BC (*FGrHist / BNJ* 566 F 42)] because in it there was once a large number of cattle, and that the ancient Greeks used to call bulls *itali*, from which the term *vituli* [Lat. "the young of cattle"] appears to be derived.

F 75 Paradoxographus Palatinus 21 (p. 360 Giannini)

Κάτων φησίν, ἐν ταῖς Κτίσεσιν, ἐπὶ τῶν Ἄλπεων λευκοὺς μὲν λαγωοὺς γίνεσθαι, μῦς δ' ἑνδεκαλίτρους,[1] ὗς δὲ μονοχήλους καὶ κύνας δασεῖς καὶ βόας ἀκεράτους.

[1] *μῦς δ' ἑνδεκαλίτρους Giannini: μηδὲν δεκαλίτρους codd.*

BOOK 4 (F 76–86)

The fourth book is the first of the "historical books" (4–7), which, altogether, cover the period from the First Punic War (264–241 BC) to Cato's death (149 BC). This book is said to contain the First Punic War (T 26). Therefore, an episode from the time of the First Punic War (258 BC; F 76) is assigned to this book, although the sources do not give a book number for this narrative. Further fragments transmitted for this book show that it also included the outbreak of the Second Punic War (218–201 BC; F 77) and

F 76 Gell. *NA* 3.7

Historia ex annalibus sumpta de Q. Caedicio tribuno militum; verbaque ex Originibus M. Catonis apposita quibus Caedici virtutem cum Spartano Leonida aequiperat.—[1] pulcrum, dii boni, facinus Graecarumque facundiarum magniloquentia condignum M. Cato libris Originum de Q. Caedicio tribuno militum scriptum reliquit. [2] id profecto est ad hanc ferme sententiam. [3] imperator Poenus in terra Sicilia bello Kartaginiensi primo obviam Romano exercitu progreditur, colleis locosque idoneos prior occupat. [4] milites Romani, uti res nata est, in locum insinuant

F 75 Paradoxographus Palatinus

Cato says, in the *Foundations*, that in the Alps white hare-like animals are born, mice weighing eleven-pound, solid-hoofed pigs, shaggy dogs, and cattle without horns.[1]

[1] On assigning this fragment to Cato's *Origines* (and possibly to Book 2), see Mazzarino 1982–1987, 464–66.

BOOK 4 (F 76–86)

Hannibal's conduct after the victory in the Battle of Cannae (216 BC; F 78–79). A comment on the Carthaginian way of life (F 84) confirms that the conflict with Carthage was a topic. Several fragments point to descriptions of fighting between hostile armies (F 76, 81, 82). That in another passage (F 80) Cato seems to have distinguished what he would like to write about from what is covered by the pontifical tablets might suggest a second proem.

F 76 Gellius, *Attic Nights*

A story taken from the annals, about Q. Caedicius, a military tribune [258 BC (*MRR* 1:207)]; and words from the *Origines* of M. Cato appended, in which he likens Caedicius' valor to that of the Spartan Leonidas.—[1] A glorious deed, by the gods, and well worth the grandiloquence of accomplished Greek oratory, has been recorded and transmitted by M. Cato in the books of his *Origines*, concerning Q. Caedicius, a military tribune. [2] That [story] is undoubtedly roughly along the following lines: [3] in Sicily in the First Punic War the Carthaginian general advances

fraudi et perniciei obnoxium. [5] tribunus ad consulem venit, ostendit exitium de loci importunitate et hostium circumstantia maturum. [6] "censeo," inquit "si rem servare vis, faciundum ut quadringentos aliquos milites ad verrucam illam"—sic enim Cato locum editum asperumque appellat—"ire iubeas, eamque uti occupent imperes horterisque; hostes profecto ubi id viderint, fortissimus quisque et promptissimus ad occursandum pugnandumque in eos praevertentur unoque illo negotio sese alligabunt. atque illi omnes quadringenti procul dubio obtruncabuntur. [7] tunc interea occupatis in ea caede hostibus tempus exercitus ex hoc loco educendi habebis. alia nisi haec salutis via nulla est." [8] consul tribuno respondit consilium quidem † istuc quidem †[1] atque[2] providens sibi viderier; "sed istos" inquit "milites quadringentos ad eum locum in hostium cuneos quisnam erit qui ducat?" [9] "si alium" inquit tribunus "neminem repp<er>eris,[3] me licet ad hoc periculum utare; ego hanc tibi et rei publicae animam do." [10] consul tribuno gratias laudesque agit. [11] tribunus et quadringenti ad moriendum proficiscuntur. [12] hostes eorum audaciam demirantur; quorsum ire pergant in exspectando sunt. [13] sed ubi apparuit ad eandem[4] verrucam occupandam iter intendere, mittit adversum illos imperator Karthaginiensis peditatum equitatumque, quos in exercitu viros habuit strenuissimos. [14] Romani

[1] istuc quidem *vel* istuc quid *vel* istud *vel* istuc utile *vel* fidum *vel om. codd.*: fidelem istud *Madvig* [2] atque *vel* aeque *codd.* [3] repp<er>eris *Hertz*: repperis *vel* reperis *vel* reppериris *codd.* [4] ad eandem *vel* eandem *vel* eadem *vel* adem *codd.*: ad eam *Gronovius*

against the Roman army and is the first to take possession of the hills and strategic points. [4] As a result of this situation, the Roman soldiers make their way to a place exposed to danger and destruction. [5] The tribune comes to the consul [A. Atilius Caiatinus, cos. 258 BC] and points out that destruction is imminent from the unfavorable nature of the location and the encircling by the enemy. [6] "I recommend," he says, "that, if you wish to save the day, you should order some four hundred soldiers to advance to that wart"—for that is what Cato calls a high and rough place—"and command and urge them to occupy it. Undoubtedly, as soon as the enemy have seen that, all their bravest and keenest men will be intent upon attacking and fighting with them and will devote themselves to that one task. And beyond a doubt all those four hundred will be slaughtered. [7] Then, in the meantime, while the enemy is engaged in that slaughter, you will have time to lead the army out of this place. There is no other way to safety but this." [8] The consul replied to the tribune that this plan seemed good [?] and wise to him; "but who," he says, "will there be to lead those four hundred men to that place against the formations of the enemy?" [9] "If you should find no one else," the tribune says, "you may use me for that dangerous task. I give this life of mine to you and to the *res publica*." [10] The consul offers thanks and praise to the tribune. [11] The tribune and the four hundred march forth to death [cf. F 114]. [12] The enemy marvel at their audacity; they are waiting to see where they might proceed to go. [13] But when it became apparent that they were on their way to occupy that very wart, the Carthaginian commander sends against them the strongest men from infantry and cavalry whom he had in the army. [14]

milites circumveniuntur, circumventi repugnant; fit proelium diu anceps. [15] tandem[5] superat multitudo. [16] quadringenti omnes <in> tumulo[6] perfossi gladiis aut missilibus operti cadunt. [17] consul interibi, dum ea pugna <pugnatur>,[7] se in locos tutos atque editos subducit. [18] sed quod illi tribuno, duci militum quadringentorum, divinitus in eo proelio usu[8] venit, non iam nostris, sed ipsius Catonis verbis subiecimus: [19] "dii inmortales tribuno militum fortunam ex virtute eius dedere. nam ita evenit: cum saucius multifariam ibi factus esset, tamen volnus capiti[9] nullum evenit, eumque inter mortuos, defetigatum volneribus atque quod sanguen ei[10] defluxerat, cognovere. eum sustulere, isque convaluit, saepeque postilla operam rei publicae fortem atque strenuam praehibuit,[11] illoque facto, quod illos milites subduxit, exercitum ceterum servavit. sed idem bene factum quo in loco ponas nimium interest. Leonides Laco,[12] qui simile apud Thermopylas fecit, propter eius virtutes omnis Graecia gloriam atque gratiam praecipuam claritudinis inclitissimae decoravere monumentis: signis, statuis, elogiis, historiis aliisque rebus

[5] tandem *vel* tamen *codd.* [6] <in> tumulo *Holford-Strevens (post Cohee)*: cum uno *vel* tum una *codd.*: ad unum *Pricaeus* [7] pugna <pugnatur> *Bergk*: pugna *vel* puga *vel* <fit> pugna *vel* pugna <fit> *vel* pugnatur *codd.* [8] usu *de Buxis*: usus *codd.* [9] capiti *codd.*: capitale *Mommsen*: capitis *Pianezzola 1975 (for a justification of the transmitted text, with further references, see Calboli 1996, 17–22)* [10] ei *Lion*: eius *vel om. codd.* [11] praehibuit *Quicherat*: per(h)ibuit *vel* exhibuit *codd.* [12] Laco *Gronovius*: lacu *vel* lacn *vel* lacii *vel* laudatur *codd.*

The Roman soldiers are surrounded; surrounded, they fight back; a battle uncertain for a long time takes place. [15] Finally, the weight of numbers wins out. [16] All four hundred fall <on> the hill, run through with swords or overwhelmed with missiles. [17] The consul meanwhile, while that battle <is being fought>, withdraws to safe positions on high ground. [18] But what, divinely, happened to that tribune, the leader of the four hundred soldiers, in that battle, we have appended, no longer in our words, but in those of Cato himself: [19] "The immortal gods gave the military tribune good fortune on account of his valor. For it happened like this: although he had been wounded in many places there, still no injury to his head occurred, and they recognized him among the dead, exhausted from wounds and because some of his blood had flowed out. They lifted him up, and he recovered, and often afterward rendered brave and vigorous service to the *res publica*; and by that act, that he drew off those soldiers, he saved the rest of the army. But for the same good service, there is a great difference in the status that you accord [cf. Sall. *Cat.* 8]. As regards Leonidas, the Laconian, who performed something similar at Thermopylae, because of his deeds of valor, all Greece adorned his glory and outstanding esteem with memorials of the highest distinction; by pictures, statues, honorary inscriptions, histories, and other things they recognized that deed of his as most

gratissimum id eius factum habuere; at tribuno militum parva laus pro factis reddita,[13] qui idem fecerat atque rem servaverat." [20] hanc Q. Caedici tribuni virtutem M. Cato tali suo testimonio decoravit. [21] Claudius autem Quadrigarius Annali tertio non Caedicio nomen fuisse ait, sed Laberio.

[13] reddita *Watt*: relicta *codd.*

Cf. Non., p. 187.20–23 M. = 276 L.

F 77a Non., p. 100.9–13 M. = 142 L.

DUOETVICESIMO,[1] ita ut duodecimo. . . . Cato in IV Originum: "deinde duoetvicesimo anno post dimissum bellum, quod quattuor et viginti annos fuit, Carthaginienses sextum de foedere decessere."[2]

[1] duoetvicesimo (duodevicesimo) *codd. Gell. NA 5.4*: duodevicesimo *codd.*: duovicesimo *Iunius*

[2] decessere *codd. Gell. NA 10.1.10*: decernere *codd.*

Cf. Gell. *NA* 5.4.5: ‹* * *›[1] hic ita scripsit: "mortuus est anno duovicesimo; rex fuit annos XXI." ‹Cato in IIII Originum "deinde duovicesimo post dimissium bellum, quod quattuor et viginti annos fuit, Carthaginienses sextum de foedere decessere."›[2]

[1] *ante* hic *lac. statuit Thysius* [2] *post* XXI *lac. statuit Hosius; nam etiam Catonis mentio quaeritur*

---

[1] I.e., at the beginning of the Second Punic War (218–201 BC), marked by the siege of Saguntum in 219 BC, which can be described as happening in the twenty-second year after the end of the First Punic War (264–241 BC). For discussion of the dating, the potential identification of the preceding treaty breaks,

deserving of gratitude; but the tribune of the soldiers, who had done the same thing and had saved the day, received only modest praise relative to his deeds." [20] With such high personal testimony did M. Cato honor this valorous deed of Q. Caedicius the tribune. [21] But Claudius Quadrigarius [Q. Claudius Quadrigarius (*FRHist* 24 F 42)], in the third book of the *Annals*, says that his name was not Caedicius, but Laberius.[1]

[1] Allusions to and variations of this story are transmitted by a number of ancient authors (Liv. 22.60.11; *Epit.* 17; Plin. *HN* 22.11; [Aurel. Vict.] *Vir. ill.* 39; Flor. 1.18[2.2].12–14; Oros. 4.8.1–3; Ampel. *Lib. mem.* 20.5; Zonar. 8.12), assigning different names to the tribune (Frontin. *Str.* 1.5.15). The tribune's behavior recalls the Roman ritual of *devotio*, with the crucial difference that the individual willing to sacrifice themselves for the common good survives. On this passage, see Pianezzola 1975; Mariotti 1991 (on *verruca*); Calboli 1996; Courtney 1999, 74–78; Krebs 2006 (suggesting influence of Herodotus); von Albrecht 2012, 28–36 (on style).

F 77a Nonius Marcellus

duoetvicesimo ["in the twenty-second"], just like *duodecimo* ["in the twelfth"]. . . . Cato in [Book] 4 of the *Origines*: "then in the twenty-second year after the end of the war, which lasted for twenty-four years, the Carthaginians withdrew from the treaty for the sixth time."[1]

and the impact of the implied views on the Roman perception of history, see Nenci 1964; Hoyos 1987; 1998, 144–49, 220–21n4 (with further references). On such statements in the context of the concept of *Punica fides* in Rome (cf., e.g., Cic. *Off.* 1.38: *Poeni foedifragi*, "treaty-breaking Carthaginians"), see Waldherr 2000.

F 77b Gell. *NA* 10.1.10

in M. autem Catonis quarta Origine ita scriptum[1] est: "Carthaginienses sextum de foedere decessere." id verbum significat quinquies ante eos fecisse contra foedus et tum sextum.

[1] scriptum *vel* perscriptum *codd.*

F 78 Gell. *NA* 10.24.6–7

suppetit etiam Coelianum illud ex libro Historiarum secundo: "si vis mihi equitatum dare et ipse cum cetero exercitu me sequi, diequinti Romae in Capitolium curabo tibi cena sit cocta." [7] et historiam autem et verbum hoc sumpsit Coelius ex Origine <IIII>[1] M. Catonis, in qua ita scriptum est: "igitur dictatorem Carthaginiensium magister equitum monuit: 'mitte mecum Romam equitatum; diequinti in Capitolio tibi cena cocta erit.'"

[1] <IIII> *Holford-Strevens*: <IV> *Hertz*

Cf. Macrob. *Sat.* 1.4.26; Liv. 22.51.1–4; Val. Max. 9.5.ext.3; Flor. 1.22.19–21; Amm. Marc. 18.5.6; Sil. 10.375–79; Plut. *Fab.* 17.1–2; Zonar. 9.1.

F 79 Gell. *NA* 2.19.9

M. Cato in quarto[1] Originum: "deinde dictator iubet postridie magistrum equitum arcessi: 'mittam te si vis cum equitibus.' 'sero est,' inquit magister equitum: 'iam rescivere.'"

[1] quarto *codd.*: quinto *Nipperdey*

F 77b Gellius, *Attic Nights*

In the fourth book of M. Cato's *Origines*, however, it is written as follows: "The Carthaginians withdrew from the treaty for the sixth time [*sextum*]." This word [*sextum*] indicates that they had acted against a treaty five times before and then for the sixth time.

F 78 Gellius, *Attic Nights*

There comes to mind also the following passage of Coelius from the second book of the *Histories* [L. Coelius Antipater (*FRHist* 15 F 22)]: "If you are willing to give me the cavalry and to follow me yourself with the rest of the army, I will make sure that on the fifth day [*diequinti*] dinner will have been cooked for you on the Capitol at Rome." [7] But Coelius took both the story and this word [*diequinti*] from the ‹fourth› book of M. Cato's *Origines*, in which the following is written: "Then the master of the horse advised the dictator of the Carthaginians [Hannibal]: 'Send the cavalry with me to Rome; on the fifth day [*diequinti*] dinner will have been cooked for you on the Capitol.'"[1]

1 According to some ancient authors, this master of the horse was Maharbal. On this individual as well as the sources for his life and this incident, see Geus 1994, 194–96.

F 79 Gellius, *Attic Nights*

M. Cato [says] in the fourth [book] of the *Origines*: "Then, on the following day, the dictator orders the master of the horse to be summoned: 'I will send you, if you wish, with the cavalrymen.' 'It is too late,' the master of the horse says; 'they have already found out.'"

F 80 Gell. *NA* 2.28.4–7

sed de lunae solisque defectionibus, non magis[1] in eius rei causa reperienda sese exercuerunt. [5] quippe M. Cato, vir in cognoscendis rebus multi studii, incerte[2] tamen et incuriose super ea re opinatus est. [6] verba Catonis ex Originum quarto haec sunt: "non lubet scribere, quod in tabula apud pontificem maximum est, quotiens annona cara, quotiens lunae aut solis luminē caligo aut quid[3] obstiterit." [7] usque adeo parvi fecit rationes veras solis et lunae deficientium vel scire vel dicere.

1 magis *Watt (1994, 279)*: minus *codd.*: nimis *Ciacconius*: {non} minime *Laughton* 2 incerte *vel* incerta *codd.*
3 <aliud> quid *Teuffel (cf. Schröder 1990, 584–85)*

F 81 Gell. *NA* 5.21.17

<. . . idem Cato>[1] in IIII Originum eodem in loco ter hoc verbum posuit: "compluriens eorum milites mercennarii inter se multi alteri alteros <in castris>[2] occidere, compluriens multi simul ad hostis transfugere, compluriens in imperatorem impetum facere."

1 *corruptissime ab Nonio traditum hic inseruit Hertz*
2 <in castris> *Nonius Marcellus*: *om. codd. Gell.*

Non., p. 87.13–17 M. = 124 L.: CONPLURIENS, frequenter. Cato suasione in legem Popili [*Orat.* F 227]: "quod conpluries usu venit omni tempore anteventum esse rem publicam credimus."—idem Originum lib. IV: "conpluries eorum milites mercennarii inter se multi[1] alteri alteros in castris occidere."

1 multi *etiam codd. Gell.*: inulti *Mercerus*

F 80 Gellius, *Attic Nights*

But as regards eclipses of the moon and the sun, they [the ancient Romans] concerned themselves not particularly with discovering the causes of that phenomenon. [5] In fact, M. Cato, although a man of great eagerness in investigating things [*FRHist* 5 T 14d], nevertheless held an opinion on that matter without certain foundations and without careful consideration. [6] Cato's words from the fourth [book] of the *Origines* are as follows: "I do not feel like writing what is on the tablet with the chief pontiff: how often grain was dear, how often darkness or something obscured the light of the sun or the moon." [7] Of so little importance did he consider it to know or to tell the true causes of eclipses of the sun and the moon.[1]

[1] In the absence of any context it is difficult to determine how Cato's comment on the pontifical chronicles might have been intended: Cato could have characterized these records in a tendentious way in order to distinguish his own writing from them. At any rate the remark seems to be a statement on recording the occurrences of eclipses rather than on the question of whether or not their causes should be investigated (as suggested by the transmitting author Gellius).

F 81 Gellius, *Attic Nights*

<. . . The same Cato>, in [Book] 4 of the *Origines*, used this word [adverb *compluriens* (cf. *Orat*. F 227, 251)] three times in the same passage: "several times [*compluriens*] their mercenary soldiers have killed each other in large numbers <in the camp>; several times [*compluriens*] many have deserted at the same time to the enemy; several times [*compluriens*] they have made an attack on the general."

F 82 Gell. *NA* 11.1.6–7

cum autem usus et mos sermonum is sit ut ita et nunc loquamur, ut plerique veterum locuti sunt,[1] "multam dixit" et "multa dicta est," non esse ab re putavi notare quod M. Cato aliter dixit. nam in quarto Originum verba haec sunt: "imperator noster, si quis extra ordinem depugnatum ivit, ei multam facit." [7] potest autem videri consulta elegantia mutasse[2] verbum, cum in castris et in exercitu multa fieret, non in comitio nec ad populum diceretur.

[1] sunt *vel* sint *codd.* [2] mutasse *vel* vitasse *codd.*

F 83 Gell. *NA* 11.3.1–2

quod genus est praepositio "pro": [2] aliter enim dici videbam "pontifices pro conlegio decrevisse," aliter "quempiam testem introductum pro testimonio dixisse," aliter M. Catonem in Originum quarto "proelium factum depugnatumque pro castris" scripsisse et item in quinto "urbes insulasque omnis pro agro Illyrio esse,"[1] . . .

[1] esse *vel* <est> esse *codd.*

F 82 Gellius, *Attic Nights*

Furthermore, since there is that usage and custom in language so that even now we say in the same way as the majority of the ancients said, "he pronounced a fine" [*multam dixit*] and "a fine was pronounced" [*multa dicta est*], I have thought it not out of place to note that M. Cato spoke otherwise. For in the fourth [book] of the *Origines* are these words: "If anyone has gone to fight out of line, our commander imposes a fine [*multam facit*] upon them." [7] But it can be seen that he changed the word [*dicere* vs. *facere*] out of studied fastidiousness, since the fine was imposed in the camp and in the army, not pronounced in an assembly or before the People.

F 83 Gellius, *Attic Nights*

Of that kind [i.e., Latin particle with a variety of uses] is the preposition *pro*: [2] for I saw that it was used in one way in "the priests passed a decree in the name of [*pro*] the priestly college," in another way in "that some witness who had been called in said by way of [*pro*] testimony," that in yet another way M. Cato had written in the fourth [book] of the *Origines*: "the battle [was] joined and fought out in front of [*pro*] the camp," and likewise in the fifth [book] [F 94]: "that the cities and islands are all in front of [*pro*] the Illyrian land [on the Balkan peninsula]," . . .

F 84a Fest., p. 132.8–13 L.

MAPALIA casae Poenicae appellantur: in quibus quia nihil est secreti, solet solute viventibus obici id vocabulum. Cato Originum libro quarto: "mapalia[1] vocantur ubi habitant; ea quasi cohortes rotundae sunt."

[1] Originum libro quarto mapalia *vel* Originum libro IIII ait mapalia *codd.*: libro IIII Originum mapalia *ed. princ.*

F 84b Serv. auct. ad Verg. *Aen.* 1.421

"magalia quondam": Cato Originum quarto magalia aedificia quasi cohortes rotundas dicit. alii . . .

F 85 Prisc., *GL* II, p. 254.6–13

quidam tamen veterum et "hoc ossu" et "hoc ossum" proferebant . . . Cato tamen "os" protulit in IIII Originum: "si quis membrum rupit aut os fregit, talione proximus cognatus ulciscitur" . . .

F 86 Prisc., *GL* II, p. 382.3–4

Cato in IIII Originum: "duo exules lege publicati et execrati,"[1] passive, καταραθέντες.[2]

[1] lege publicati et execrati *Wagener*: lege publica . . . et execrari *Peter*: lege publica <condemnati> et execrati *Mommsen ap. Jordan*: lege publica execrari *Hertz* lege *vel* legem *codd.* publica *vel* publicam *vel* puplicam *codd.* execrari *vel* exsecrari *vel* et execrassi *vel* et execrari* *vel* et exsecrari *vel* et execrari *vel* execrati *codd.* [2] καταραθέντες *vel* καταραθῆντες *vel* καταραθῆτες *vel* καταπραθέντης *vel* καταραθήεναι *codd.*: καταραθῆναι *Hertz*

F 84a Festus

mapalia[1] is what Punic huts are called: since in those there is nothing segregated, it is customary to use this word as abuse against those living a loose life. Cato [says] in the fourth book of the *Origines*: "the places where they live are called *mapalia*; these are like round pens as it were."

[1] *mapalia / magalia / magaria* is generally interpreted as a Punic word denoting "huts" or "yurts" (cf. Sall. *Iug.* 18.8; for a linguistic discussion of the term, see Lippi 1984).

F 84b Servius Danielis, *Commentary on Virgil*

"*magalia* once": Cato says in the fourth [book] of the *Origines* that *magalia* are buildings almost like round pens. Others . . .

F 85 Priscian

Yet some of the ancients regularly used both *hoc ossu* and *hoc ossum* [unusual declension of *os*, "bone"] . . . yet Cato used *os* [standard form, acc. sg.] in [Book] 4 of the *Origines*: "if anyone has maimed a limb or broken a bone [*os*], the nearest relative [i.e., of the victim] takes revenge by retaliation in kind" [on these principles cf. *Twelve Tables* 8.2–3] . . .

F 86 Priscian

Cato in [Book] 4 of the *Origines*: "two exiles by law having been deprived of their property and cursed," in the passive [rather than deponent], "having been cursed" [in Greek].[1]

[1] The text of the fragment is uncertain; the translation follows one of the possible conjectures. On the potential contexts considered for this passage, see Ferrary 2001.

BOOK 5 (F 87–102)

*The fifth book is said (T 26) to include the Second Punic War (218–201 BC). What can be identified from the extant fragments is Cato's speech on behalf of the Rhodians of 167 BC (*Orat. *F 163–71), which he is known to have inserted*

F 87 Gell. *NA* 6.3.14

Cf. *Orat.* F 163

F 88 Gell. *NA* 6.3.16

Cf. *Orat.* F 164.

F 89 Gell. *NA* 6.3.26

Cf. *Orat.* F 165.

F 90 Gell. *NA* 6.3.36

Cf. *Orat.* F 166.

F 91 Gell. *NA* 6.3.37

Cf. *Orat.* F 167.

F 92 Gell. *NA* 6.3.38

Cf. *Orat.* F 168.

F 93 Gell. *NA* 6.3.48–50

Cf. *Orat.* F 169.

BOOK 5 (F 87–102)

into this book of his historiographical work (F 87–93), as well as mention of geographical features of the area of Illyria (F 94, 99), and descriptions of fighting (F 95, 96, 97).

F 87 Gellius, *Attic Nights*

Cf. *Orat.* F 163.

F 88 Gellius, *Attic Nights*

Cf. *Orat.* F 164.

F 89 Gellius, *Attic Nights*

Cf. *Orat.* F 165.

F 90 Gellius, *Attic Nights*

Cf. *Orat.* F 166.

F 91 Gellius, *Attic Nights*

Cf. *Orat.* F 167.

F 92 Gellius, *Attic Nights*

Cf. *Orat.* F 168.

F 93 Gellius, *Attic Nights*

Cf. *Orat.* F 169.

F 94 Gell. *NA* 11.3.1–2

Cf. F 83.

F 95 Gell. *NA* 15.9.4–5

"immo" inquam "potius nos et quam audaces et quam licentes sumus, qui 'frontem' inprobe indocteque non virili genere dicimus, cum et ratio proportionis, quae analogia appellatur, et veterum auctoritates non 'hanc,' sed 'hunc frontem' debere dici suadeant. [5] quippe M. Cato in quinto[1] Originum ita scripsit: 'postridie signis conlatis, aequo fronte, peditatu, equitibus[2] atque alis[3] cum hostium legionibus pugnavit.'[4] 'recto' quoque 'fronte' idem Cato in libro eodem dicit."

[1] quinto *vel* quinta *vel* primo *codd.*
[2] equitibus *del. Hertz* [3] alis *vel* aliis *codd.*
[4] pugnavit *vel* pugnavimus *codd.*

F 96 Gell. *NA* 15.9.4–5

Cf. F 95.

F 97 Gell. *NA* 15.13.5

M. Cato in quinta Origine "exercitum" inquit "suum pransum paratum cohortatum[1] eduxit foras atque instruxit."

[1] cohortatum *codd. rel.*: cohortavit *cod. unus*: et hortatum *cod. unus*

F 94 Gellius, *Attic Nights*

Cf. F 83.

F 95 Gellius, *Attic Nights*

"On the contrary," I ["GELLIUS," in conversation with a grammarian] said, "it is rather we who are as bold and as liberal as possible when, improperly and ignorantly, we use *frons* ['front'] not in the masculine gender, while both the principle of regularity, which is called analogy, and the authority of the ancients indicate that one ought to say, not *hanc frontem* [fem.], but *hunc frontem* [masc.]. [5] Indeed, M. Cato, in the fifth[1] [book] of the *Origines*, wrote as follows: 'On the following day, when battle was joined, with a level front line [*aequo fronte*: masc.] he fought with infantry, cavalry, and auxiliary troops against the enemy's legions.' Cato also says 'with a straight front line' [*recto fronte*: masc.; cf. *Orat.* F 47; *Op. cet.* F 24] in the same book [F 96]."

[1] One group of manuscripts assigns this fragment to Book 1, but this indication is not regarded as reliable.

F 96 Gellius, *Attic Nights*

Cf. F 95.

F 97 Gellius, *Attic Nights*

M. Cato says in the fifth book of the *Origines*: "He led forth his army, fed, prepared, and exhorted [used in passive sense], and drew it up in order of battle."

F 98 Fest., p. 268.25–27 L.

PILATES[1] lapidis genus, cuius meminit[2] Cato Originum lib. V: "lapis candidior quam pela{s}tes."[3]

[1] Pellates (Φελλάτης) *Leutsch* [2] m. (*sic*) *cod.* (*i.e.* meminit *vel* Marcus) [3] quam pilates *Epit.*

Cf. Paul. *Fest.*, p. 273.5–6 L.: PILATES genus lapidis. Cato: "lapis candidior quam pilates."

F 99 Non., p. 151.6–8 M. = 221 L.

PISCULENTUM positum piscosum, ut pulverulentum. Cato Originum lib. V: "origine[1] fluvium Naronem magnum, pulchrum, pisculentum."—et lib. VII: . . . .

[1] *del. Mercier*

F 100 Non., p. 363.1–13 M. = 576 L.

PROTELARE est percutere, perturbare. . . . Cato Originum lib. V: "sed protelo trini boves unum aratrum ducent."

F 98 Festus

pilates, a kind of stone [probably a kind of pumice], which Cato mentions in Book 5 of the *Origines*. "a stone brighter than *pilates*."

F 99 Nonius Marcellus

pisculentum is used for "rich in fish," like *pulverulentum* ["rich in dust"]. Cato [says] in Book 5 of the *Origines*: "from the source[1] the river Naro [mod. Neretva, in the eastern part of the Adriatic basin], large, beautiful, rich in fish [acc.]."—And in Book 7: . . . [F 111].

[1] The first word of the quotation (*origine*) is often deleted as a scribal error, interpreted as repeating the indication of the work from which the excerpt is taken; if the word is correct and part of the fragment, it presumably indicates that the characteristics of the river apply from its source.

F 100 Nonius Marcellus

protelare ["drive before one, beat back, beat off"] is "to strike," "to upset."[1] . . . Cato [says] in Book 5 of the *Origines*: "but in a tandem arrangement of draft animals [*protelum*] three oxen each will pull one plow."

[1] The examples given for this lemma include not only uses of the verb but also instances of the noun *protelum* ("tandem arrangement of draft animals").

F 101 Prisc., *GL* II, p. 475.20–25

frequenter tamen antiquissimi neutro participio futuri addebant "esse" et infinitum futuri significabant, "oraturum esse" pro "oratum ire" dicentes et "facturum esse" pro "factum ire." Cato in V Originum: "illi polliciti sese facturum omnia," per ellipsin "esse" pro "factum ire," quod Graeci dicunt ποιήσειν, quod est infinitum futuri.

F 102 Prisc., *GL* II, p. 510.16–23

. . . "nosco novi notum"—similiter ex eo composita: "ignosco ignovi ignotum." . . . unde et participium futuri "ignoturus." . . . Cato in V Originum: "quod eorum nemo quisquam quicquam mihi ignoturus est"; quidam tamen contra regulam a praesenti tempore hoc derivatum protulerunt, "ignosco ignosciturum."

BOOK 6 (F 103)

A single fragment explicitly attributed to Book 6 survives, and this is generic. (On its quotation in a discussion on "translation," see Gamberale 1969, 167–68.) Therefore, it

F 101 Priscian

Yet, the very early [writers] frequently added *esse* to the neuter future participle and [thus] indicated the future infinitive, saying *oraturum esse* instead of *oratum ire* ["to be going to say"] and *facturum esse* instead of *factum ire* ["to be going to do"]. Cato [says] in [Book] 5 of the *Origines*: "those promised that they would do everything," with an ellipsis of *esse* [only *facturum*], instead of *factum ire*, what the Greeks express as "to be going to do" [in Greek], which is the future infinitive.

F 102 Priscian

. . . *nosco, novi, notum* ["I get to know," "I know," "known"] —similarly the compounds formed from that: "*ignosco, ignovi, ignotum* ["I forgive," "I have forgiven," "forgiven"]. . . . whence also the future participle *ignoturus* ["about to forgive"]. . . . Cato [says] in [Book] 5 of the *Origines*: "that / because no one of them is going to forgive me anything"; some, however, have used against the rule this [form of the future participle] derived from the present tense, *ignosco, ignosciturum*.

BOOK 6 (F 103)

is impossible to define the historical period covered by this book. It is usually assumed that the two final books of the Origines *(6 and 7) describe contemporary history.*

F 103 Gell. *NA* 20.5.13

hoc ego verbum *ξυνετοὶ γάρ εἰσιν* uno itidem verbo[1] dicere aliud non repperi quam est scriptum a M. Catone in sexta Origine: "itaque ego" inquit "cognobiliorem cognitionem esse arbitror."

[1] verbo *vel* versu *codd.*

BOOK 7 (F 104–12)

The seventh book must cover the most recent history described in the Origines. *It included Cato's speech against Ser. Sulpicius Galba concerning the latter's treatment of the Lusitanians in 149 BC (the year of his death), which*

F 104 Gell. *NA* 13.25.15

Cf. *Orat.* F 196.

F 105 Gell. *NA* 1.12.17

Cf. *Orat.* F 197.

F 106a Fronto, *Ad M. Caes.* 3.21.4 (p. 52.1–4 van den Hout)

Cf. *Orat.* F 199.

F 106b Quint. *Inst.* 2.15.8

Cf. *Orat.* F 198C.

F 103 Gellius, *Attic Nights*

To express this word ξυνετοὶ γάρ εἰσιν ["for they are intelligible," in a letter by Aristotle] by a single word in the same way, I have found nothing other than what is written by M. Cato in the sixth book of the *Origines*: "therefore," he says, "I believe the idea [*cognitio*] to be more intelligible [*cognobilior*]."

BOOK 7 (F 104–12)

Cato is known to have inserted in the Origines *(F 104–7; cf. T 34;* Orat. *F 196–99A). In addition, mention of geographical features in the Iberian peninsula (F 111) and a comment on women's ornaments (F 109) can be discerned.*

F 104 Gellius, *Attic Nights*

Cf. *Orat.* F 196.

F 105 Gellius, *Attic Nights*

Cf. *Orat.* F 197.

F 106a Fronto, *Correspondence*

Cf. *Orat.* F 199.

F 106b Quintilian, *The Orator's Education*

Cf. *Orat.* F 198C.

F 106c Val. Max. 8.1.absol.2

Cf. *Orat.* F 198B [*FRHist* 5 T 13c].

F 107a Cic. *Brut.* 89–90

Cf. *Orat.* F 198 [*FRHist* 5 T 13a].

F 107b Cic. *De or.* 1.227–28

Cf. *Orat.* F 198A [*FRHist* 5 T 13b].

F 108 Fest., p. 128.3–8 L.

MULLEOS genus calceorum aiunt esse; quibus reges Albanorum primi, deinde patricii sunt usi. M. Cato Originum lib. VII: "qui magistratum curulem cepisset calceos mulleos † allitaciniatos †,[1] ceteri perones."[2]

[1] allitaciniatos *vel* alita ciniatos *codd.*: allutaciniatos *ed. princ.*: aluta laciniatos *Mueller*: aluta cinctos *Haupt*: aluta vinctos *Mommsen* [2] perones *edd.*: peronei *vel* pernei *codd.*

F 109 Fest., p. 320.17–23 L.

RUSCUM est, ut ait Verrius, amplius paullo herba, et exilius[1] virgultis fruticibusque,[2] non dissimile iunco; cuius coloris rebus uti mulieres solitas[3] commemorat Cato Originum lib. VII: "mulieres opertae[4] auro purpuraque;

[1] exilius *Ursinus*: exirius *cod.* [2] fruticibusque *Ursinus*: fructibusque *cod.* [3] solitas *edd.*: solitae *cod.*
[4] opertas *Scaliger*

F 106c Valerius Maximus, *Memorable Doings and Sayings*

Cf. *Orat.* F 198B [*FRHist* 5 T 13c].

F 107a Cicero, *Brutus*

Cf. *Orat.* F 198 [*FRHist* 5 T 13a].

F 107b Cicero, *On the Orator*

Cf. *Orat.* F 198A [*FRHist* 5 T 13b].

F 108 Festus

mullei ["red high-soled shoes"][1] are a type of shoe, they say; these were used first by the Alban kings, then by the patricians. M. Cato [says] in Book 7 of the *Origines*: "someone who had obtained a curule magistracy [wore] red high-soled shoes . . . [perhaps: fastened by a leather strap?], others thick boots."

[1] On this kind of shoe, see Isid. *Orig.* 19.34.10; on the form of these types of shoes and their potential to mark social and political status in Rome, see Goette 1988; Ryan 1998, 55–59.

F 109 Festus

ruscum ["butcher's broom"] is, as Verrius [M. Verrius Flaccus] says, slightly fuller than a grassy plant and thinner than brushwood and shrubs, not dissimilar to a rush; that women were accustomed to use things of its color is mentioned by Cato in Book 7 of the *Origines*: "women covered

arsinea,[5] rete, diadema, coronas aureas, ruscea † facile †,[6] galbeos, lineas,[7] pelles, redimicula."

[5] arsinea *Scaliger*: ars inheret *cod.* [6] rusceas fascias *Mueller* [7] galbas lineos *Jordan*: galbeas lineas *Mueller*

F 110 Fest., p. 374.11–17 L.

SOCORDI>AM quidam <pro ignavia posuerunt . . .>[1] M. Cato pro <stultitia posuit Originum lib.>[2] VII, cum ait: . . . mensam ti . . . ne quid neg . . . retur[3]

[1] *suppl. Epit.* [2] *suppl. Epit.* [3] <ob im>mensam ti<miditatem et socordiam causa erat> ne quid neg<oti publici . . . gere>retur *Mueller (post Ursinum)*

Cf. Paul. *Fest.*, p. 375.1–2 L.: socordiam quidam pro ignavia posuerunt; Cato pro stultitia posuit.

F 111 Non., p. 151.6–9 M. = 221 L.

PISCULENTUM positum piscosum, ut pulverulentum. Cato Originum lib. V: . . . .—et lib. VII: "fluvium Hiberum; is oritur ex Cantabris,[1] magnus atque pulcher, pisculentus."

[1] Cantabris *Iunius*: catinatis *codd.*

F 112 Charis., *GL* I, p. 93.18–21 = p. 119.1–5 B.

alia autem singulariter quidem per omnes casus declinantur, sed pluraliter nominativo tantum et accusativo et vocativo, ut maria rura aera iura; quamvis Cato Originum VII genetivo casu dixerit "iurum legumque cultores," et . . .

Cf. Charis., *GL* I, p. 135.7–9 = p. 171.24–27 B.

with gold and purple; headdresses, hairnet, ornamental headband, golden wreaths, ribbons in the color of the butcher's broom [?], armbands, necklaces, furs, hairbands."

F 110 Festus

Some <have used *socordia* ["sluggishness"] instead of *ignavia* ["idleness"] . . .> M. Cato <used it> instead of <*stultitia* ["stupidity"] in Book> 7 <of the *Origines*>, when he says:[1] . . . [?].

[1] The quotation of the passage in which Cato used *socordia* in the sense of *stultitia* has mostly been lost.

F 111 Nonius Marcellus

pisculentum is used for "rich in fish," like *pulverulentum* ["rich in dust"]. Cato [says] in Book 5 of the *Origines*: . . . [F 99].—And in Book 7: "the river Hiberus [mod. Ebro (cf. Plin. *HN* 3.21)]; it originates among the Cantabrians [people in northern Iberia], large and beautiful, rich in fish."

F 112 Charisius

Yet other [words] are declined in all cases in the singular, but in the plural only in the nominative, accusative, and vocative, like *maria* ["seas"], *rura* ["country estates"], *aera* ["copper coins"], *iura* ["legal codes"]; even though Cato said in [Book] 7 of the *Origines*, with a genitive case "observers of legal codes and laws [gen. pl.]," and . . .

UNCERTAIN BOOKS (F 113–28)

These fragments are assigned to the Origines *in the transmission, but not to a particular book, and are too vague for potential attributions to specific books or historical contexts. Some of them are just individual words; others*

F 113a Cic. *Tusc.* 4.3

nam cum <et> carminibus soliti illi esse dicantur {et}[1] praecepta quaedam occultius tradere et mentes suas a cogitationum intentione cantu fidibusque ad tranquillitatem traducere, gravissumus auctor in Originibus dixit Cato morem apud maiores hunc epularum fuisse, ut deinceps qui accubarent canerent ad tibiam clarorum virorum laudes atque virtutes; ex quo perspicuum est et cantus tum fuisse descriptos[2] vocum sonis et carmina.

[1] et *transp. Giusta*

[2] descriptos *vel* rescriptos *codd.*: discriptos *Seyffert*: praescriptis *Bouhier*

UNCERTAIN BOOKS (F 113–28)

point to metaliterary comments and to descriptions of geographical features, population developments, customs, and military activities.

F 113a Cicero, *Tusculan Disputations*

For, as they are said to have had the habit <both> to convey {both} certain instructions more guardedly in verse and to withdraw their minds from the exertion of their thoughts to calmness by song and the music of the lyre, Cato, a writer of the greatest authority, said in the *Origines* that there had been this custom at banquets among the ancestors, that those who reclined at the table would sing in turn, to the accompaniment of the flute, of the praiseworthy and glorious deeds of famous men.[1] From this it is clear that both songs for the sounds of voices and poems had then been written down.

[1] Churchill (1995) suggests that the statement in Cato, alluded to several times by Cicero (cf. F 113c), comes from the prologue of the *Origines* and forms part of the justification for this work (thus also Cugusi 1994, 269–70; Cugusi and Sblendorio Cugusi 2001, 2:290–91). On the practice mentioned, see also Cic. *De or.* 3.97; Varro, *Vit. pop. Rom.* F 84 Riposati (ap. Non., p. 77.2–5 M. = pp. 107–8 L.); Val. Max. 2.1.10; Quint. *Inst.* 1.10.20; Hor. *Carm.* 4.15.25–32.

F 113b Cic. *Tusc.* 1.3

Cf. *Orat.* F 149.

F 113c Cic. *Brut.* 75

"recte," inquam [Cicero], "Brute, intellegis. atque utinam exstarent illa carmina, quae multis saeclis ante suam aetatem in epulis esse cantitata a singulis convivis de clarorum virorum laudibus in Originibus scriptum reliquit Cato! . . . "

F 114a Cic. *Sen.* 74–75

["Cato":] moriendum enim certe est, et incertum an hoc ipso die: mortem igitur omnibus horis impendentem timens, qui poterit animo consistere? [75] de qua non ita longa disputatione opus esse videtur, cum recorder non . . . sed legiones nostras, quod scripsi in Originibus, in eum locum saepe profectas alacri animo et erecto, unde se redituras numquam arbitrarentur.

F 114b Cic. *Tusc.* 1.101

[M.:] talis innumerabilis nostra civitas tulit. sed quid duces et principes nominem, cum legiones scribat Cato saepe alacris in eum locum profectas unde redituras se non arbitrarentur?

F 113b Cicero, *Tusculan Disputations*

Cf. *Orat.* F 149.

F 113c Cicero, *Brutus*

"You understand this correctly, Brutus," I [CICERO] said. "And if only there were still extant those songs, of which Cato in the *Origines* has recorded in writing that many generations before his time they were regularly sung by individual guests at banquets on the praiseworthy deeds of famous men! . . . "

F 114a Cicero, *On Old Age*

["CATO":] For one certainly has to die, and it is uncertain whether [it will happen] on this very day: therefore, how will anyone be able to be steadfast in their mind if they are fearing death hanging over them at all hours? [75] About that [issue] such a long discussion does not seem to be necessary, when I recall, not . . . , but that our legions, as I have written in the *Origines*, have often set out with cheerful and confident spirit to a place whence they thought they would never return.

F 114b Cicero, *Tusculan Disputations*

[M.:] Such [virtuous men] our community has produced in countless numbers. But why should I name commanders and leaders, when Cato writes that legions often set out cheerfully to a place whence they thought they would not return?

F 115 Plin. *HN* 8.11

Cf. T 43.

F 116 Gell. *NA* 2.22.28–29

sed quod ait ventum qui ex terra Gallia flaret, "Circium" appellari, M. Cato in libris Originum eum ventum "Cercium" dicit, non "Circium." [29] nam cum de Hispanis scriberet qui citra Hiberum colunt, verba haec posuit: "set in his regionibus ferrariae, argentifodinae pulcherrimae, mons ex sale mero magnus; quantum demas, tantum adcrescit.[1] ventus Cercius, cum loquare, buccam implet, armatum hominem, plaustrum oneratum percellit."

[1] adcrescit *vel* adorescit *vel* adorrescit *codd.*

Cf. Apul. *Mund.* 14.

F 117 Gell. *NA* 18.12.1, 7

id quoque habitum est in oratione {facienda}[1] elegantiae genus, ut pro verbis habentibus patiendi figuram agentia ponerent ac deinde haec vice inter sese mutua verterent. [2] . . . [7] M. Cato in Originibus: "eodem convenae[2] conplures ex agro accessitavere. eo res eorum auxit."

[1] *del. Rutgers* [2] conven(a)e *vel* convene ut *vel* covenit *vel* covenid *vel* convenere *codd.*

F 115 Pliny the Elder, *Natural History*

Cf. T 43.

F 116 Gellius, *Attic Nights*

But as to his [Favorinus'] statement that the wind that blows from Gaul is called *Circius*, M. Cato, in the books of the *Origines*, calls that wind *Cercius*, not *Circius* [north-northwesterly wind, named after Cape Circe]. [29] For when he was writing about the Iberians who live on this side of the Hiberus [mod. river Ebro], he set down these words: "But in these regions are the finest iron and silver mines, and a large mountain of pure salt; as much as you might take from it, it grows back again to the same extent. The *Cercius* wind, when you speak, fills your cheek; it overturns an armed person or a loaded cart [cf. Sen. *Q Nat.* 5.17.5; Plin. *HN* 2.121]."

F 117 Gellius, *Attic Nights*

This also was regarded as a type of elegance in {composing} discourse, that they put, in place of verbs having a passive form, the actives and then in turn substituted these for each other. [2] . . . [7] M. Cato [says] in the *Origines*: "many newcomers kept arriving from the country at the same place. Thereby their community enlarged [rather than 'was enlarged']."

F 118 Non., p. 229.8–9 M. = 339 L.

TRIBUTUM neutro. masculino Cato Originum libris: "ne praedia in lubricum derigerentur,[1] cum tributus exigeretur."

[1] in ludibrium diriberentur *Mueller*

F 119a Charis., *GL* I, p. 101.14–16 = p. 128.23–25 B.

hinc muliebre ministerium cinerarius dicitur. nam Cato in Originibus "mulieres" inquit "nostrae capillum cinere unguitabant,[1] ut rutilus esset crinis."[2]

[1] iungitabant f. inungitabant *Cauchii ex deperdito cod. excerpta*: inungitabant *Putschen* [2] et rutilus esse cinis *cod., corr. cod. descr.*: et[or] utilius esse crinis *Cauchii ex deperdito cod. excerpta*

F 119b Serv. et Serv. auct. Verg. ad *Aen.* 4.698

"flavum crinem": matronis numquam flava coma dabatur, sed nigra: unde Iuvenalis [6.120] "et nigro flavum crinem abscondente galero." huic ergo dat quasi turpi: vel quia[1] in Catone legitur de matronarum crinibus: "flavo cinere unctitabant ut rutili[2] essent."

[1] turpi flavum vel quia *unus cod.*: huic quasi turpi dat crinem flavum vel quia in catone legitur . . . essent *unus cod. in marg.*: turpi. aut flavum quia *Daniel*

[2] rutili *Thilo*: rutuli *vel* rutilae *codd.*

F 118 Nonius Marcellus

tributum ["levy, tribute"], in the neuter. [It is used] in the masculine [by] Cato in the books of the *Origines*: "that estates would not be directed onto a slippery slope [to financial ruin] when tribute [*tributus*] was exacted."

F 119a Charisius

Hence an attendant for women is called hairdresser [*cinerarius*, lit. "ashman"]. For Cato says in the *Origines*: "our women were in the habit of treating their hair with ash [*cinis*, *cineris*] so that the hair would be red."

F 119b Servius and Servius Danielis, *Commentary on Virgil*

"blond hair": Blond hair was never attributed to married women, but rather black: hence Juvenal [6.120] [says]: "and with a black hat hiding the blond hair." Thus, he [Virgil] gives [it] to her [Dido] as if dishonorable, or because one reads in Cato about the hair of married women: "they used to treat it with yellow ash so that it would be red."

F 120 Charis., *GL* I, p. 124.1–3 = p. 158.1–4 B.

biber τό πίειν G. Fannius annalium VIII: "domina eius, ubi ad villam venerat, iubebat biber dari"; Cato quoque Originum *[1] sed et Titinius in Prilia . . .

[1] *lac. statuit Keil*

F 121 Charis., *GL* I, p. 131.16–18 = p. 167.15–18 B.

glis Varro in Admirandis: "in silva mea est glis nullus." sed et Cato in Originibus ita est locutus. quidam enim hic ‹glir huius›[1] gliris putant dici.

[1] *add. Keil ex Charis.*

Cf. Charis., *GL* I, p. 90.3–4 = p. 113.20–22 B.: gliris nominativus est hic glis, non glir, ut quidam volunt. nam Varro in Admirandis: ait "in silva mea glis nullus," et Cato in Originibus.

F 122 Serv. auct. ad Verg. *G.* 1.75

"tristisque lupini": . . . nonnulli proprie calamos lupinorum alas dici putant, ut Aelius[1] alae ex lupino s*liis,[2] Cato in Originibus alae ex[3] lup* leg*[4] de lingua Latina alam culmum fabae dic*[5]

[1] ut Aelius *Daniel, sed potest legi* caelius *(Thilo)*

[2] *post* s *XII fere litterae evanuerunt.* surculi sine foliis *Daniel*

[3] ex *Daniel, sed dubitari potest utrum* ex *an* et *scriptum fuerit (Thilo)* [4] *post* lup *quattuor, post* leg *decem litterae deletae sunt*: lupino lugium . . . tamen Varro *Daniel. scribendum videtur* alae ex lupino legumine. Varro. *(*lupino legumine *C. L. Rothii est coniectura) (Thilo)* [5] *post* dic *septem fere litterae interierunt*: dicere . . . *Daniel*: dicit . . . *Masvicius*: *fort.* dici docet *Thilo*

F 120 Charisius

biber, "to drink" [in Greek; shortened form of infinitive in Latin]: G. Fannius [says] in [Book] 8 of the *Annals* [C. Fannius (*FRHist* 12 F 2)]: "his mistress, as soon as she had come to the villa, ordered that she be given something to drink"; Cato too in the *Origines* *,[1] but also Titinius in *Prilia* [Tit. *Tog*. 78 R.[3]] . . .

[1] The quotation from Cato's *Origines* that must have included a form of the verb *biber(e)* seems to have dropped out.

F 121 Charisius

glis ["dormouse"]: [M. Terentius] Varro [uses it] in *Admiranda* [Logist. F 57 Bolisani]: "in my wood there is no dormouse." But also Cato in the *Origines* spoke thus [i.e., used the form *glis*].[1] For some believe that one says *hic* <*glir, huius*> *gliris* [nom., gen.; different form of nom.].

[1] On this note and its potential point of reference in Cato's *Origines*, see Mazzarino 1982–1987, 461–64.

F 122 Servius and Servius Danielis, *Commentary on Virgil*

"and of the bitter lupin": . . . Some believe that the shoots of lupins are properly called wings, as Aelius [L. Aelius Stilo (F 5 *GRF*)] [says]: "wings from the lupin . . ." [?], Cato in the *Origines*:[1] "wings from the lupin . . ." [?] about the Latin language the wing the stem of the bean plant . . . [?]

[1] Like other parts of the passage, the transmission of the quotation from Cato is corrupt, so that its content and extent cannot be determined precisely.

F 123 Serv. ad Verg. *Aen.* 1.95

"quis": et quis et quibus significat: secundum artem enim sic dicimus. ab eo enim quod est "a qui" in "bus" mittit, ab eo quod est "a quo" in "is" mittit, sed a tertia declinatione in usu sunt dativus et ablativus plurales, licet antiqui omnibus usi sint casibus. denique Cato in Originibus ait "si ques sunt populi." et declinavit "ques quium," ut "puppes puppium."

F 124 Serv. et Serv. auct. ad Verg. *Aen.* 3.637

"Argolici clipei aut Phoebeae lampadis instar": unum magnitudinis est, quia Graecorum clipei rotundi, ut Cato Originum ait; aliud splendoris.

F 125 Serv. auct. ad Verg. *Aen.* 10.541

"immolat": . . . sane immolari proprie dicuntur hostiae, non cum caeduntur, sed cum accipiunt molam salsam: Cato in Originibus ita ait Lavini boves immolatos,[1] prius quam caederentur profugisse in † siciliam.[2]

[1] immolatos *Masvicius*: immolatus *cod.*
[2] in silvam *Brissonius*

F 123 Servius, *Commentary on Virgil*

"for/by whom": It denotes both *quis* and *quibus* [different forms of dat. and abl. pl.]: for according to the grammatical system we say so. For what is derived from *a qui* ends in *-bus*, what is from *a quo* ends in *-is*, but from the third declension the dative and ablative plural are in use [i.e., *quibus*], even though the ancients used all cases. Finally, Cato in the *Origines* says "if there are any [*ques*] peoples" [cf. F 1, 32]. And he declined *ques*, *quium* [nom. and gen. pl., third decl.], like *puppes*, *puppium* ["stern of a boat, ship"; nom. and gen. pl.].

F 124 Servius and Servius Danielis, *Commentary on Virgil*

"like the Argolic shield or the Phoebean light" [of the Cyclops' eye]: one [likeness] is of size, because the shields of the Greeks are round, as Cato says in the *Origines*; the other [likeness is] of splendor.

F 125 Servius Danielis, *Commentary on Virgil*

"he immolates": . . . in fact sacrificial victims are properly said to be immolated [*immolari*], not when they are killed, but when they receive the sacrificial salted grain [*mola salsa*]: Cato in the *Origines* says as follows: that at Lavinium [town in Latium] immolated cattle fled into the forest [?] before they could be killed.

F 126 SHA (Flav. Vopisc.), 28 *Prob.* 1.1

certum est, quod Sallustius Crispus quo<d>que[1] Marcus Cato et Gellius historici sententiae modo in litteras rettulerunt, omnes omnium virtutes tantas esse qua<n>tas[2] videri eas voluerint eorum ingenia, qui unius cuius<que>[3] facta descripserint.

1 quoq; *cod.*[1] 2 quãtas *cod. corr.*: euatas *cod.*[1]
3 cuiusque *codd. rec.*: cuius *cod.*

F 127 Macrob. *Sat.* 1.14.5

hinc et Ateius Capito annum a circuitu temporis putat dictum, quia veteres "an" pro "circum" ponere solebant, ut Cato in Originibus: "arator[1] an terminum," id est circum terminum, et "ambire" dicitur pro "circumire."

1 arator *Jan*: oratorum *codd.*: arato <agro>rum *Schröder*

F 128 Prisc., *GL* II, p. 293.5–12

inveniuntur tamen quaedam pauca feminini generis, quae et masculinis transfigurantur non habentibus neutra, quae et animalium sunt demonstrativa, naturaliter divisum genus habentia, quae differentiae causa ablativo singulari "bus" assumentia faciunt dativum et ablativum pluralem, quod nulla alia habet declinatio in "bus" terminans supra

F 126 *Historia Augusta* (Flavius Vopiscus), *Life of Probus*

It is certain, as Sallustius Crispus [C. Sallustius Crispus (*ORF*^{4} 152); cf. Sall. *Cat.* 8.2–3] and as Marcus Cato and Gellius [Cn. Gellius (*FRHist* 14 F 31)], the historiographers,[1] have recorded in their writings in the style of a maxim, that all the virtues of all individuals are as great as the talents of those who have described the deeds of each individual wanted them to appear.

[1] Since Cato is defined as a historiographer, the passage has been attributed to the *Origines*, although the work referred to is not identified.

F 127 Macrobius, *Saturnalia*

Hence Ateius Capito [C. Ateius Capito (F 15 Strzelecki)] also thinks that the year [*annus*] is named after a temporal cycle, because the ancients were accustomed to use *an* instead of *circum* ["around"], as Cato in the *Origines*: "the plowman *an terminum* ["around the boundary marker"], that is, *circum terminum*, and *ambire* is used instead of *circumire* ["to go around"].[1]

[1] On the various proposed readings and interpretations of this fragment, see Neuhauser 1958, 140–41; Schröder 1990, 589–90.

F 128 Priscian

Yet a small number of certain [words] of feminine gender are found which are developed from masculine [words] that do not have neuter forms, which are also indicators of living beings, naturally having a divided gender, which, for the sake of distinguishing, form the dative and ablative plural adding *-bus* to the ablative singular, since no other declension has the above-mentioned cases ending in *-bus*,

dictos casus, ut a longam in eis paenultimam habeat, ut "his natabus," "filiabus," "deabus," "equabus," "mulabus," "libertabus," "asinabus." M. Cato in Originibus: "dotes filiabus suis non dant."

POSSIBLE FRAGMENTS (F 129–56)

These fragments have been transmitted for Cato but are not assigned to a specific work in the sources. Because of their content, they might come from the Origines *(as suggested in* FRHist*). At least some of them could equally belong to other works (alternative potential attributions*

F 129 Cic. *Verr.* 2.2.5

itaque ad omnis res sic illa provincia semper usi sumus ut, quicquid ex sese posset efferre, id non apud eos nasci, sed domi nostrae conditum putaremus. quando illa frumentum quod deberet non ad diem dedit? quando id quod opus esse putaret non ultro pollicita est? quando id quod imperaretur recusavit? itaque ille M. Cato sapiens cellam penariam rei publicae nostrae, nutricem plebis Romanae Siciliam nominabat. nos vero experti sumus Italico maximo difficillimoque bello Siciliam nobis non pro penaria cella, sed pro aerario illo maiorum vetere ac referto fuisse; nam sine ullo sumptu nostro, coriis, tunicis, frumentoque suppeditando, maximos exercitus nostros vestivit, aluit, armavit.

so as to have a long *a* in them as the penultimate [syllable], like *natabus* ["to female children"], *filiabus* ["to daughters"], *deabus* ["to goddesses"], *equabus* ["to mares"], *mulabus* ["to she-mules"], *libertabus* ["to freedwomen"], *asinabus* ["to she-asses"]. M. Cato in the *Origines*: "they do not give dowries to their daughters [*filiabus*]."

POSSIBLE FRAGMENTS (F 129–56)

are indicated in notes where appropriate). Thus, if the information in the transmission is taken as the basis, these pieces would have to be assigned to the category of Incertorum operum reliquiae *(see Introduction to* Incertorum operum reliquiae*).*

F 129 Cicero, *Verrine Orations*

Therefore, for all purposes, we have always treated that province [Sicily] in such a way that we regarded whatever it could produce from its own resources not as growing among them, but as kept in store in our home. When has it not provided punctually the grain that it owed? When has it not spontaneously promised what it believed was needed? When has it refused [to supply] what was demanded? Therefore, that famous M. Cato, the "Wise," called Sicily the granary of our *res publica*, the nurse of the Roman People [*Op. cet.* F 41]. Indeed, we have found out, in the most serious and most critical Italic war [Social War, 91–88 BC], that for us Sicily was not like a granary, but like that ancient and well-filled state treasury of the ancestors; for, without any cost to us, it supplied us with hides, shirts, and grain, to clothe, feed, and equip our very large armies.

F 130a Cic. *Rep.* 1.27

[Scipio:] . . . quam est hic fortunatus putandus . . . ; qui denique ut Africanum avum meum scribit Cato solitum esse dicere, possit idem de se praedicare, numquam se plus agere quam nihil cum ageret, numquam minus solum esse quam cum solus esset.

F 130b Cic. *Off.* 3.1

P. Scipionem, Marce fili, eum qui primus Africanus appellatus est, dicere solitum scripsit Cato, qui fuit eius fere aequalis, numquam se minus otiosum esse quam cum otiosus, nec minus solum quam cum solus esset. magnifica vero vox et magno viro ac sapiente digna!

Cf. Non., p. 236.1–3 M. = 352 L.; Plut. *Mor.* 196B (*Apophth. reg. et imp.*, *Scipio the Elder* 1); Ambros. *Off. ministr.* 3.2; *Ep.* 49.1; Hieron. *Adv. Iovin.* 1.47; Grillius, ad Cic. *Inv. rhet.* 1.1 (pp. 10.43–11.1 Jakobi).

F 131 Cic. *Rep.* 2.1–3

hic ‹. . . cupidi›tate[1] audiendi, ingressus est sic loqui Scipio: Catonis hoc senis est . . . [2] is dicere solebat, ob hanc causam praestare nostrae civitatis statum ceteris civitatibus, quod in illis singuli fuissent fere quorum[2] suam quis-

[1] *huius vocabuli in principio libri vestigia dispexisse Powellio videtur, cetera usque ad* -tate (*id est tres versus codicis*) *evanuerunt*: ut omnis igitur vidit incensos cupiditate *Mai*: cum omnes flagrarent cupiditate *Heinrich* [2] quorum *cod.*[2]: qui *cod.*[1]

F 130a Cicero, *On the Republic*

[SCIPIO:] . . . how fortunate is such a person to be considered . . . ; who, finally, could declare the same thing about themselves that, according to what Cato writes, my grandfather Africanus [P. Cornelius Scipio Africanus maior, cos. 205, 194, censor 199 BC (*ORF*[4] 4)] was accustomed to say, that he was never doing more than when he was doing nothing, that he was never less alone than when he was alone.[1]

[1] Because of the similarity to F 2, it is sometimes assumed that this comment and the similar one in F 130b might belong to the introduction of the *Origines* (e.g., Cugusi 1994, 267–68; Cugusi and Sblendorio Cugusi 2001, 2:290–91).

F 130b Cicero, *On Duties*

Cato, my son Marcus, who was approximately his contemporary, writes that P. Scipio, he who was the first to be called Africanus [P. Cornelius Scipio Africanus maior, cos. 205, 194, censor 199 BC (*ORF*[4] 4)], was accustomed to say that he was never less at leisure than when he was at leisure, that he was never less alone than when he was alone. An admirable utterance, in truth, and worthy of a great and wise man!

F 131 Cicero, *On the Republic*

Then, [when he saw the interlocutors full of] eagerness to hear [?], SCIPIO [P. Cornelius Scipio Aemilianus Africanus minor (*ORF*[4] 21)] began to speak as follows: "This is a statement by Cato of old . . . [T 10] . . . [2] He [Cato] used to say [*Op. cet.* F 46] that the situation of our community was superior to other communities for this reason that in

que rem publicam constituisset[3] legibus atque institutis suis, ut Cretum Minos, Lacedaemoniorum Lycurgus, Atheniensium (quae persaepe commutata esset) tum Theseus, tum Draco, tum Solo, tum Clisthenes, tum multi alii, postremo exsanguem iam et iacentem doctus vir Phalereus sustentasset Demetrius; nostra autem res publica non unius esset ingenio sed multorum, nec una hominis vita sed aliquot constituta saeculis et aetatibus; nam neque ullum ingenium tantum exstitisse dicebat, ut quem res nulla fugeret quisquam aliquando fuisset; neque cuncta ingenia collata in unum tantum posse uno tempore providere ut omnia complecterentur, sine rerum usu ac vetustate. [3] quamobrem, ut ille solebat, ita nunc mea repetet oratio populi Romani originem (libenter enim etiam verbo utor Catonis); . . ."

[3] constituisset *cod.*[2]: constituissent *cod.*[1]

F 132 Cic. *Div.* 1.28

[Quintus Cicero:] itaque multa auguria, multa auspicia, quod Cato ille sapiens queritur, neglegentia collegi amissa plane et deserta sunt.

those there had virtually been single individuals, each of whom had established their state by their laws and institutions, like Minos that of the Cretans, Lycurgus that of the Lacedaemonians, and that of the Athenians (which was changed very frequently) first Theseus, then Draco, then Solon, then Cleisthenes, then many others, and finally, when it was already bloodless and lying flat out, that learned man of Phalerum, Demetrius, had propped it up. Our state, however, was established by the mental powers, not of a single individual, but of many, not in the lifetime of a single man, but over several centuries and ages. For he used to say that no talent had existed that was so great that there would ever have been anyone whom nothing could escape, nor could all talents combined into a single place at a single time have the foresight to cover everything, without the aid of experience and without the passage of time. [3] For that reason, as he [Cato] was accustomed to do, so my discourse will now trace 'the origin' of the Roman People (for I gladly use also a term of Cato's);[1] . . ."

[1] These historical reflections are sometimes linked to the introduction of the *Origines* (e.g., Cugusi 1994, 268–69; Cugusi and Sblendorio Cugusi 2001, 2:292–93). The final comment alludes to the word regarded as the title of Cato's historical work.

F 132 Cicero, *On Divination*

[QUINTUS CICERO:] Thus, many auguries, many auspices, as the famous Cato, the "Wise," laments, through the negligence of the college [of augurs], have been entirely lost and abandoned.

F 133 Liv. 34.15.9

Valerius Antias supra quadraginta milia hostium caesa eo die scribit; Cato ipse, haud sane detractator[1] laudum suarum, multos caesos ait, numerum non adscribit.[2]

[1] detractator *unus cod.*: detractor *codd. rel.*
[2] adscribit *codd. rel.*: scribit *unus cod.*

F 134 Frontin. *Str.* 4.1.16

M. Cato memoriae tradidit, in furto conprehensis inter commilitones dextras esse praecisas, aut, si lenius[1] animadvertere voluissent, in principiis sanguinem missum.

[1] si lenius *Lipsius*: silentius *vel* ut silentius *vel* si levius *codd.*

F 135 Plut. *Cat. Mai.* 10.3–5

Cf. *Orat.* F 55; *Op. cet.* F 65.

F 136 Plut. *Cat. Mai.* 14.2

Cf. T 59.

F 137 Plut. *Mor.* 276C (*Quaest. Rom.* 49)

διὰ τί τοὺς παραγγέλλοντας ἀρχὴν[1] *ἔθος ἦν ἐν ἱματίῳ τοῦτο ποιεῖν ἀχίτωνας, ὡς Κάτων ἱστόρηκε;*

[1] *ἀρχὴν Bachet de Meziriac*: *ἄρχειν codd.*

Cf. Plut. *Coriol.* 14.2–3.

F 133 Livy, *History of Rome*

Valerius Antias [*FRHist* 25 F 40] writes that over forty thousand of the enemy were killed on that day [at the battle of Emporiae in 195 BC]. Cato himself, certainly not a belittler of his own achievements [*FRHist* 5 T 21a], says that many were killed, but does not add a number.

F 134 Frontinus, *Stratagems*

M. Cato has handed down to posterity [cf. *Op. cet.* F 18] that those caught in theft had their right hands cut off among their fellow soldiers or, if they had wished to punish them more leniently, had their blood let in the headquarters section of the camp [on this punishment, cf. Gell. *NA* 10.8].

F 135 Plutarch, *Life of Cato the Elder*

Cf. *Orat.* F 55; *Op. cet.* F 65.

F 136 Plutarch, *Life of Cato the Elder*

Cf. T 59.

F 137 Plutarch, *Moralia* (*Roman Questions*)

Why was it the custom for those canvassing for office to do this in the toga without a tunic, as Cato has recorded?

F 138 Fest., p. 166.2–7 L.

NATI<NATIO dicebatur negoti>atio:[1] et natinatores <ex eo seditiosa negotia>[2] gerentes. M. Cato in . . . : "<tu>multu[3] Macedoniae Etruriam, Samnites, Lucanos inter se natinari atque factiones esse."

[1] *suppl. ex Epit.* [2] *suppl. Mueller (ex Epit.)*
[3] <Originum libro V scripsit: "audito tu>multu" *Mueller*

F 139 Fest., p. 186.2–4 L.

. . . cuntur noma[1] . . . unde Cato in o[2] . . . multam vivunt . . .

[1] <Numidae di>cuntur Noma<des> *Ursinus*
[2] o *vel* e *vel* c *cod.*: O<riginibus *Lindsay (in Gloss. Lat.)*

F 140 Paul. *Fest.*, p. 519.14–15 L.

VIRITIM dicitur dari, quod datur per singulos viros. Cato: "praeda quae capta est, viritim divisa."

F 138 Festus

nati‹natio [abstract noun] was used for *negoti›atio* ["business"]: and *natinatores* [personal noun], ‹on that basis,› for people carrying out ‹seditious business›. M. Cato in . . . :[1] "that in the tumult of Macedonia Etruria, the Samnites, and the Lucanians [Italic peoples] carried out seditious business [*natinari*; verb] among themselves and there were factions."

[1] The identification of the work from which the quotation has been taken has been lost. Since the fragment suggests a historical context, it could come from the *Origines*.

F 139 Festus

. . . [?] . . . , whence Cato in o . . . they live a lo . . .[1]

[1] The word indicating the work of Cato quoted from seems to start with the letter *o*; therefore, it could be the *Origines*. The text of the quotation is too lacunose to enable a restoration and thus a translation or an identification of the content.

F 140 Paul the Deacon, *Epitome of Festus*

To be given *viritim* ["man by man"] is said for what is given to men individually. Cato: "the booty that was captured, divided among men individually."[1]

[1] Such a comment could occur in a historical narrative. Since Cato is known to have delivered speeches on booty and to have made statements on booty (e.g., *Orat.* F 98, 173, 224–26; *Op. cet.* F 58, 65), it could come from another context too.

F 141 Fronto, *Ad M. Caes.* 2.11.3 (p. 31.15–16 van den Hout)

[M. Aurelius Caesar:] id vespera et concubia nocte, dum se intempesta nox, ut ait M. Porcius, praecipitat, eodem modo perseverat.

F 142 Charis., *GL* I, p. 102.8–11 = p. 130.2–7 B.

ergo lacte sine vitio dicemus. nam et Cato sic dixit "et in Italia atras capras lacte album habere." . . . at consuetudo tamen aliud sequitur.

F 143 Charis., *GL* I, p. 215.20–23 = pp. 278.24–79.2 B.

primo pedato[1] Cato senex, "in his duobus bellis alteras stipendio agrique parte multati, alteras oppidum vi captum, alteras primo pedato et secundo," ut Maximus notat; hodieque nostri per Campaniam sic locuntur.

[1] pedato *Cauchii ex deperdito cod. exerpta, Putschen*: pedatu *cod.*

F 144 Serv. ad Verg. *Aen.* 1.726

Cf. *Orat.* F 144.

F 141 Fronto, *Correspondence*

[M. Aurelius Caesar:] That [lowering of temperature] persists in the same way in the evening and the early part of the night, until the dead of night descends, as M. Porcius [Cato] says.

F 142 Charisius

Thus, we will say *lacte* ["milk"; acc. instead of more common *lac*] without a fault. For Cato too said so: "and that in Italy black goats have white milk [*lacte*]." . . . But still usage acts in accordance with something else.

F 143 Charisius

primo pedato[1] ["at the first stage / attack"; cf. *Orat.* F 57; *Orig.* F 20] [is used by] Cato of old: "in these two wars at one time they were punished by a tribute payment and by [the loss of] part of the territory, at another time the town was captured by force, at yet another time at the first and the second attacks," as Maximus [Statilius Maximus, F 9 Zetzel] notes; and today our people speak so throughout Campania.

[1] On the expression *pedato*, see Briscoe 2010, 156.

F 144 Servius, *Commentary on Virgil*

Cf. *Orat.* F 144.

F 145 Serv. auct. ad Verg. *Aen.* 3.64

"caeruleis vittis": Cato ait, deposita veste purpurea feminas usas caerulea cum lugerent. veteres sane caeruleum nigrum accipiebant.

F 146 Serv. et Serv. auct. ad Verg. *Aen.* 3.707

"Drepani portus": Drepanum civitas est non longe a monte Eryce, trans Lilybaeum . . . Cato pluraliter "haec Drepana" dicit.

F 147 Serv. ad Verg. *Aen.* 4.293

"quae mollissima fandi": Cato "qua[1] mollissimum est adoriantur."[2]

[1] qua *Commelinus*: quam *unus cod.* [2] adoriuntur *Daniel primus*

F 148 Serv. auct. ad Verg. *Aen.* 4.682

"populumque patresque urbemque tuam": "patres" id est senatum; "urbem tuam" quam tu extruxisti. et quidam hoc loco volunt tres partes politiae conprehensas, populi, optimatium, regiae potestatis: Cato enim ait de tribus ipsis partibus ordinatam fuisse Carthaginem.

F 145 Servius Danielis, *Commentary on Virgil*

"with dark bands": Cato says that, having taken off their purple garments, women used dark ones when they were mourning. The ancients certainly understood "dark" as black.

F 146 Servius and Servius Danielis, *Commentary on Virgil*

"the port of Drepanum": Drepanum [mod. Trapani] is a settlement not far from mount Eryx, beyond Lilybaeum [on Sicily] . . . Cato says, in the plural, "Drepana."

F 147 Servius, *Commentary on Virgil*

"which [times are] easiest for speaking": Cato: "where it is easiest, let them attack."

F 148 Servius Danielis, *Commentary on Virgil*

"the People, the fathers and your city [Carthage]": "fathers," this is the Senate; "your city," which you have built. And some want in this passage the three parts of a political system to be included, those of the People, of the nobility, and of monarchic power: for Cato says that according to these three parts Carthage had been organized.[1]

[1] On the constitution of Carthage, see, e.g., Arist. *Pol.* 2.8, 1272b–73b; Polyb. 6.51.1–2. The comment is often seen as a reference to the concept of the "mixed constitution" (as presented, e.g., in Cicero's *De re publica*). Catalano (1974, 688–90) cautions that the fragment shows Cato listing simply three elements in the Carthaginian political structure; Catalano also argues that, in contrast to other ancient authors, Cato might have welcomed the involvement of the People and less so that of the nobility.

F 149 Serv. auct. ad Verg. *Aen.* 8.694

"telisque volatile": Cato "sub tela volantia."

F 150 Serv. ad Verg. *Aen.* 10.13

"Alpes inmittet apertas": emphasis est; non enim dixit "per Alpes inmittet exercitum"; sed "ipsas Alpes," quas patefecit non sibi tantum sed omnibus gentibus, quae secundum Catonem et Livium muri vice tuebantur Italiam: quas Hannibal post bella Hispaniae, quae XVII annis confecit, ante exustas aceto infuso rupit: Iuvenalis "et montem rupit aceto." denique loca ipsa quae rupit, Poeninae Alpes vocantur.

F 151 Amm. Marc. 15.12.4

vini avidum genus affectans ad vini similitudinem multiplices potus et inter eos humiles quidam obtunsis ebrietate continua sensibus (quam furoris voluntariam speciem

F 149 Servius Danielis, *Commentary on Virgil*

"and [iron] flying with arrows": Cato: "under flying arrows/javelins."

F 150 Servius, *Commentary on Virgil*

"it [Carthage] will cause the Alps to open": This is emphasis; for he [Virgil] did not say "it will send the army through the Alps [and thus open it up]"; but "the Alps themselves," which it has opened not only for itself, but for all nations, and which, according to Cato and Livy [Liv. 21.35.8–9], used to protect Italy like a wall: after the wars in the Iberian peninsula, which he completed in 17 years [Second Punic War, 218–201 BC], Hannibal cracked them [the Alps] open, first having burned them, by pouring in vinegar:[1] Juvenal [10.153] [says]: "and he cracked open the mountain with vinegar." Thus, the very places that he cracked open are called Punic Alps [cf. F 57].

[1] Ancient historiographers report that Hannibal cleared the path through the Alps with fire and vinegar (Liv. 21.37.2–3; App. *Hann.* 4.15; Amm. Marc. 15.10.11). Apparently, a combination of heat and acid can soften certain types of stone (esp. limestone), so that they can then be worked upon with tools more easily. In antiquity there seems to have been the belief that Hannibal applied this method when crossing the Alps.

F 151 Ammianus Marcellinus

A nation [i.e. the Gauls] desirous of wine, striving for many kinds of drinks similar to wine, and among them some people of the baser sort, their senses, blunted by continuous drunkenness (a state that a statement of Cato's defines

esse Catoniana sententia definivit) raptantur discursibus vagis, . . .

Cf. Sen. *Ep.* 83.18.

F 152 Prisc., *GL* II, p. 87.15–17

. . . ; vetustissimi tamen comparativis etiam huiuscemodi sunt {est quando}[1] usi. Cato {dixit}:[2] "quod iter longius arduiusque erat a curia." . . . .

[1] sunt *vel* sunt est quando *vel* est sunt quando *vel* est quando *vel* * * est quando (st?) *codd.* [2] dixit *om. unus cod.*

F 153 Prisc., *GL* II, p. 227.12–13

idem "nulli" pro "nullius": "qui tantisper nulli rei sies,[1] dum nihil agas."

[1] sies *codd. p. 266*: est *codd. hoc loco*

Cf. Prisc., *GL* II, p. 266.12–13: idem:[1] "qui tantisper nulli rei sies, dum nil agas," "nulli" pro "nullius."; Columella, *Rust.* 11.1.26: nam illud verum est M. Catonis oraculum: "nihil agendo homines male agere discunt."

[1] idem in secundo *unus cod.*[2]: idem in II. *edd.*

F 154 Prisc., *GL* II, p. 260.6–7

Cf. *Orat.* F 127.

as a voluntary type of madness [*Op. cet.* F 80; cf. 58.16]), are swept along in random movements in different directions, . . .

F 152 Priscian

. . . ; the very early [writers], though, used comparatives of this type too {it is when}. Cato {said}: "since the route was longer and more arduous from the Senate house." . . . [*Orat.* F 19, 186, 178, 161, 182].

F 153 Priscian

The same [Cato] [used] *nulli* ["of not any / none"; less common form of gen. sg.] instead of *nullius*: "you who would be of no worth for as long as you are doing nothing" [cf. F 25].

Cf. Columella: For this is a true divine pronouncement of M. Cato: "By doing nothing men learn to act badly."[1]

[1] Columella's comment might be based on the statement attested for Cato, having been adapted or quoted from memory (on this saying, see Otto 1890, 9, s.v. *agere* 1). If the correction in one manuscript of Priscian in one of the places where the passage is quoted is regarded as reliable, it could point to a location in the second book.

F 154 Priscian

Cf. *Orat.* F 127.

F 155 Lydus, *Mag.* 1.47

ἀδωράτωρας οἱ Ῥωμαῖοι τοὺς ἀπομάχους καλοῦσιν (ἀδωρέα γὰρ κατ᾽ αὐτοὺς ἡ τοῦ πολέμου λέγεται δόξα ἀπὸ τῆς ζειᾶς καὶ τῆς τιμῆς τῶν ποτε τιμηθέντων αὐτοῖς), βετερανοὺς δὲ τοὺς ἐγγεγηρακότας τοῖς ὅπλοις (μάρτυρες Κέλσος τε καὶ Πάτερνος καὶ Κατιλίνας, οὐχ ὁ συνωμότης ἀλλ᾽ ἕτερος, Κάτων <τε>[1] πρὸ αὐτῶν ὁ πρῶτος καὶ Φροντῖνος, μεθ᾽ οὓς καὶ Ῥενᾶτος, Ῥωμαῖοι πάντες· . . .) . . .

[1] *add. Wünsch*

F 156 Isid. *Orig.* 19.2.11

parastatae stipites sunt pares stantes quibus arbor sustinetur. Cato: “malum deligatum, parastatae vinctae.”

F 155 Lydus, *On the Magistracies of the Roman Republic*

The Romans call *adoratorai* those unfit for military service [e.g., because of wounds] (for among them *adorea* [Lat. *adorea* or *adoria*, "glory, distinction"] is a term for the fame of war, from spelt [Lat. *adoreum*, "spelt"], and the honor of those once honored by them [since a reward of valor originally consisted of grain or possession of a large amount of grain was regarded as an honor]) and veterans [Lat. *veterani*] those who have grown old [Lat. *vetus*] in arms (witnesses are Celsus [A. Cornelius Celsus] and Paternus [P. Taruttienus Paternus] and Catilina, not the conspirator, but another one, and Cato the Elder before them, and Frontinus [Sex. Iulius Frontinus], with them also Renatus [P. Vegetius Renatus], all of them Romans; . . .) . . .

F 156 Isidore, *Origins*

parastatae ["square posts"] are matching upright stakes by which a ship's mast is supported. Cato [says]: "the mast fastened, the square posts bound together."